THE SOVIET UNION AND THE ARABIAN PENINSULA

The Soviet Union and the Arabian Peninsula

Soviet Policy Towards the Persian Gulf and Arabia

ARYEH Y. YODFAT

CROOM HELM
London & Canberra

ST. MARTIN'S PRESS
New York

© 1983 Aryeh Y. Yodfat
Croom Helm Ltd, Provident House, Burrell Row,
Beckenham, Kent BR3 1AT

British Library Cataloguing in Publication Data

Yodfat, Aryeh Y.
  The Soviet Union and the Arabian peninsula.
  1. Soviet Union — Foreign relations — Persian
    Gulf region   2. Persian Gulf region —
    Foreign relations — Soviet Union
  I. Title
  327.470536   DK68.7.P/

  ISBN 0-7099-2904-8

All rights reserved. For information write:
St. Martin's Press, Inc., 175 Fifth Avenue, New York, N.Y. 10010
First published in the United States of America in 1983

Library of Congress Cataloging in Publication Data

Yodfat, Aryeh, 1923-
  The Soviet Union and the Arabian Peninsula

  1. Arabia — Foreign relations — Soviet Union.
2. Soviet Union — Foreign relations — Arabia. 3. Persian
Gulf Region — Foreign relations — Soviet Union. 4. Soviet
Union — Foreign relations — Persian Gulf Region.
I. Title.
DS228.S65Y53   1983   327.47053   82-42717
ISBN 0-312-74907-4

Photoset by Pat Murphy Composition
296b Lymington Road, Highcliffe, Dorset
Printed and Bound in Great Britain by
Billing & Son Ltd., Worcester

CONTENTS

PREFACE

This book attempts to review and analyze relations between the USSR and the countries of the Persian Gulf and Arabian peninsula.

Chapter 1 summarizes events from the beginning of the Soviet regime up to 1975. In Chapter 2, we review events of the years 1975–8. Chapter 3 is more detailed, and opens with a description of the impact on the Gulf region of events starting in January 1979 in Iran, with the Shah's downfall and the rise of Ayatollah Khomeyni. Chapter 4, also quite detailed, describes the situation in the region from the outbreak of the Iran-Iraq war in September 1980 until early 1982.

We have based the book mainly on primary sources of Soviet, Arab, Iranian, Western and other origins. Quotations and references are given to enable the reader to reach his own conclusions and focus attention on events and their background, both in the Gulf countries and the USSR.

The author wishes to thank the documentation centres and libraries of the Shiloah Centre for Middle Eastern and African Studies, Tel Aviv University, and of the Harry S. Truman Research Institute, Jerusalem, and their staffs, whose help has been of inestimable value.

Aryeh Y. Yodfat

ABBREVIATIONS

ADN	East German News Agency, East Berlin
AFP	Agence France Presse, Paris
BBC	British Broadcasting Corporation
BNLF	Bahrain National Liberation Front
CENTO	Central Treaty Organization
CIA	Central Intelligence Agency, USA
CMEA	Council for Mutual Economic Assistance (Comecon)
CP	Communist Party
CPSU	Communist Party of the Soviet Union
DPK	Democratic Party of Kurdistan, Iraq (Kordestan, Iran)
ELF	Eritrean Liberation Front
FBIS	Foreign Broadcast Information Service, USA
GCC	Gulf Co-operation Council
GDR	German Democratic Republic
ICP	Iraqi Communist Party
IISS	International Institute for Strategic Studies, London
INA	Iraqi News Agency, Baghdad
IRP	Islamic Republican Party, Iran
KGB	Komitet Gosudarstvennoy Bezopasnosti, Committee for State Security, USSR
KUNA	Kuwait News Agency, Kuwait
ME	Middle East
NATO	North Atlantic Treaty Organization
NDF	National Democratic Front, YAR
NF	National Front
NLF	National Liberation Front, PDRY
NVOI	National Voice of Iran
NY	New York
OPEC	Organization of Petroleum Exporting Countries
PDFLP	Popular Democratic Front for the Liberation of Palestine

PDP	People's Democratic Party, Afghanistan
PDRY	People's Democratic Republic of Yemen (South Yemen)
PDU	People's Democratic Union, PDRY
PFLB	Popular Front for the Liberation of Bahrain
PFLO	Popular Front for the Liberation of Oman
PFLOAG	Popular Front for the Liberation of Oman and the Arabian Gulf
PFLP	Popular Front for the Liberation of Palestine
PLO	Palestine Liberation Organization
PNF	Progressive National Front, Iraq
PRC	People's Republic of China
PRSY	People's Republic of South Yemen
PUK	Patriotic Union of Kurdistan, Iraq
PVP	People's Vanguard Party, PDRY
QNA	Qatar News Agency, Doha
RDF	Rapid Deployment Force
RUSI	Royal United Services Institute, UK
SACP	Saudi Arabian Communist Party
SNLF	Saudi National Liberation Front
SPA	Saudi Press Agency, Riyadh
TASS	Telegraph Agency of the Soviet Union
UAE	United Arab Emirates
UAR	United Arab Republic
UN	United Nations
UPONF	Unified Political Organization National Front, PDRY
US, USA	United States, United States of America
USSR	Union of Soviet Socialist Republics
YAR	Yemen Arab Republic (North Yemen)
YSP	Yemeni Socialist Party, PDRY

1 ARABIA AND THE GULF — SOVIET APPROACHES, SUCCESSES AND FAILURES (1917–1975)

The Arabian Peninsula — Initial Ties

In the first years of the Soviet regime there was very little, if any, Soviet interest in the Persian Gulf-Arabian peninsula countries. The USSR's attempts at penetration were more a part of its confrontations with Britain — at that time its principal enemy — or as bargaining points for negotiations with Britain, rather than as an aim in itself.

Diplomatic relations were established between the USSR and Hejaz in August 1924, during a period of strained relations between the latter's ruler, Sharif Husayn al-Hashimi of Mecca and Medina, and Britain.[1] At that time, the Soviets exaggerated the role of Hejaz, assuming that it had strong influence on other Muslim states because of its guardianship of the Muslim holy places. The Soviets believed that ties with Husayn would moderate the attitude of the Soviet Muslims to the Soviet regime and contribute to Soviet relations with Muslim states. In actual fact, Husayn had no power or influence, even in his own country.

When Ibn Sa'ud replaced Husayn and became 'King of Hejaz, Sultan of Nejd and its Dependencies' in 1926, the USSR was the first foreign power to accord him recognition. In 1927 two Soviet trade delegations visited Hejaz and an exhibition of Soviet goods was organized in Jidda. The British saw this as a danger to their position and exerted pressure to put an end to Soviet interference.[2]

Yemen's opposition to British rule in Aden and South Arabia brought it closer to Britain's enemy — the Soviet Union. Yemen proposed the establishment of diplomatic relations and purchased Soviet goods. In May 1928 a Soviet trading ship loaded with Soviet goods visited the port of Hodeida and on 1 November of the same year, a 'Treaty of Friendship and Trade between the USSR and Yemen' was signed, marking the first treaty between the Soviet Union and an Arab country. The USSR sold Yemen kerosene, soap, sugar, timber and flour and provided it with medical aid, buying coffee in return. In 1939 the treaty was extended for ten more years.[3] However, as the USSR's preoccupation with Europe

1

grew, together with its desire to improve relations with Britain, it lost interest in that distant region, and withdrew its personnel, ending activities there for a time.

Renewed Soviet interest in Saudi Arabia became evident in the mid-1950s as part of the USSR's activities against the British-sponsored Baghdad Pact, and its establishment of ties with Egypt. At that time the Soviets were under the illusion that they would be able to renew their ties with Saudi Arabia. However, the Saudis exploited the occasion to bring pressure to bear on Britain and the USA rather than to turn towards the Soviets.

The Soviets were more successful in Yemen, with which they renewed relations, and a USSR-Yemen treaty of friendship was signed on 31 October 1956.[4] Accordingly, the Soviets provided economic and technical assistance and limited quantities of arms. In April 1961, with Soviet aid and having involved about 500 Soviet experts, the construction of the port of Hodeida was completed.[5] Crown Prince Muhammad al-Badr of Yemen visited the USSR in June 1956 and was accorded a friendly welcome.[6] When his father Imam Ahmad died on 19 September 1962, a telegram of condolences, signed by N. S. Khrushchev and L. J. Brezhnev was sent to Prince Muhammad. They also sent him a message of congratulations on his accession as Imam.[7]

North Yemen — the Civil War and After

A military coup staged on 26 September 1962 led to the establishment of a Yemen Arab Republic (YAR) with President 'Abdallah as-Sallal at its head. On 29 September Sallal asked the USSR to continue the friendly relations existing between the two countries. Khrushchev's reply of 1 October affirmed recognition of the YAR, stating that any foreign intervention in internal Yemeni affairs was inadmissible.[8]

Soviet economic and technical aid gradually increased. In September 1962 there were about 60 Soviet technicians in Yemen. By June 1963 their number had reached between 900 and 1,000.[9] Military aid was provided by the Soviets indirectly, through Egypt, which at that time was gradually improving its relations with the USSR. The Soviets attached great importance to this development, whereas the Egyptians, in an effort to prevent any direct military deals between Soviets and Yemenis, insisted that Soviet arms intended for Yemen should be supplied through them.

President Sallal visited the USSR between 16 and 24 March 1964. While there he signed a treaty of friendship and an economic and technical co-operation agreement comprising a Soviet loan of 65 million roubles (about $39 million).[10] Sallal also tried to reach an agreement with the Soviets to receive direct military supplies, but Egyptian pressure on the USSR frustrated these efforts.

In the aftermath of the Arab-Israeli Six-Day war in June 1967, Egypt could not afford to continue to keep forces in Yemen, having a greater need of them at home. Egypt was also interested in improving its relations with the conservative Arab states, and ending its military involvement in Yemen would contribute greatly toward this. The result was that withdrawal of the Egyptian forces led to Soviet-Yemeni contacts and the beginning of direct Soviet military supplies.

President 'Abdallah as-Sallal was overthrown by a military coup on 5 November 1967, while in Iran on his way to Moscow. Qadi 'Abd ar-Rahman al-Iryani was appointed Head of State and Muhsin al-'Ayni as Prime Minister.

As fighting intensified, the Soviets became directly involved in attempting to prevent the downfall of the republic. Substantial amounts of arms were flown to the YAR and as royalist pressure on San'a grew, the Soviets increased their supplies, bringing in equipment and technicians. Soviet pilots were reported to have flown combat missions for the republicans.[11]

This was the first time that direct Soviet participation in the Yemeni civil war was made public, but the scope of the USSR's involvement was limited. The number of Soviet pilots was small and their presence was intended to continue only as long as the republicans had none of their own, or other Arab pilots for the newly arriving planes. When the news became known, the Soviets had to restrict their presence even more, since it led to sharp Saudi and American reactions. Saudi Arabia declared that it had concluded an agreement with Egypt to end foreign intervention and was not going to bring about the replacement of Egyptians by Soviets. It threatened that if such a situation were to continue, it might cease restraining royalist activities and perhaps reconsider the provision of financial assistance to Egypt. There were reports that the USA had made clear to the Soviets that direct involvement would not be tolerated. Thus the Soviets decided to acquiesce, and their pilots were replaced by Syrian and other Arab pilots.

Nevertheless, at the end of October 1968 royalist forces again neared San'a. Their positions were attacked by Soviet planes, one of which was shot down, and its pilot was reported to be a Russian.[12]

The lifting of the royalist siege of San'a brought with it the rise of Yemen's 'Third Force' and a gradual cessation of the civil war.[13] The YAR's policy now became pragmatic. The need for financial aid, to terminate the civil war and to curb the power of the tribes, drove the Third Force republican leaders to seek aid from the West and make peace with Saudi Arabia.

Relations between the YAR and Saudi Arabia improved after a Marxist wing of the republican movement was crushed in 1968.[14] Although they were opposed to the re-establishment of the Imam's dynasty, the republican leaders were willing to allow his supporters to participate in the government. Agreement was facilitated by Saudi Arabia's decision to phase out its support of the royalists and this in turn led to the establishment of a united government which included moderates from both the republican and royalist camps.

Seven years of civil war had left North Yemen destroyed and poor and in need of extensive aid from any available source. Saudi Arabia was willing to help it overcome its economic difficulties, realizing that such a policy was bound to strengthen the YAR conservatives and limit the country's dependence on the USSR and the People's Republic of China (PRC).

Soviet military aid continued to arrive, although on a limited scale.[15] In border clashes between the YAR and South Yemen, the USSR supported the latter, leading to its even greater rejection by the YAR and the improvement of the latter's relations with Western countries. American Secretary of State William Rogers visited the YAR in July 1972 and soon afterwards diplomatic relations were re-established between the two countries.

It was at this time that President Anwar al-Sadat asked the Soviets to withdraw their military forces from Egypt. The YAR was also reported to have asked the USSR to recall Soviet experts (about 100) working there.[16] Most of them were engaged in training the air force which flew MiG-17 jets.[17] YAR officials, fearing that the Soviet officers would pass on information to their countrymen in South Yemen, barred them from military camps and head-quarters, and refused all facilities.

A ship carrying Soviet arms, *en route* to Hodeida, was reported to have changed course after armed clashes broke out between the two Yemens, and eventually it docked in Aden.[18] Only about a dozen Soviet military advisers now remained in North Yemen, and according to Prime Minister Muhsin al-'Ayni the YAR had not received any new weapons or spare parts from the USSR since 1970.[19]

Both sides tried, however, to pretend that friendly relations still existed. The North Yemenis wanted to continue receiving Soviet aid, even if it was limited, while the Soviets, for their part, were interested in keeping a foothold in the YAR in order to prevent an increase of other presences — in other words, the Western powers or China. The Chinese were giving aid by building roads from San'a to Sa'da and Hodeida, and from Imram to Hajjah. They had also built a textile plant in San'a and were undertaking other projects.[20] The Soviets had established a strategic infrastructure in the YAR which they believed could serve them, if needed. This included a modern port at Hodeida (which the Soviets planned to extend still further), a modern airport near Hodeida and a highway from Hodeida to Taiz.

The military coup of 13 June 1974 in North Yemen was reported in the Soviet media without comment, but greetings from Kosygin and Gromyko expressed confidence that the friendly relations between the two countries would continue to develop.[21] This, however, was just a pretence. The leader of the coup, the Chairman of the Command Council, Lt.-Col. Ibrahim al-Hamdi, was considered quite acceptable to Saudi Arabia and went, at the beginning of July 1974, to Ta'if to receive King Faysal's blessing. The YAR became quite dependent on Saudi Arabia for assistance.

The great powers' interest in Yemen began to wane. Since it had no oil or other natural resources, their interest was not in the country as such, but rather to maintain a presence in the region. The Soviets, however, concentrated their interest in this area on neighbouring South Yemen, where they saw greater possibilities.

South Yemen — a Soviet Listening-post and Focus

On 30 November 1967 South Arabia was proclaimed an independent state and named the People's Republic of South Yemen (PRSY). (On 30 November 1970 the name was changed to the People's Democratic Republic of Yemen (PDRY).) The new state was ruled by the National Liberation Front (NLF), to whom Britain had transferred all power. Its leader Qahtan ash-Sha'bi became President, Prime Minister and Supreme Commander of the Armed Forces. The PRSY was proclaimed a unitary state (and not federal as South Arabia had been), having a presidential form of government and only one legal ruling party, the NLF.

The PRSY was immediately accorded recognition by the Soviet Union, [22] and gradually Soviet experts and technicians replaced the British, who had remained there training the armed forces, until asked to leave. Small quantities of obsolete military equipment were given by the Soviets as grants (or almost grants) since the PRSY could hardly afford to pay for them. Some Soviet economic aid was given, but too little to solve the country's difficulties.

The relatively moderate and pragmatic President Qahtan ash-Sha'bi was forced by the ruling NLF radical wing to resign on 22 June 1969. He was replaced by a Presidential Council headed by Salim Rubay'i 'Ali. The NLF ideologist and Secretary-General 'Abd al-Fattah Isma'il emerged as its 'strong man'. Rivalry between the two already began to appear at this stage. Both were radical and militant, advocating extreme social and economic reforms and politicization of the armed forces. Isma'il, a North Yemeni (and therefore having no local tribal support), was against tribal allegiances, but in favour of a union with North Yemen (although on his terms) and closer relations with the USSR. For a time Rubay'i inclined towards the PRC, but later moved closer to the USSR.[23]

The regime leaned heavily on the USSR. Soviet economic and technical aid was not copious, but it covered many fields, making it much more effective and giving the Soviets a relatively broad presence. The Soviets paid attention to the development of fishing and ports, thus bolstering their naval presence in the region. There were numerous exchanges of low-level delegations and a great number of South Yemenis underwent training in the USSR. Military aid included supplies of equipment and study in Soviet military schools, while Soviet instructors and advisers held posts in the PDRY. It was reported that the port of Aden was being used by the Soviets as a submarine base and the British-built airfield outside Aden was being used for reconnaissance flights. Soviet activity also increased around the island of Socotra in the Gulf of Aden, where the airstrip had been improved and Soviet marines had carried out amphibian landing exercises.[24]

The Soviets paid particular attention to inter-party co-operation between the Communist Party of the Soviet Union (CPSU) and the National Liberation Front (NLF). A party school was established with Soviet instructors, using Soviet experience as a model, who taught not only Marxist-Leninist theory but also organizational methods and techniques for controlling both the civilian and military apparatus.

Ruling parties in the radical Arab states were generally dominated either by the military in uniform or, more often, by former senior military officers now appearing as civilians. The situation in the PDRY was an exception. From the beginning, civilians had full control over the military. In the armed forces, party commissars, whose loyalty was more to the party than to their military commanders, were nominated at each level of command.

In December 1967 the NLF changed its name to National Front (NF), thus signifying that the liberation stage was over and that the PDRY had become 'fully liberated'. Then in October 1975 it united with two small groups: the communist People's Democratic Union (PDU) and a group called the People's Vanguard Party (PVP), a faction of the local Ba'thists (who were closer to the Iraqi rather than the Syrian Ba'th Party). They formed themselves into a Unified Political Organization National Front (UPONF). In practice, the NF dominated the united party and the partners were given minor positions.[25]

The Soviets, with an interest in strengthening the party role, tried to bring it closer to them, treating it as if it were a communist party in all but name, and hoping that it would become so in time. They had learned from experience that their relations with less developed countries lasted longer when based not only on a temporary merging of interests, but on ideological ties as well. Also needed was a ruling Marxist-Leninist party which followed Soviet doctrine and accepted the role of the USSR as leader in the communist world. All this came at a time of increasing Soviet interest and activity in the region. The Soviet presence in the PDRY served as a listening-point and a focus.

Saudi Arabia — the Soviets Wait for Changes

Until the 1960s the Soviet media maintained an ambivalent attitude towards Saudi Arabia. On the one hand the country was described as a symbol of 'reaction, backwardness, feudalism, serving imperialism', but at the same time the Soviets described the Saudi rulers as 'victims of colonialism', exploited by the 'imperialist oil monopolies' and forced to serve them. Then again, when King Faysal came to power in 1964, he was described as 'a willing servant of imperialism'.

The Soviet attitude towards Saudi Arabia changed somewhat after the June 1967 Six-Day war, when Saudi Arabia undertook to provide financial support to Egypt and other Arab countries which had suffered in the war. At that time the Soviets again tried to re-establish diplomatic relations with Saudi Arabia, but to no avail.

Even if certain aspects of Saudi policy served Soviet aims, in general it was against the USSR's interests, and so the Soviets preferred not to react directly. Although, for the most part, the Soviet media ignored them, there were from time to time Soviet outbursts against Saudi Arabia and its policy.[26] Occasionally the Soviets attempted to point out the advantages to the Saudis of closer ties with the Soviet Union, or at least the establishment of diplomatic relations between the two countries. They accused 'the imperialists' of having an interest in relations not being established.[27]

The tone of Soviet approaches to Saudi Arabia again became friendly during and after the October 1973 war, when King Faysal supported the use of the Arab 'oil weapon' against any country friendly to Israel, especially the USA.

A message of congratulations sent in 1973 by King Faysal to the Chairman of the Supreme Soviet, N. Podgorny, on the occasion of the anniversary of the October revolution, led to much speculation regarding its meaning and intention.[28] In Moscow this message aroused hopes and great interest. Rumours circulated concerning the possibility of an improvement in relations between the two countries. 'Informed diplomatic sources' in Beirut were quoted as saying that contacts were taking place between Saudi Arabia and the USSR, aimed at establishing relations and an exchange of ambassadors. It was also said that an invitation to King Faysal to visit Moscow had, in principle, been accepted.[29] The rumours may have originated in Riyadh during a period of Saudi pressure on the United States. Alternatively, this could have been a Soviet attempt to test Saudi reactions.

If the Soviets still had any illusions at the end of 1973 regarding the possibility of changes in Saudi policy, these had disappeared shortly after the beginning of 1974. First, the Soviets were dissatisfied with Saudi Arabia's oil policy, which aimed at squeezing advantages from the West while compromising with it. Secondly, they strongly disapproved of King Faysal's role in the arrangement of an Egyptian-Israeli separation agreement, and in Egypt's swing away from the USSR. From April 1974 they resumed attacking Saudi Arabia in their broadcasts.

King Faysal's assassination on 25 March 1975 received extensive Soviet coverage. Soviet commentators were careful, however, not to appear to be presenting their own positions. They attributed their remarks to quotations from the 'Western press', the 'Arab press' or 'what was being said in Riyadh'. This enabled them to change their positions as developments required. The questions the Soviets asked were: Who stood behind the assassination? What were their motives? Who would benefit from it? The answers to all these questions were usually: the USA and the American oil companies.[30] The Soviets viewed the assassination as a Saudi-American plot to bring to power someone more amenable to their wishes. For their part, although relieved to be rid of their worst Middle East enemy, the Soviets feared that his successor would be even worse.

Kuwait — the Soviets Enjoy Ties while Expecting the Regime's Downfall

Although Kuwait proclaimed its independence in June 1961, the USSR viewed this as being in name only. They saw that the country was still politically and militarily dependent on Britain and economically controlled by the Western oil companies.[31] Nevertheless, in March 1963 the Soviets were concluding an agreement to establish diplomatic relations with Kuwait, while the Ba'thist regime in Iraq was persecuting communists, disregarding Soviet protests.

In fact there was no change in the Soviet attitude to Kuwait. This could be seen from Khrushchev's reference to Kuwait in his speech at a Cairo meeting of 20 May 1964:

Kuwait. There is some little ruler sitting there, an Arab of course, a Muslim. He is given bribes, he lives the life of the rich, but he is trading in the riches of his people. He never had any conscience and he won't ever have any.[32]

Soviet officials were not so outspoken after 1967, at least outwardly. Their delegations visited Kuwait and trade relations were established between both countries. Their attitude to Kuwait was also greatly influenced by the ups and downs in Soviet-Iraqi relations.

The Soviets soon discovered Kuwait's importance both as an oil producer and because of its position in the Gulf. Kuwait's internal situation — limited democracy, a large immigrant population, loud proclamations of anti-Western slogans — made the Soviets believe that sooner or later the regime would change. Soviet visitors described the growth of the Kuwaiti workers' 'class consciousness', noting that they had 'displayed a considerable degree of organization and resolve', established trade unions and struck against the oil companies.[33]

The Soviet-Iraqi friendship treaty of 9 April 1972 aroused Kuwait's suspicions, making it fear Soviet intentions in the region. This brought the country closer than ever (although not formally) to the USA, Saudi Arabia and Iran. However, because of internal and inter-Arab considerations Kuwait accompanied this move with sharp verbal attacks on the USA and a refusal to join Western-initiated defence treaties. This was evident mainly during sessions of parliament which included noisily radical anti-American members.

The Soviets watched this process carefully; it was not unexpected. According to them, Kuwait, which before the development of its oil industry had been in a patriarchal pre-capitalist stage, was now entering the period of capitalism. The existing anti-Americanism reflected a process which they believed was only just beginning, resulting from social contradictions which are characteristic of the capitalist world. The greater the number of workers, the sooner their class-conscious vanguard would appear. Privileges and benefits were accorded to the local population but not to immigrants. Immigrants could not attain citizenship, their rights were restricted and they experienced discrimination. This, according to a Soviet commentator well acquainted with the Gulf countries, was a source of friction, reminiscent of class struggle:

The oil boom attracted immigrant workers from all over the Middle East, many of them Palestinians. But these people could not buy property or start up a business. They had no rights at all, and social tensions between the educated immigrants — engineers, doctors, economists, lawyers and clerks — and the native population, not so well educated, were growing. The less well paid immigrants — manual labourers, servants and porters — were 'social dynamite'. Measures had been taken by the ruling regime to preserve stability by social benefits and some bourgeois-democratic freedoms, but these mainly affected the native population.[34]

For the time being the Soviets were interested in maintaining good relations with Kuwait's rulers, and so refrained from intervening in its internal affairs. Moscow radio denied that the Soviet Union developed relations only with those Arab countries 'which raise the slogan of building socialism', and that co-operation between the USSR and Arab countries 'which follow another direction' could not be expected 'to produce any results or benefits'. As an example, the commentary referred to the economic, technical and cultural co-operation 'which had been fruitfully developing' between the USSR and Kuwait. Soviet-Kuwaiti relations were broadening. The Soviet Union occupied first place as Kuwait's supplier of ships and shipping equipment. Soviet automobiles, television sets, refrigerators and bicycles were sold in Kuwait. Soviet experts were working in Kuwait and their work '[had] been receiving the fullest appreciation of the Kuwaiti government'.[35] However, although the Soviets attempted to increase economic co-operation with Kuwait, they had little to offer that could compare with Western or Japanese goods, either in quality or in price.[36]

The Soviet media kept referring to the existence of friendly relations. On the occasion of a visit by a delegation of the USSR Supreme Soviet to Kuwait in March 1974, they praised the latter's policy of non-alignment, its 'non-affiliation with military pacts', the similarity of its views with those of the USSR on most important international problems, and its co-operation with the Soviet Union.[37] This, however, was mere lip-service, since the Soviets were expecting changes in Kuwait's regime and believed they were imminent.

Bahrain, Qatar and the UAE — No Diplomatic Relations

When on 16 January 1968 the British announced that they would cease to maintain military forces 'east of Suez' after the end of 1971, the Soviets doubted their sincerity. They did not believe that Britain would simply abandon such important positions without being forced to do so. In the Soviet view, Britain only wished to change the form of its presence, to share control over the region jointly with the Americans and 'feudal regimes'.[38]

Although the Soviets opposed plans to establish a federation of Gulf states,[39] support was given to these plans by Arab states friendly to the USSR such as Egypt, Iraq and Algeria (although Syria and South Yemen continued to oppose the idea). This made the Soviets stop their attacks on the proposed federation and the Gulf states involved in it. Instead, Soviet propaganda now turned against the 'imperialist defence plans' and 'plots'.

Arab and Western efforts to establish a Gulf federation met with great difficulties, due to the divergent interests of the local rulers, especially their fear of Bahrain's relatively large size and its 'progressive' character. Bahrain's refusal to join was followed by Qatar. What remained was only a plan for a mini-federation and this too was put together only after great efforts and concessions on many issues, such as the centralization principle and sovereignty.

When *Bahrain* was formally proclaimed independent on 16 August 1971 it immediately concluded a defence agreement with Britain. Although the USSR was severely critical of this, it could ill afford not to recognize Bahrain. The Soviet position became even more uncomfortable after the PRC recognized the newly independent Gulf states. Nevertheless, Saudi Arabian pressure prevented the establishment of diplomatic relations and the exchange of diplomatic missions.

Generally, the Soviets regarded Bahrain as more advanced than the other Gulf countries. The early discovery of oil and Bahrain's introduction of welfare services and Western education had produced a strong, politically conscious intelligentsia and proletariat. Even before independence, the country emerged as a centre for radical elements and political ferment which then brought an upsurge of labour unrest and demonstrations. Bahrain also became the headquarters of a wide spectrum of radical, nationalist and Marxist movements, whose significance the Soviets exaggerated.[40]

Qatar proclaimed its independence in early September 1971. On 10 September Podgorny sent a telegram to the Emir, recognizing the new state.[41] He said nothing, however, about diplomatic relations, and in fact no such relations were established.

The United Arab Emirates (UAE) proclaimed its establishment on 2 December 1971 and included the Shaykhdoms of Abu Dhabi, Dubai, Ajman, Fujairah, Sharjah and Umm al-Quwain. Shortly afterwards they were joined by Ras-al-Khaimah. Again, the USSR was quick to give them recognition and request the establishment of diplomatic relations, to which the UAE promptly agreed.[42]

A Soviet delegation arrived in Abu Dhabi on 29 January 1972, and on 14 February the parties announced that they had agreed to exchange diplomatic representatives at embassy level.[43] But in a counter-move, pressure exerted by Saudi Arabia, Iran, Oman, Qatar and other Arab countries upon the UAE in general, and each member of the UAE in particular, succeeded in preventing the establishment of relations.[44]

Oman-Soviet Support of the Revolt in Dhofar

The Sultanate of Muscat and Oman (whose name was changed to Oman in August 1970) had no relations with the USSR and received only negative appraisals in the Soviet media, which considered the country to be nominally independent but actually serving British, and in later years also American, interests.

The Dhofar Liberation Front, which was active in the south-western province of Dhofar and was attempting to overthrow the Sultan and drive out the British, was occasionally referred to in the Soviet media. In September 1968 the Front changed its name to the Popular Front for the Liberation of Oman and the Arabian Gulf (PFLOAG). Neighbouring South Yemen's attainment of independence at the end of 1967 gave them both a spring-board for their movement, and a pipeline to the outside world. Material aid for the Front began arriving, mainly from the PRC, but the Soviets then made efforts to attract them by providing military equipment, training and financial aid (though on a very modest scale), to be channelled through South Yemen. When writing about the Front, Soviet commentators described it more as they would wish to see it than as it actually was.

As the date for formal British withdrawal from the Gulf area drew nigh and the Soviets saw that their attempts to penetrate the region by diplomatic means (establishing relations with the newly, or soon-to-be, independent Emirates) had failed, they intensified their support for revolutionary elements acting against existing regimes. The Soviets believed that the events in the PDRY would be repeated in the Gulf area, with the PFLOAG playing the same role as the PDRY's NLF. They considered that since the situation in Oman was fairly similar, it should therefore yield similar results.[45] But things were not the same. The character of the population, the economy, the society and the regimes — all of them were different.

A change in the Soviet attitude to the PFLOAG came around 1971, when the USSR began to provide active aid, exploiting Chinese attempts to dissociate themselves at that time from guerrilla movements. At the same time, Soviet influence in the PDRY increased.

Soviet aid to the PFLOAG came mainly through South Yemen and as part of Soviet aid to that country. There was little, if any, direct arms supply, because this would adversely influence Soviet relations with the Gulf states, including Iran. Soviet arms also arrived from Iraq.

A. Vasil'yev, a frequent visitor to the Gulf countries, described 'the liberated areas of Dhofar', where he was impressed by seeing 'fighters' reading Lenin's works in Arabic, and a school named after Lenin.[46] He said that the PFLOAG conference in June 1975 'set the task of intensifying efforts to unite all the principal patriotic groups in the British protectorates. . . . Formation of a vanguard revolutionary party within the framework of the Popular Front was put on the order of the day.' It reflected a Soviet wish for an extension of the Front's activities to even more Gulf states. Turning the Front into a political party could raise Soviet hopes that such a party might become pro-Soviet, although it might also adopt the Chinese brand of communism. Vasil'yev hinted at this. He said that during his visits to Dhofar he had observed 'that Arab translations of Lenin's works were eagerly read'. However 'it is to be regretted that the teachings of Marxism-Leninism sometimes reach the PLF [PFLOAG] activists at second hand, in distorted versions'.[47] This was a clear hint at the spreading of Mao's *Little Red Book* and other Chinese literature among the PFLOAG.

Direct Chinese arms supplies ceased at the beginning of the 1970s. The Chinese wished to develop bilateral relations with the Gulf states and understood that identification with opposition groups would seriously harm this effort. The Chinese Foreign Minister, Chi Peng-lei, on a visit to Iran, gave assurances on 16 June 1973 that China had no hand in the subversive activities across the Persian Gulf and did not support the left-wing guerrillas there.[48]

The competition between the Chinese and the Soviets over the PFLOAG was won by the the USSR. This came, however, at a time of a decline in the power and activities of the PFLOAG. The movement was restricted to the Dhofar province which had no strategic or economic importance, and no oil; it was far from the more populated coast of the Gulf of Oman and from the Persian Gulf oilfields. British, Pakistani and Jordanian officers, joined in 1973 by Iranians, all assisted in reorganizing the Sultan of Oman's forces.[49]

A TASS report of 9 August 1974 described 'a special congress of the Oman and Persian Gulf People's Liberation Front', held 'in the liberated territory of Dhofar'. The purpose was to change the Front's name to Popular Front for the Liberation of Oman (PFLO). The change in name, from PFLOAG to PFLO, was made to give the impression that the Front's aims were being restricted to Oman itself, abandoning its previously declared wish to act in the whole Gulf area.

Moscow radio broadcasts in Arabic calling for support of the PFLO intensified in early 1975 in the wake of reports concerning American plans to use the former British military base on the island of Masirah, belonging to Oman. Soviet commentators compared the situation in Dhofar to that in South Vietnam.[50]

The main Soviet effort in the area was concentrated on maintaining or establishing good relations with the existing regimes. Thus it would seem to have been contrary to Soviet interests to publicize its aid to the PFLO, since this would impede those efforts. However, the USSR also wished to appear as the leader of the communist world and of the world's 'national liberation movement', and this required that it give maximum publicity to its aid to the PFLO. Officially, the USSR, as a state, chose the former course, while the second was proclaimed to be a matter of 'Soviet public opinion' and 'the Soviet people'. In fact, it was no more than a division of functions, with the same people trying to act in both ways.

Iraq — between Identification and Conflict of Interests, Friendship and Suspicion

Diplomatic relations were established between the USSR and Iraq in September 1944.[51] They were, however, restricted to the presence of a few diplomatic representatives in each country. The Soviets considered Iraq a semi-colonial state, nominally independent, but actually subject to British domination. They had an interest in a presence, however limited, in Iraq, for the following reasons: Iraq's proximity to the USSR; the existence, since 1934, of an Iraqi Communist Party; and a large Kurdish minority whose leadership maintained ties with the Soviet Union.

Western plans in the early 1950s to establish a 'Middle East Command' or a 'Middle East Defence Organization' (MEDO), allied to NATO and including Iraq, brought Soviet protests. A Soviet note to a number of Middle East countries on 21 November 1951 stated that their signature to such a treaty would cause 'serious harm' to their existing relations with the Soviet Union.[52]

Iraq ignored such Soviet appeals and decided to break relations with the USSR. On 6 November 1954 it announced its decision 'to save expenses' and close its legation in Moscow. Iraq added that the decision was also in accord with its internal policy of opposition to communism, and so the Soviet Union was asked to close its legation in Baghdad.[53] On 24 February 1955 a Western-sponsored mutual defence treaty known as the Baghdad Pact was signed between Turkey and Iraq. That same year Pakistan, Iran and Britain joined the pact.

The Baghdad Pact evoked considerable anxiety in the USSR. The Soviets felt that it endangered vital parts of their country, exposing it to Western penetration, so they sought ways to circumvent or end it by establishing a presence to the south and west. The Soviet-Egyptian arms deal of September 1955 (announced as an Egyptian-Czechoslovak deal) was a step in the circumvention process.[54]

The Iraqi revolution of 14 July 1958, headed by General 'Abd al-Karim Qassim, brought the re-establishment of diplomatic relations with the USSR.[55] Agreements were signed on trade, and on economic and technical co-operation.[56] Iraq withdrew from the Baghdad Pact and abrogated the 1955 Anglo-Iraqi agreement. Thus on 30 May 1959 the last British soldiers left Iraq. Iraq also abrogated the 1954–5 and subsequent agreements with the USA for American aid to the country.

Egypt was pressing for a union of the Arab world under its leadership and in 1959 Iraq was asked to join the United Arab Republic (UAR) of Egypt and Syria. However, the Iraqi government had no intention of undermining its independence by joining a union dominated by Egypt. It was supported in this by the Iraqi Communist Party (ICP), which now emerged from underground as the most highly organized political force in the country. In the strained relations that now developed between Egypt and Iraq, the Soviets preferred to side with the latter, despite the difficulties such an attitude brought in their relations with Egypt.[57]

Officially, the ICP was illegal; in practice it acted openly, either directly or through 'mass organizations', trade unions and professional bodies, student and youth organizations, in the 'republican vigilance committees', in the ministries, and so on. In early 1959 the ICP claimed cabinet seats and the more militant among the party members demanded and attempted to seize power.

There was a fairly good chance of success for the communists, and the temptation for the Soviets to support such attempts was great. Had the ICP succeeded, the Soviets could have reached the Persian Gulf, outflanked Turkey and Iran and menaced Western oil supplies. But the dangers were also great: success was not fully assured. It might have worsened Soviet relations with other Arab countries and perhaps led to a confrontation with Western powers. The Soviets decided to be cautious. They told the Iraqi communists to drop their demands and make peace with Qassim. Gradually the communists' position deteriorated, they were removed from leading positions and their influence declined, although they continued to be a power in Iraqi politics.

Soviet-Iraqi relations were, however, not governed by Qassim's domestic policy. The Soviet Union was interested in maintaining as strong a presence as possible in Iraq, so Soviet aid — economic, technical and military — continued, even though the Soviet leadership did not approve of Qassim's policies and his attitude to the Iraqi communists.

The Ba'th Party's rise to power in February 1963 met with a sharp Soviet response. The Ba'thist regime immediately began persecuting the communists amid sharp protests from the Soviet Union. Soviet economic and military aid ceased almost entirely. The Iraqi Army, which deployed Soviet arms, remained without spare parts, ammunition and instructors, just at a time when it was fighting the Kurdish revolt. Soviet aid, however, did not stop completely. Some spare parts and other military supplies continued to arrive via East Germany, Hungary and Czechoslovakia.

Following a coup led by the President, General 'Abd al-Salam 'Arif, in November 1963, Soviet-Iraqi relations improved. They remained relatively friendly even after the President's death in a helicopter accident in April 1966, when he was succeeded by his brother 'Abd al-Rahman 'Arif.

Soviet interest in Iraq increased after the 1967 Arab-Israeli war. Iraq's 'anti-imperialist' foreign policy — breaking diplomatic relations with the USA, Britain and West Germany, followed by an anti-Western oil boycott some months later — received considerable Soviet praise. Naturally, the Soviets were anxious that this situation and the regime which brought it about should continue.[58]

The 'Arif regime was overthrown on 17 July 1968, and power passed to a group of army officers headed by General Ahmad Hassan al-Bakr, a Ba'th Party leader who had also held power during the party's rule in 1963. The 1963 Ba'thist regime was well remembered by the Soviet leadership and they were worried that what had happened then might be repeated. But the Soviets soon learned that the 1968 Ba'thist regime was different from that of 1963, and certainly no worse than 'Arif's.[59] As long as the Iraqi government followed, on the whole, the foreign policy of its predecessors, the USSR cared little about Iraq's internal affairs.

The Ba'thists achieved little inside the country and so directed more effort and attention towards foreign policy. They spouted extreme anti-Western slogans and attempted to show themselves as the 'most revolutionary' of the Arab states. They tried to persuade the Soviets that, in spite of their orientation to the right (while in Syria the Ba'th Party regime leaned strongly left),[60] they could be relied upon more than the Syrian Ba'thists. In May 1969, when Syria's Chief of Staff went to Peking, Baghdad sent a military delegation, headed by its Defence Minister, to Moscow to ask for an increase in Soviet arms supplies.

About this time, the Soviets were taking a closer look at the Persian Gulf-Indian Ocean region, and this made them attach more importance to their relations with Iraq. Iraq's relative weight in the Arab world increased after the death of Egypt's President Gamal 'Abd al-Nasir (in September 1970), its interest being focused on playing a greater role in the region's policy-making. The Soviets were keen to strengthen Iraq's role, since it was the only country in the Persian Gulf with whom they had close ties. Iraq well served

Soviet interests there, by reacting strongly against Western pressures and by taking very negative stands against local conservative regimes.

Soviet aid to Iraq was mainly in the form of arms supplies. Here the USSR had a relative advantage, while in other fields they could not compete with the superior technology and resources of the West. Moreover, Iraq, in contrast to Egypt or Syria, could pay for all her purchases. The USSR also provided economic and technical aid for the establishment of industrial enterprises, irrigation and navigation of the Euphrates and Tigris, the creation of a fishing fleet and the development of the oil industry.[61] This was paid for in part with Iraqi oil.[62]

Iraq's isolation in the region, its fear of Iran and its domestic difficulties also contributed to its gravitation towards the Soviet Union. At the same time it was conducting a war against the revolt of its Kurdish minority and struggling against the Western oil companies. Iraq also came out strongly against Western arms supplies to the Gulf countries and the West's strengthening of the region's conservative regimes.

A Soviet-Iraqi treaty of friendship and co-operation was signed in Baghdad on 9 April 1972 by Soviet Prime Minister Alexei Kosygin and Iraq's President, Ahmad Hassan al-Bakr.[63] The treaty specified 'unbreakable friendship', calling for regular consultations and contacts and also co-operation between the parties. The military clause of the treaty (Article 9) specified mutual aid in strengthening 'defence capability', seeking to demonstrate that the treaty was between equals. It gave contractual authorization for the stationing of Soviet forces in Iraq or for Soviet use of Iraqi sea and air bases. Article 10 included an obligation not to enter into a pact for action against the other side, nor to allow use of the territory of either country for activities (military or otherwise) potentially harmful to the other.

The signing of the treaty gave the Soviets a prestige and propaganda advantage, since it was a kind of declaration that Iraq was to be included among the USSR's allies. In practical terms, the treaty was more an expression of the existing relations between the two countries at that time rather than a long-term obligation. The worsening of Egyptian-Soviet relations, less than a year after the signing of a similar treaty between them, showed that a treaty by itself could not determine relations between states. Soviet-Iraqi relations continued to develop according to current wishes and interest rather than in accordance with the terms of the treaty as such. The views expressed at that time about Iraq's becoming a Soviet satellite were greatly exaggerated. It seems, however, that the Soviets did not sufficiently consider the wider impact that the treaty would have on the regional situation. It aroused hostile reactions among Iraq's neighbours — Iran, Saudi Arabia, the Gulf Emirates — and other Arab states.

The strained relations between Iraq and its neighbours made it seek further Soviet aid and protection. This had both advantages and disadvantages for the Soviets. For one thing, it involved the risk that the Soviet Union's good relations with certain other countries, such as Syria, might suffer. For another, there was the danger that the Soviet Union might find itself being drawn into a local conflict in which it had no direct interest.

Such a conflict exists between Iraq and Iran. Baghdad was the headquarters of a movement whose declared aim was to detach Khuzestan province from Iran. In turn, Iran supported the uprising of the Iraqi Kurds headed by Mustafa al-Barzani who had enjoyed Soviet support during periods when Iraqi regimes were out of favour with Moscow. This was so, for example, during the first period of Iraqi Ba'th rule in 1963 which the Soviets regarded as 'fascist' or 'Nazi'.[64] But times had changed: the Ba'thists had become friends of the Soviet Union and there seemed a possibility that the Kurdish struggle might bring about the regime's downfall. Accordingly, the Soviets stopped supporting the Kurds and pressed them to accept what the authorities were ready to offer. The Kurds' foreign relations were being conducted through Iran, but the Iraqi-Iranian agreement of 6 March 1975 to settle the differences between the two countries effectively closed the border to the Kurds, ending Iran's aid.

Officially the Soviets 'expressed satisfaction' with the agreement,[65] hoping that it would leave Iraq free to pursue an active policy in the Gulf and, in particular, to form a radical bloc with Syria to counter the American-oriented Arab states. In fact, things turned out otherwise. Iraq used its new freedom to sharpen its differences with Syria. Furthermore, after the end of the Kurdish revolt, Iraq had less need for Soviet military aid and thus became less dependent on the Soviets. It could now afford to reject Soviet advice and requests.

The Soviets took issue with the Iraqis over their treatment of Iraqi communists. They now pressed for an agreement between the

Ba'th Party and the Iraqi Communist Party, providing for co-operation between them. Such an agreement, establishing a 'National Front', was signed on 17 July 1973. It was warmly welcomed by the Soviets,[66] who hoped that it would at least end persecution of the communists, and make it unnecessary for the USSR to intervene on their behalf. The Soviets therefore pressured the communists to make concessions and accept Ba'thist approaches and policies.

There appeared to be a certain meeting of Soviet-Iraqi interests, but there were still differences and even clashes. Each side was trying to use the other to gain an advantage, often to the detriment of the other side's interests.

Iran — Soviet Attempts to Attract and Control

Iran has had a long history of relations both with the Soviet Union and, much earlier, with Russia's Tsarist regime. It had stood in the way of Russian nineteenth-century advances in Central Asia and Transcaucasia, but later gradually came under Russian control. A Russian-British convention of 31 August 1907 partitioned Persia into Russian and British spheres of influence with a neutral zone between them. The richer northern part was in the Russian sphere — it was in fact under Russian control and only nominally ruled by the Persians.

The Soviet regime which came to power in November 1917 renounced all claims of the old regime pertaining to Persia, and a Soviet-Persian friendship treaty was signed on 26 February 1921.

In Article 5 of the treaty the parties undertook not to permit a third party hostile to one of them 'to import or to convey in transit across their countries, material which could be used against the other party'. They also agreed not to permit the presence within their territories of forces of a third party which 'would be regarded as a menace to the frontiers, interests or safety of the other contracting parties'.

Article 6 declared that in case a third party attempted 'to use Persian territory as a base of operations against Russia' thereby threatening the frontiers of Soviet Russia or its federated associates, and if the Persian government was unable to remove the danger itself, the Soviet government 'shall have the right to advance her troops into the Persian interior for the purpose of carrying out the military operations necessary for its defence'.[67] On 1 October 1927 a Soviet-Persian treaty of non-aggression and neutrality was signed.[68]

With the outbreak of the Second World War Iran declared its neutrality but strongly tended in favour of Germany. The large number of Germans and the German influence in Iran were seen by the USSR and Britain as a danger to them both. So on 25 August 1941, after the Iranian government had rejected an ultimatum to expel the Germans from its territory and to permit the transportation of allied war materials for the USSR over its roads and railways, Soviet and British troops entered Iran.

Iran was once again — as it had been before the First World War — divided into Soviet and British spheres, with the Soviets again occupying the northern provinces. The pro-German Reza Shah was forced to abdicate, being succeeded by his son, Muhammad Reza Pahlavi.

After the end of the war Soviet military forces remained in Iran. In December 1945 two autonomous republics were established, with Soviet backing, in the Soviet-occupied areas: the Autonomous Republic of Azerbaijan and a Kurdish People's Republic. The Soviet military authorities supported their establishment and forestalled any action by the central Iranian authorities against them. But strong American pressure brought a withdrawal of Soviet troops from Iran on 9 May 1946, and the Azerbaijan and Kurdish republics collapsed a few months later, when the entry of Iranian troops met no local or Soviet resistance.

When in 1955 Iran joined the Western-sponsored Baghdad Pact, the USSR viewed the move with much disfavour. It was the same when in March 1959 Iran signed a bilateral security pact with the USA. The Soviets sharply protested, claiming that this was inconsistent with the Soviet-Iranian treaties of 1921 and 1927. A strong Soviet propaganda campaign against Iran was mounted, but Iran, for the most part, ignored it.

When J. F. Kennedy's administration took office in early 1961, the President initiated a process of withdrawal from the region and reduced aid to Iran, considering that the country could well afford to take care of itself. The Shah protested at the move, although there was little he could do to prevent it. He therefore decided to end Iran's sole dependence on the USA and began to improve relations with USSR. In September 1962 the Shah pledged to the Soviets that he would never allow American missiles to be based in

Iran.[69] Agreements were concluded regarding Soviet-Iranian economic and technical co-operation, followed by frequent reciprocal high-level visits.

However, the Shah's fears of Soviet advances in the region made him turn once more to the USA. In May 1972, a few weeks after the Soviet-Iraqi friendship treaty was concluded, President Richard Nixon visited Tehran. He informed the Shah that the US would sell him F-14 and F-15 aircraft and that 'in the future the US would, in general, sell Iran any conventional weapon systems that it wanted'.[70]

This marked the beginning of a boom in American arms sales to Iran. In fact, it began only after the increase in oil prices in 1973 provided Iran with the means to buy what it desired. From 1972 to 1978 Iran ordered about $20 billion worth of US arms, and with the strengthening of Iran's military forces the Shah abandoned his earlier attempts to steer a more or less neutral course between East and West. He became more and more aligned with the USA.

The Soviet media were critical of the Iranian-American connection, but their attacks at this stage were directly primarily against the USA — and even these were mild and indirect, in order not to harm Soviet-American relations. They were also careful not to attack Iran or the Shah directly and their criticism was more in the form of 'friendly advice'. They continued to pretend that friendly relations existed, hoping that the pretence might lead to the real thing.

Factors behind Soviet Successes and Failures

Soviet successes in the Middle East from the mid-1950s to the early 1970s were due in no small measure to the temporary identity of Soviet and local factors which the Soviets could use to their advantage. They saw such an identity as more than temporary, quoting those in the Arab world (such as Iraq's 'strong man' and later President, Saddam Husayn) who termed Arab-Soviet co-operation 'strategic', and described themselves as 'natural allies' of the Arab world.

The following factors are among those that worked to the Soviet advantage:

(1) Anti-Western Arab leaders who wished to rid themselves of

Western presence and influence remembered the earlier colonial or semi-colonial dependence and wanted to demonstrate its end by their anti-Westernism.

(2) The communist model was viewed as appropriate to their needs. Radical Middle East leaders looking for suitable models on which to base their own regimes rejected the capitalist example because they identified it with imperialism and the hated West. The same was true for Western multi-party parliamentary democracy and economic liberalism. Fascism was not fashionable any more either. The communist model, with its centralized rule and state-controlled economy, seemed to suit them best. It would ensure that the regime would stay in power and would give them legitimacy. It gave the cover of a 'progressive' ideology to military dictatorships and enabled them to mobilize the masses. Thus new possibilities of receiving Soviet aid opened up.

(3) Expansionist regimes hoped to export revolutions and revolutionize the region (Nasirism, the Syrian and Iraqi Ba'th Parties, the PDRY regime). Those who opposed them were conservatives leaning on the West. The radicals needed a great power who could help them and found the USSR suited to this purpose.

(4) The Soviets projected an image of being strong, technologically advanced, successful, winning, and ready to help friends and allies.

And yet, in spite of all the above, the more the Soviets became involved in the region, the more differences became apparent between them and their local friends. Complications were due in no small measure to the significant psychological, cultural and social differences between the Soviets and the Arabs. The Soviets had failed to appreciate the impact of factors such as nationalism, religion, tribal and family allegiances, illiteracy and economic backwardness. They discovered that the Arab approach to problems could be very different from their own way of thinking and that, although they often used the same terms, each side interpreted them differently.

Arab leaders wanted Soviet arms but not Soviet advice. They were sensitive to any Soviet interference in their internal affairs or attempts to attach strings to their aid. Arab nationalism, even when radical and socialist, was basically different from communism. It was self-centred, anti-communist and opposed to class struggle, and it stressed the importance of religion.

Among the factors complicating Soviet-Arab relations and underlining Soviet-Arab differences we note:

(1) *The problem of the Arab communist parties.* The USSR established relations with Arab states which, even though they spouted communist slogans and furthered Soviet aims, were anti-communist in their internal policies. Although the Soviet leaders tried to ignore this, they could not remain completely indifferent to the persecution of Arab communists, and intervention on their behalf often worsened relations between the USSR and the Arab states.

(2) *Divisions in the Arab world.* The Soviets were in favour of Arab unity as long as it was directed against the West, but when it was based on local issues common to all Arabs (such as Islamic solidarity) and accompanied by a tendency to turn away from the USSR, then the Soviets pushed for a unity of radical Arab forces to be held together by 'anti-imperialism'. They also worked for a division between 'progressives' and 'reactionaries'.

(3) *Involvement in local conflicts.* The Soviets encouraged disputes and differences between Middle East states which they were able to exploit to their own advantage. However, they became no less involved in local conflicts in which they had no interest at all. Moreover, the more the Soviets committed themselves to helping a particular state, the more obstinate such states became in their local disputes and the more they expected the Soviets to help them. When such aid was not forthcoming, these countries turned their backs on the Soviets.

(4) *Extensive aid did not automatically bring friendship and influence.* The Soviets were now looked on as suppliers of arms and lenders of money. The more aid they provided, the more the local leaders demanded of them. Similarly, the stronger the recipients of Soviet aid became, the less ready were they to accept Soviet advice. Increased Soviet aid did not, therefore, mean increased Soviet influence, and the high costs of this aid usually yielded the Soviets few gains. The question of debt repayment also arose and sharpened relations between borrower and lender.

(5) *The fluidity of Middle East politics.* The Soviets (and they were not alone in this) had great difficulty adapting themselves to the constant changes in the region. Very often policy would be decided on for a situation which existed at the time of its consideration, but by the time a course of action had been determined that situation no longer existed.

As they faced increasing difficulties in the Arab world, the Soviets were forced to devote more efforts towards consolidating their past achievements. This they did by attempting to make the radical states more dependent on them. They sought long-range connections, and attempted to set up states having regimes ideologically closer to their own. This meant additional interference in local affairs, an action which was often strongly resisted by Middle East leaders.

Decline of Soviet Influence and Status

The mid-1970s saw a decline in Soviet influence and status in the Middle East compared to the situation during the early years of the decade. There were many reasons for this, most of them because of changes in the Middle East over which the Soviets had no control:

(1) A new generation of leaders had arisen in the Arab world — less ideological, more pragmatic, and unimpressed by Soviet slogans which they felt belonged in the past. On the other hand, these leaders found much in common with the Western world.

(2) Arab leaders rediscovered the advantages of Western organization and technology. Liberalization began in Egypt in the mid-1970s (a so-called 'open door' policy), and Syria and Iraq applied to Western countries for more advanced technology and in order to diversify their sources of arms.

(3) The Arab world appears to have a pro-Western cultural orientation. Arab consumers prefer Western goods, books and movies, as well as to travel in the West. When able to choose, Arab students prefer to study in Western countries rather than in the Soviet Union. In the Middle East frequent changes in regimes take place, and those who lose power — even the radicals and pro-Soviets — generally seek refuge in Western countries. Communists are an exception, but even among these there are many who prefer Western Europe or Latin America to the communist countries.

The processes described above took place in varying degrees in such Soviet-oriented countries as Egypt, Syria, Iraq, the Sudan, North Yemen and Somalia.

Egypt under Gamal 'Abd al-Nasir was the centre of Soviet

activities in the region until the mid-1970s, when it became disenchanted with the Soviets and moved more and more into the American orbit. Then Egypt became dependent on aid from the conservative Arab states and fell under their influence rather than influencing them, as it had done in the past.

Syria was, to a certain extent, dependent on the Soviets because of the considerable aid it was receiving from them. It was also isolated in the Arab world, so that when in 1975 it became involved in the Lebanese civil war, the Soviets found themselves in a delicate position due to the support that they were giving Syria in Lebanon.

Jordan maintained 'correct' relations with the Soviet Union, but the Soviets, for their part, were not interested in being identified with a regime that they did not believe would last long. Every time the USA refused aid or military supplies to Jordan, King Husayn threatened to turn to the USSR. The Soviets would have been happy to increase their presence there but it was clear to them that the King was insincere, since Soviet aid would have brought with it a strengthening of those forces in Jordan wishing to overthrow him and end the monarchy.

Iraq received extensive Soviet supplies of modern arms, and economic and technical aid. This was no burden for the Soviets as Iraq paid in hard currency or crude oil. But it diminished the advantages to the Soviets of such co-operation, giving the transactions more of a commercial than a political, character.

The Shah's Iran worked against the Soviet presence, activating the region and acting as a barrier against a Soviet advance towards the Gulf. Iran had undertaken to safeguard the free flow of oil through the Gulf, thus maintaining the *status quo* and helping to preserve the conservative regimes in the region. It also took into consideration the possibility of an Iranian-Arab conflict, which would turn Arab nationalism against it. Therefore it tried to strengthen ties with those Arab states who could help to prevent such an eventuality. In the same way it worked to prevent the Iraqi-Iranian dispute from turning into a broader Arab-Iranian confrontation.

The likelihood of an Arab-Iranian conflict was expressed in the differences over naming the Gulf: should it be the Persian Gulf, as is generally accepted, or the Arabian Gulf, as the Arab states call it? Another source of tension, leading to press and radio attacks on Iran, was the involvement of Iran, a non-Arab country, in Oman, an Arab country, since 1972 until the end of the Shah regime in

Iran. In general terms, Iran's growing military power, its control over navigation in the Gulf and its command of the Straits of Hormuz all increased Arab resentment. The Soviets, although expecting a conflict, hoped it would not occur, since anything they did then would be to their disadvantage.

Lower Soviet Priority Given to the Middle East, but not to the Gulf Region

The mid-1970s was also a time of increasing Soviet efforts to give priority in foreign affairs to relations with the developed capitalist world — the USA and Western Europe — and to pay less attention to other arenas. The Soviets paid lip-service to the Third World countries, perhaps as a substitute for doing little for them. This was also the situation during Stalin's time, and some members of the Soviet leadership have continued to share such views throughout the years since then. By the mid-1970s it seemed that the position of this group was gaining increasing consideration. The huge Soviet investments and efforts in the Third World, they argued, had brought the USSR very few gains. They raise the old Bolshevik question of 'Who used whom?' and concluded that in general the Arabs had succeeded in using the Soviets more than the Soviets had used the Arabs.

Developments in the Third World and the Arab countries now became less important to the Soviets. Although they described their aid to the Arabs as part of aid to national liberation movements, such movements lost much of their attraction for the USSR because some, after achieving their aims, turned against the Soviets, or at least did not side with them. The Soviets, believing that they would succeed in turning Arab countries onto a 'non-capitalist path of development' leading to socialism, had invested a great deal of effort and resources in some of them, but with little success.

The importance of the Middle East was now much lower on the Soviet scale of priorities. But this applied less to the Gulf and Arabian peninsula region, as pointed out above, because of its close proximity to the USSR, its rich oil resources and the opportunities that the Soviets believed might open up for them there.

Notes

1. USSR, Ministry of Foreign Affairs, *SSSR i Arabskiye Strany, 1917–1960*

gody. Dokumenty i Materyaly (The USSR and Arab Countries, 1917–1960, Documents and Records) (Moscow, 1961), pp. 60, 797.

2. For Soviet-Saudi relations at that time, see ibid., pp. 61–4, 77–80, 797–8; A. Y. Yoffe, *Narody Azii i Afriki*, no. 6 (1965), pp. 57–66; *Mizan* (March–April 1966), pp. 87–91; Stephen Page, *The USSR and Arabia* (Central Asian Research Centre, London, 1971), pp. 13–24.

3. USSR, *SSSR*, pp. 64–77; 798; A. Stupak, 'Carrying out Lenin's Legacy. Memoirs of a participant in the first Soviet mission in Yemen', *Aziya i Afrika Segodniya*, no. 5 (May 1969), pp. 5–7.

4. USSR, *SSSR*, pp. 124–5.

5. G. Y. Pyasetski, *Na Pustynnym Beregu Tihamy* (On the Desert Coast of the Tihama) (Moscow, 1967). The author was from 1958 to 1961 head of a group of Soviet experts who built the port of Hodeida.

6. USSR, *SSSR*, pp. 124–5, 131, 137–9.

7. *Pravda*, 21 Sept. 1962.

8. Ibid., 2 Oct. 1962.

9. *New York Times*, 16 June 1963.

10. *Pravda*, 25 March 1964.

11. *Al-Hawadith* (Beirut), 15 Dec. 1967; *New York Times*, 14, 15 Dec. 1967. A royalist broadcast said on 3 December 1967 that their anti-aircraft guns had shot down near San'a a Tupolev plane with a Soviet pilot who was raiding royalist positions.

12. *Al-Hayat*, 9 Nov. 1968.

13. *Reuters*, 1 May 1969.

14. F. Halliday, 'Counter-Revolution in Yemen', *New Left Review*, no. 63 (Sept.–Oct. 1970), pp. 3–25.

15. Hanson W. Baldwin, *International Herald Tribune*, 9 March 1969.

16. *Akhbar al-Yawm*, 2 Aug. 1972.

17. *An-Nahar Arab Report*, 14 Aug. 1972.

18. Ibid., 20, 27 Nov. 1972; *Daily Telegraph*, 7 Aug. 1972; *Financial Times*, 4 Oct. 1972.

19. *The Times*, 23, 24 Oct. 1972; *Ath-Thawrah* (San'a), 31 July 1973.

20. *Le Monde*, 12 Oct. 1970; *New Middle East* (Feb. 1971), p. 43; *Reuters*, 14 Aug. 1972; *Ath-Thawrah* (San'a), 11 July 1973.

21. Moscow radio in Arabic, 27 June 1974.

22. *Izvestia*, 3 Dec. 1967.

23. A. Yodfat and M. Abir, *In the Direction of the Gulf. The Soviet Union and the Persian Gulf* (Frank Cass, London, 1977), pp. 103–16; Mordechai Abir, *Oil, Power and Politics. Conflict in Arabia, the Red Sea and the Gulf* (Frank Cass, London, 1974), pp. 75–118.

24. *New York Times*, 8 March 1975.

25. For Soviet comments on the establishment of the UPONF, see J. Alexandrov, 'Democratic Yemen: Towards Unity of the National Forces', *New Times*, no. 42 (Oct. 1975), pp. 16–17; *Pravda*, 11, 14 Oct., 4 Nov. 1975.

26. See, for example, D. Volsky, 'King Faisal's "Holy War"', *New Times*, no. 5 (Feb. 1973), pp. 26–7.

27. Moscow radio in Arabic, 20 Feb. 1973. In FBIS, USSR, 21 Feb. 1973, pp. B6–B7.

28. Faysal wished Podgorny health and happiness, 'and also progress and success to the friendly people of the Soviet Union'. (*Izvestia*, 14 Nov. 1973). Podgorny's reply to Faysal thanked him for the congratulations, wished him good health and happiness, and to 'the friendly people of Saudi Arabia prosperity and progress'. (Moscow radio in Arabic, 4 Dec. 1973). In FBIS, USSR, 5 Dec. 1973, p. F1).

29. *An-Nahar*, 19 Nov. 1973.

30. *Pravda* (31 March 1975) said that King Faysal generally pursued a pro-Western and in particular a pro-American course, but recently his Middle East policy — and particularly his oil policy — was disliked by Americans and he had become 'a major obstacle for some people'. The Central Intelligence Agency (CIA) 'could have been a party' to his assassination. Threats had been made against leaders of oil-producing countries. Was one of them not carried out in Riyadh?, *Pravda* asked.

31. The experience of Kuwait in gaining formal independence . . . shows that self-government alone is not enough. State sovereignty is largely illusory as long as the oil companies retain control of the entire economy of the shaykhdoms.' (Y. Andreyanov, *International Affairs*, Moscow, no. 10 (Oct. 1962), p. 79).

32. Cairo radio, 20 May 1964. For the Khrushchev visit to Egypt see Aryeh Yodfat, *Arab Politics in the Soviet Mirror* (Halsted Press, John Wiley & Sons, New York and Toronto, 1973), pp. 78–9, 227–30.

33. V. Kassis and R. Moseyev, 'The Kuwait Goldmine', *New Times*, no. 52 (30 Dec. 1969), pp. 26–8.

34. A. Vasil'yev, *Pravda*, 10 Oct. 1972.

35. Moscow radio in Arabic, 4 July 1972. In FBIS, USSR, 5 July 1972, pp. B3–B4.

36. Moscow radio stated on 3 October 1972 that Soviet trade with Kuwait amounted to $22 million per annum. About 75 per cent of Soviet exports to Kuwait comprised ships, machinery, electrical equipment, buses and lorries. Exports also included non-ferrous rolled materials, gas pipes, timber, sugar and other goods. The USSR had purchased 32,000 tons of diesel oil from Kuwait 'in the last two years'.

37. *Izvestia* and Moscow radio in Arabic, 19 March 1974.

38. *Pravda*, 14, 20 Jan. 1968.

39. Ibid., 28 Feb. 1969.

40. 'Abdallah Rashid (Member, Central Committee, Bahrain National Liberation Front), 'Bahrain: Fighting for Liberation', *World Marxist Review*, vol. 21, no. 10 (Oct. 1978), pp. 65–8; T. Zumbadze, 'Bahrein', *International Affairs* (Moscow), no. 8 (Aug. 1970), p. 110; A. Vasil'yev, 'Independent Bahrein', *New Times*, no. 35 (Sept. 1971), p. 24.

41. *Izvestia*, 12 Sept. 1971.

42. TASS, 27 Dec. 1971.

43. *Le Monde*, 1 Feb. 1972; Dubai radio, 15 Feb. 1972.

44. *An-Nahar*, 17 Feb., 11 March 1972; *Al-Hayat*, 17 Feb., 25 April 1972; Amman radio, 25 April 1972.

45. An early 1969 Soviet comment said that the Front's activities, formerly confined only to Muscat and Oman, 'have now been extended to the whole of the Gulf area . . . the aim is to eliminate all vestiges of British colonialism and drive the foreign monopolies out'. (*New Times*, no. 1, 1 Jan. 1969, p. 25).

The Front recognizes 'scientific socialism', said a Soviet comment a few months later. It aimed to overthrow the existing regimes before the British withdrawal and to establish its power from the frontier of South Yemen to the Trucial Oman principalities and later to Qatar and Bahrain, excluding only Kuwait. 'The liberation fighters are inspired by the example of South Yemen, whose peoples succeeded in overthrowing their feudalist rulers and uniting their country before they won their independence.' (*International Affairs*, no. 4, April 1969, p. 89).

46. *Pravda*, 1, 3 Aug. 1971.

47. *New Times*, no. 38 (Sept. 1971), pp. 27–30.

48. *Echo of Iran* (Tehran), 17 June 1973.

49. R. P. Owen, 'Developments in the Sultanate of Muscat and Oman', *The World Today* (Sept. 1970), pp. 379–83; R. M. Burrell, 'Rebellion in Dhofar: The Spectre of Vietnam', *New Middle East*, no. 42–3 (March–April 1972), pp. 55–8;

D. L. Price, *Oman: Insurgency and Development*, Conflict Studies (London), no. 53 (Jan. 1975); Penelope Tremayne, 'End of Ten Years' War', *RUSI* (Journal of the Royal United Services Institute for Defence Studies, UK), vol. 122, no. 1 (March 1977), pp. 44–8; Bard E. O'Neill and William Brundage, 'Revolutionary Warfare in Oman: A Strategic Appraisal', *Middle East Review*, vol. 10, no. 4 (Summer 1978), pp. 48–56.

50. Moscow radio in Arabic, 17 Dec. 1974; Moscow 'Peace and Progress' in Arabic, 21 Jan. 1975; Moscow radio in Persian, 7 Feb. 1975.

51. *Izvestia*, 13 Sept. 1944.

52. Ibid., 23 Nov. 1951.

53. Ibid., 8 Jan. 1955.

54. For the Soviet-Egyptian arms deal of 1955 and its background, see Uri Ra'anan, *The USSR Arms the Third World* (MIT Press, Cambridge, Mass., and London, 1969), pp. 13–172.

55. *Izvestia*, 17, 19 July 1958.

56. *Pravda*, 13 Oct. 1958; *Vedomosti Verkhovnogo Sovieta SSSR*, 23 April, 26 Nov. 1959.

57. For Soviet views on Iraq's internal and inter-Arab policies, see Yodfat, *Arab Politics*. For Iraqi positions, see Uriel Dann, *Iraq Under Qassem: A Political History, 1958–1963* (Praeger, New York, 1963); Majid Khadduri, *Republican Iraq: A Study of Iraqi Politics since the Revolution of 1958* (Oxford University Press, London, 1969).

58. For Soviet-Iraqi relations at that time, see Aryeh Yodfat, 'Unpredictable Iraq Poses a Russian Problem', *New Middle East*, no. 13 (Oct. 1969), pp. 17–20.

59. *Pravda*, 12 Aug. 1968.

60. Aryeh Yodfat, 'The end of Syria's isolation?', *The World Today*, vol. 27, no. 8 (Aug. 1971), pp. 329–39.

61. *Pravda*, 18 Jan., 16 March, 25 July 1969.

62. See Aryeh Y. Yodfat, 'Russia's other Middle East Pasture — Iraq', *New Middle East*, no. 38 (Nov. 1971), pp. 26–9.

63. *Pravda*, 10 April 1972.

64. 'The Kurdish Question', in Yodfat, *Arab Politics*, pp. 181–91, 292–5.

65. *Pravda*, 17 April 1975; *Izvestia*, 3 June 1975.

66. *Pravda*, 28 July 1973.

67. Jacob C. Hurewitz (ed.), *Diplomacy in the Near and Middle East: A Documentary Record, 1914–1956*, vol. II. (Van Nostrand, Princeton, N.J., 1956), pp. 90–4; Leonard Shapiro (ed.), *Soviet Treaty Series: A Collection of Bilateral Treaties, Agreements and Conventions Etc., Concluded between the Soviet Union and Foreign Powers*, vol. I, 1917–1928 (Georgetown University Press, Washington, D.C., 1950), pp. 92–4.

68. Shapiro, *Soviet Treaty Series*, pp. 340–1.

69. *Pravda*, 17 Sept. 1962.

70. US Senate, 94th Congress, 2nd sess., Committee on Foreign Relations, Subcommittee on Foreign Assistance, *US Military Sales to Iran. A Staff Report . . . July 1976* (Government Printing Office, Washington, D.C., 1976), p. 5.

2 SOVIET RETREATS IN THE REGION AND ADVANCES AROUND IT (1975–1978)

Soviet Assets, Perceptions, Expectations

The years 1975–8 saw the Soviets losing ground in the Middle East, but gaining in the periphery: Afghanistan in the east, Ethiopia in the south and Libya in the west. Of the Arab countries, only the PDRY had close ties with the USSR, based not only on military co-operation but on a common ideology.

Iraq, Syria, Libya and Algeria reaffirmed their friendship with the USSR and their support for Soviet goals on the world scene. Although they were receiving Soviet military supplies, their ideological ties with Moscow were limited, finding expression in international rather than regional and domestic issues.

Another group of countries, although maintaining full relations with the USSR, were nevertheless considered pro-Western, and were the object of sustained Soviet attempts to improve relations, usually through economic or even military aid. This group included Iran, Kuwait and Jordan.

Still another category comprised countries which had once had a strong Soviet orientation but later switched to the West. The Soviets still had hopes that these would return to the fold — either from disappointment with the West or through a change in leadership. Egypt led this list, which also included Sudan and North Yemen.

The last group of countries — all in the Gulf region, and comprising Saudi Arabia, the UAE, Bahrain and Qatar — had no relations at all with the USSR, but the Soviets were anxious to develop formal ties in order to be able to influence their policies. The Soviet attitude to Oman, however, was different. Here they saw fewer opportunities to change its pro-Western orientation and therefore openly supported those acting to overthrow the regime.

The Soviets recognized the growing importance of the Gulf and their need for a presence there in order to be able to influence events, or at least to be better informed of the situation in the region. Their attempts to this end, supported by local Arab forces, were unsuccessful mainly because of American, Iranian and Saudi Arabian action. The Soviets' position was much weaker here, and the forces they did have were too weak and ineffective to be of much use.[1]

In the Gulf region the Soviets attempted to establish contact with intellectuals, to influence the leadership of labour organizations and infiltrate opposition forces. They did all this very carefully in order not to make it appear that they were interfering in the internal affairs of those countries.

The Soviets have supported the revolt in the Dhofar province of Oman since the late-1960s, considering it to be a nucleus of the revolutionary forces in all East Arabian countries. As noted previously, the Popular Front for the Liberation of Oman and the Arabian Gulf (PFLOAG), which had led the Dhofar revolt, changed its name in August 1974 to the Popular Front for the Liberation of Oman (PFLO) in order to signify that the movement was restricting its aims to Oman alone. A Soviet commentator interpreted it in another way:

> The reason for this is that all the national liberation organizations of the Persian Gulf region which were members of the PFLOAG have been granted political and organizational independence and the right to act independently in accordance with their own programmes and in regard to the local political situation. However, it is envisaged that all detachments of the liberation movement of Oman and the Persian Gulf region should co-operate closely and render one another the necessary support. . .[2]

The Soviets saw no chance, at least during the next few years, of a repetition in East Arabia of what had happened in South Arabia or of the establishment of a radical federation similar to the PDRY.

The Palestine Liberation Organization (PLO) and other Palestinian organizations were viewed by the Soviets not only in the context of the Arab-Israeli conflict, but also as influencing the situation in the Gulf. In the Soviet mind they were a revolutionary element contributing to unrest and instability, around whom all those who opposed ties with the USA and acted against existing regimes could be rallied. This was a role which, in theory, the Arab communist parties should have but did not. The PLO had attempted this in Jordan unsuccessfully and in Lebanon, and could be expected to do the same in other countries with large Palestinian communities, such as Kuwait or Abu Dhabi or even Saudi Arabia.[3]

Soviet advances in Afghanistan, the Horn of Africa and South Yemen gave rise to fears of a Soviet attempt to 'encircle' the Gulf. This led to the Gulf countries increasing their arms purchases and strengthening their ties with the West. The Soviets claimed that US arms sales to the Gulf region were a matter of concern to them since: 'the Persian Gulf countries border directly on the Soviet Union. The territory on which the Pentagon is now so suspiciously active is right near vital centers of the Soviet Union. Naturally our country cannot look on indifferently.'[4]

There was no consistency and no clear line in treatment of the Gulf region by the Soviet media. They attacked the local rulers, describing them as 'reactionary' and 'feudal', fearful of economic and social changes, and spending their petrodollars on arms purchases to suppress 'the national liberation movement' and preserve their positions.[5] At the same time the Soviets also tried to attract these rulers, to persuade those of them who had no relations with the USSR to establish such relations to their own advantage. Such a dual approach was directed primarily at Saudi Arabia.

Saudi Arabia

Saudi Arabia's Internal Situation as seen through Soviet Eyes

After King Faysal's death in 1975, it seemed as if Saudi Arabia would continue as before. Although conservative and isolationist, Saudi Arabia became different from the Gulf states in many ways. It was more aware of the outside world and had more ties with Western countries. Not only did it try to establish its importance in the inter-Arab and the Islamic arenas, but it also hoped to play a role in the Western world, of which it felt itself becoming more a part.

The Soviets watched developments carefully in Saudi Arabia. It seemed as if they knew more about the country than before, but if one can judge from what they wrote or said about it, they did not always understand what they saw concerning Saudi motivation and aims. Some sectors of the Soviet academic community, especially orientalists, seemed to have a better knowledge and understanding of Saudi Arabia, but, with few exceptions, they had little influence over the Soviet decision-making process.

The opinion prevailing in the USSR was that the existing regime would come to an end because of the following factors:

(1) Modernization.
(2) An increase in education.
(3) A rise in the urban population.
(4) Saudi military forces becoming stronger and more influential.
(5) The working class increasing in both numbers and importance, thus stressing 'class consciousness'.
(6) An increase in the strength of the dissidents.

All these, they felt, would eventually lead to a revolution such as those that had taken place in Iraq in 1958 and in Ethiopia in 1974, bringing an end to the conservative regime. They compared the situation in Saudi Arabia to those in Uzbekistan and Azerbaijan before the Soviet revolution, or in Ethiopia under Emperor Haile Selassie or other similar historical situations. These led the Soviets to draw conclusions regarding the outcome of the situation in Saudi Arabia, but they forgot or ignored the fact that things were quite different in the Saudi kingdom.

The Soviet media did what they could to refrain from attacking Saudi Arabia or reacting to Saudi 'provocation', in the hope that they could eventually establish diplomatic relations. Even so, from time to time, their patience would run out and there would then be a frank (or almost frank) outburst of criticism of the Saudi rulers and their policies.

In April 1978, a commentary by V. Kudryavtsev stated that the billions of dollars which Saudi Arabia owned afforded it the opportunity 'to take giant strides along the path of economic and cultural development' and that 'something' was indeed being done in that respect.

> However, the political superstructure is adapting to the changing economy at a snail's pace. Surviving feudal foundations and the unlimited power of the royal family, the fear of decisive steps in the sphere of education, which might lead in the opinion of the ruling clan to a radicalization of the population's opinions — all this is fraught with troubles for Riyadh within the country.

Kudryavtsev is Deputy Head of the Soviet Committee for Solidarity with Asian and African Countries, an organization which serves as a link between the Soviets and 'national liberation movements', supporting those factions in Third World countries acting against regimes with whom the Soviets would like officially to appear as being friendly, or at least not against them. He predicted that the longer the existing regime remained in power, the more radical would be the one which succeeded it:

> As history confirms, the more a country's development is held back by political restrictions and the later a country embarks on the path of progressive development, the more strong, profound and painful are the social and class cataclysms. That is why the Saudi Arabian government is devoting great attention to strengthening the internal political situation.[6]

According to a Soviet comment in mid-1978:

> The oil wealth and the immense currency reserves have impelled the Saudi rulers to modernize their kingdom technically. However, the medieval structures and autocratic rule and the entire anachronistic social and political mode of life have been preserved practically intact.[7]

New Times wrote about 'the large-scale influx of foreigners' to Saudi Arabia and the Gulf Emirates. It said that arduous working conditions and complete subservience to the employers, together with housing problems and the absence of social and political rights, 'breed discontent among migrant workers and are fraught with the danger of an explosion'.[8] The Soviets expected 'an explosion' and were ready to act and influence it when it came. But it could be carried out only by local forces, if such there were, supported by the Soviets.

A Saudi Arabian Communist Party (SACP) was established in 1975. It had only a few members, probably all outside the country, and was no more than a small debating group, whose activities were restricted mainly to issuing statements.[9] A statement by the SACP published in the Iraqi Communist Party's *Tariq ash-Sha'b* said that its creation 'came as a logical result of the growth of political consciousness of the masses, of the activity of the communists there and their bitter struggle for 20 years in a climate of repression and violence'.[10] Nothing was heard about any activities of the SACP, or of its existence at all, until the end of the 1970s.

The Soviets Desire and Expect Diplomatic Relations in Opposition to Saudi Arabia's Wishes

Saudi Arabia's declared aim was to fight communism and diminish the Soviet role in the region. It succeeded in isolating the PDRY, turning Egypt, Somalia and the YAR away from the USSR, and preventing the establishment of diplomatic relations between the Soviet Union and the Gulf Emirates. This was done primarily by providing financial aid. According to a Soviet commentator:

> Saudi Arabia finances reactionary forces not only in Arab countries but also in Africa, Asia and Western Europe. Moroccan forces . . . were transported [in 1977] to the war against the rebels in Zaire at Saudi Arabia's expense. Recently Riyadh gave major financial aid to Zaire . . . encouraged the Somali regime's departure from a progressive course and its aggression against revolutionary Ethiopia . . . Money flows from Saudi Arabia to anti-communist parties and organizations in Western Europe.
>
> . . . Saudi Arabia, when granting credits, strives to dictate a certain political course . . . it allocates resources, sometimes quite considerable resources, to countries that have suffered from Israeli aggression and to a number of Palestinian organizations. At the same time Riyadh welcomes strikes both against the revolutionary wing of the PLO and against progressive forces in Arab countries.
>
> Thus the Saudis spent billions of dollars on Egypt's return to a conservative path.[11]

A condition of Soviet-Saudi Arabian competition developed in the region, with the Soviet side often finding itself the loser.

Although generally attacking Saudi Arabia's policy, the Soviet media would, from time to time, point out the error of the Saudis' not having diplomatic relations with the Soviet Union. They argued that the USSR was anxious to have ties with Saudi Arabia and that the differences in regimes need not be an obstacle. Soviet commentators cited the example of Kuwait which, in spite of having a conservative regime, had diplomatic and trade ties with the USSR.

In the mid-1970s the Soviets saw the chance of a continuing Saudi use of the oil weapon against Western countries, putting the Saudis 'on the same side of the barricades' as the Soviet Union. They considered that in the event of a confrontation between oil producers headed by Saudi Arabia, and consumers led by the USA, the Saudis would have no choice but to ask for Soviet help. The Soviets believed that merely by being available, they strengthened the OPEC countries, enabling them to adopt a firmer position. The Western world 'did not dare' to use force against the oil producers because they had to contend with a possible Soviet reaction or OPEC requests for Soviet help. The Soviets did not believe that the existing regime in Saudi Arabia would last for long. This was another reason for their desire for diplomatic relations. They wanted to be nearby in the event of change, in order to be able to intervene to their own advantage.

A Moscow radio broadcast in 1975 welcomed Prince Fahd's comments regarding the possibility of improving relations with the Soviet Union.[12] Another Soviet broadcast said:

The imperialists made substantial efforts to hinder the normal development of Soviet-Saudi relations . . . which were ruptured through no fault of the Soviet Union . . . The imperialists are persistently scaring the Saudi ruling quarters with the fictitious communist danger . . . Far-sighted politicians in a number of Arab states have recently, and with increasing persistence, called for a settlement of Saudi Arabia's relations with the Soviet Union.[13]

The Soviet media also gave considerable publicity in November 1978 to greetings from Prince Fahd to Brezhnev on the occasion on the Soviet national holiday.[14]

Ever hopeful that relations would eventually be established, the Soviets tried to hasten the process by having their media refer as little as possible to Saudi Arabia or 'Arab reaction', avoiding all attacks on Saudi Arabia's regime, policy and leadership.

Kuwait

The Soviets See a 'Potentially Explosive' Internal Situation

In actual fact, if not formally, Kuwait was dependent on the region's conservative states and the Western powers. But at the same time it carried on a campaign of verbal attacks against the USA, refusing to join Western-initiated defence treaties and supporting Palestinian organizations. The Soviets interpreted this as an expression of the regimes's weakness and its yielding to 'popular demands'. They believed that changes were imminent in Kuwait's regime but for the time being they continued to maintain good relations with its rulers, not offending them by intervening in internal affairs.

The 1975–6 civil war in Lebanon increased Kuwait's rulers' fears of a similar threat to them. Palestinians had great influence and played a major role in Kuwait; many of them had joined the opposition, and radical Palestinian organizations enjoyed the support of Iraq and the Soviet Union. The Kuwaiti authorities decided to take preventive measures, so in August 1976 the National Assembly (the Kuwaiti Parliament) was dissolved, the constitution changed and the press restricted. The latter was in part subsidized by various foreign states or groups.

These measures were indirectly criticized in *Pravda*, which said that the dissolution of parliament (which included many left-oriented members and opposition groups), together with the control of the press, meant 'a deepening of contradictions in the country, in which real power is concentrated in the hands of the ruling oligarchy that is headed by the Emir's family'.[15] *Izvestia* stated that the measures were directed against the Palestinians, from whom there was no 'Palestinian threat', and that they aimed to split the Arab world.[16]

Another *Izvestia* comment dealt with foreign workers in Kuwait and considered the situation which had developed to be potentially explosive:

In Kuwait . . . apart from the Kuwaitis — mainly of the ruling family, the ancient trading races and the former desert bedouins — there are Pakistanis, Egyptians, Palestinians, Iranians, Indians, Yemenis and others. They sometimes serve as officials but more often do the 'dirty work' at oilfields, construction sites and the port . . . These people do not have economic privileges. The oil billions of Kuwait pass them by; they do not participate, so to speak, in the distribution of the wealth.

The clan aristocracy of Gulf countries rich in 'black gold' tolerates foreigners — a work-force to extract the oil is necessary — but is beginning to think seriously about the qualitative and quantitative composition of the work-force, which is regarded as potentially 'explosive'. Social tension, despite the barrier of the immigration laws, is manifesting itself in these countries.[17]

However, in spite of such Soviet views of Kuwait's regime, the USSR had an interest in having close, or at least correct, relations with it.

The Soviets Desire Good Relations

Official Soviet statements described the friendly relations between the two countries. A joint Soviet-Kuwaiti communiqué was issued on 2–4 December 1975, after the Kuwaiti Foreign Minister's visit to the USSR: 'Both sides expressed satisfaction with the development of relations of friendship and co-operation between the Soviet Union and Kuwait and discussed ways of cementing and developing these relations in various fields.' The Soviets were interested in expanding economic and technical co-operation, but did not have much to offer which would compete with Western or Japanese goods. A 'programme of cultural and scientific exchanges' was signed, but it had no real meaning.

Iraq had claims to Kuwait, or at least parts of it, but when Kuwait was taken under the protection of both Saudi Arabia and Iran, the Iraqi option was limited. Iraq could have tried to arouse opposition in Kuwait, but with the adoption of stricter security measures by the Kuwaiti authorities, its chances of success dwindled. Under such circumstances, the Soviets advised the Iraqis not to press their claims for the time being. The Soviet-Kuwaiti statement quoted above called for 'trust and good neighbourly co-operation between countries in the Gulf zone on the basis of non-interference in each other's domestic affairs and respect of each country's right to free and independent development'.

The Kuwaiti Foreign Minister's visit came after Kuwait had taken over, in mid-October 1975, full control of its oil industry. The Soviet side expressed support of measures taken by the Persian Gulf states 'to establish national control over the use of their national wealth, including oil'.[18]

An agreement was concluded to supply Soviet arms in small quantities on a commercial basis, but with no Soviet advisers attached. The Kuwaiti side was interested in the pact in order to satisfy its leftist opposition and to neutralize Soviet support of Iraq against it. The only condition that the Soviets attached was that the arms should not be turned over to third parties without prior Soviet consent. They had proposed sending instructors and technicians to help absorb the arms, but the Kuwaitis rejected the offer, preferring to invite Egyptian and Syrian instructors who were familiar with Soviet equipment. The arms deal was reported to be worth about $400 million and included the most up-to-date Soviet 'Luna' anti-aircraft missiles, SAM-7 missiles, surface-to-surface missiles and anti-aircraft artillery.[19]

Both sides pretended that friendly relations existed between them and exchanged friendly wishes and greetings. Brezhnev sent best wishes to the Emir and the 'friendly Kuwaiti people'. The Emir thanked him and wished happiness and success 'to the friendly Soviet people'.[20] The Soviets were interested in correct working relations with Kuwait to show other countries in the region that they had nothing to fear from establishing relations with the Soviet Union and that they would even gain advantages in establishing such relations.

Bahrain, Qatar and the UAE

Bahrain, Qatar and the United Arab Emirates (UAE) had no diplomatic relations with the USSR, mainly because of Saudi pressure. The Soviets, ever hopeful that relations would be established, tried not to attack their regimes and ruling families openly. But indirectly they encouraged attempts to bring about changes through Iraq, the PDRY, the Popular Front for the Liberation of Oman (PFLO), radical Palestinian organizations and others.

In Bahrain, the Soviets saw that because of its relatively more modernized society, there were more chances for a change of regime, which could lead to the establishment of relations. There were also many nationalist and Marxist organizations with whom the Soviets tried to establish contact.[21]

A Marxist-Leninist Bahrain National Liberation Front (BNLF) was established in the 1950s. In fact, it was a communist party in all but name. A Ba'th Party was set up in 1956, and a Bahrain People's Front in 1973. The workers' trade unions were under communist influence, organizing strikes and leading political activities.

In the National Assembly elections of 1973 the communists formed a bloc with representatives of other leftist forces and won eight seats. Together with independent radical deputies they had a majority in the Assembly.[22]

In August 1975 the National Assembly rejected a government request to put Bahrain's port installations at the disposal of the US Navy, whereupon the Emir issued a decree dissolving the Assembly and returning all power to himself, or to the Council of Ministers appointed by him.[23] From time to time the Soviet media referred to American use of the Ras al-Jufayr naval base,[24] but generally kept clear of the subject of Bahrain altogether.

Qatar took up even less time in the Soviet media. One Soviet commentator described it as 'a country where, despite the radical changes of recent years, the Middle Ages live side by side with the tempestuous twentieth century'.[25]

In the UAE, according to one Soviet commentator, there were 'tribal and clan strife and social contradictions . . . [The country was] suffering from lack of literate leaders and qualified specialists . . . [and] the need to step from desert feudalism into the modern world of capitalist relations'.[26]

Another Soviet commentator said that the UAE authorities, 'finding a common language with the reactionary rulers of Saudi Arabia', supported their policy in the international arena. He also claimed that they had attempted to establish a Gulf countries' military bloc, 'with the aim of suppressing the national liberation movement in the area', and that the UAE joined those who led 'a provocative campaign' against PDRY.[27]

Declarations such as these reflected Soviet thinking, but were of no help in establishing ties with local rulers. The Soviets therefore preferred not to express themselves at all regarding those countries.

Oman: the Soviets Oppose Regime, Ruler and Policy

Oman had no relations with the USSR and the Soviets continued their sharp criticism of its regime and ruler. From time to time the Soviet media referred to the revolt of the Popular Front for the Liberation of Oman (PFLO) in the Dhofar province. The Sultan's forces, aided by forces from Iran and other countries, succeeded at least in containing the revolt, if not ending it. Soviet commentators, however, denied that the war had ended and continued to describe battles and even PFLO victories.

The PFLO was described as 'the largest, best organized and most active detachment of the region's liberation forces', succeeding in creating 'liberation regions' in Dhofar and fighting the Sultan's troops. The PFLO 'relies on the moral and other help of a number of Arab countries', particularly the PDRY, Iraq and other states. Their struggle 'meets with the understanding and support of the peoples of the socialist community'.[28] This statement was carefully worded, expressing support but making no concrete promises of aid or anything else from the Soviet Union.

Similar language was used in an 'unofficial' Soviet broadcast describing PFLO activities. It said, 'As for Soviet citizens, they have been, and still are, by the side of the patriots since the start of their struggle.'[29] Private 'Soviet citizens' may have been on the 'side' of the revolt, but official Soviet aid was not forthcoming.[30]

'Abd al-Fattah Isma'il, the Secretary-General of the PDRY ruling party, was more open about this support. He said in his speech to the 25th CPSU Congress in Moscow on 2 March 1976 that acceptance of Soviet support enabled the PDRY 'to continue to provide support and aid to revolutionaries in Oman'.[31]

A Soviet broadcast to Iran quoted Brezhnev as saying that the USSR supported national liberation movements, regarding them as 'friends in the struggle'. He added, 'These remarks . . . can be applied to the Dhofar national liberation movement.'[32]

The revolt in Dhofar became localized and drew to an end. In 1976, according to Sultan Qabus, there were still about 200 to 300 Dhofari rebels in South Yemen, being trained by experts from Cuba, the USSR, North Korea and others.[33] But by October 1977 it was reported that the last remaining PFLO group had surrendered to the Sultan's forces. The Front was reputed now to be made up only of a few leaders sitting in the PDRY, paid by and under the strict control of its authorities, doing nothing but publishing occasional statements or announcements.

The PFLO failed not only because of intervention by Iranian forces, but also because massive PDRY support dried up after it came to an agreement with Saudi Arabia to receive economic aid. The Soviet Union, unwilling to endanger its good relations with other Arab states in the region, was prepared to aid the PFLO only indirectly, through third parties. Any direct help would have an adverse effect, involving others in the conflict and gaining increased support for the Sultan. So the Soviets continued to give political backing to the PFLO, but no significant military aid.

In early 1977 the Soviets conducted a press campaign against Oman's allowing the United States Navy and Air Force to use the former British base on Masirah island, off the coast of Oman.[34]

Later that year Oman's support of Egyptian President Sadat's peace initiative with Israel was one more reason for sharp Soviet criticism of Oman's policy. Even more frowned upon were the ties established between Oman and the PRC. There had been a time when China supported the PFLOAG, but that had been many years previously. At the end of May 1978 diplomatic relations were established between the PRC and Oman,[35] soon followed by exchange visits and declarations of friendship. The Soviets, who were trying to remove the PRC presence from the region, saw these developments as directed against them and so initiated a noisy propaganda campaign against Sultan Qabus, Oman's regime and its policies.

North Yemen: Instability and Internal Struggles Used by Neighbours and More Distant Powers

The Yemen Arab Republic (YAR) pursued an increasingly independent policy, especially from the time that Lt.-Col. Ibrahim al-Hamdi came to power in mid-1974. The trend away from Soviet influence also continued, encouraged by Saudi Arabia. The latter provided aid in increasing quantities in order to ensure that the Yemenis remained within their sphere of influence. Much of this aid was given in the form of subsidies to tribes. Although the Soviets reportedly offered military aid, no arms deals were concluded.[36]

Al-Hamdi wished to strengthen the authority and power of the weak central government and diminish that of the tribes. He was sincere in calling for unity with South Yemen; his arguments were more than mere slogans requiring lip-service without action. As a first step towards the goal of unity, he tried to reach an agreement towards stronger relations with the PDRY. In order to be less dependent on Saudi Arabia's economic aid he called for an international development conference and asked world finance bodies to assist in the economic development of his country.

Such a policy led to clashes between al-Hamdi and those tribes opposed to a strong central government. He was also opposed by some army officers, as well as by Saudi Arabia. On 11 October 1977 he was assassinated and replaced by Lt.-Col. Ahmad Husayn al-Ghashmi, Command Council Deputy Chairman and Chief of the General Staff. An 'unofficial' Soviet broadcast accused Saudi Arabia of al-Hamdi's assassination.[37]

Al-Ghashmi was more conservative than al-Hamdi. He immediately sought reconciliation with the tribal leaders. In this he was
supported by Saudi Arabia, on whose aid he relied heavily, thus
reducing the need to request international economic assistance.

This was a time of increasing Soviet interest in the region.
Fighting between Ethiopia and Somalia intensified, with Ethiopia
moving closer to the Soviets and Somalia turning away from them.
Moscow had plans for a federation or a confederation of Red Sea
states, including the YAR, so this made the Soviets even more
anxious than before to diminish the Saudi role there and increase
their own. With this aim in mind they acted both directly and
through the PDRY, aided by Yemeni leftist groups and using
slogans of a united North and South Yemen. Responding to
increasing Soviet influence in South Yemen,[38] the USA also began
to pay more attention to North Yemen, and stepped up its military
aid to the country.

President al-Ghashmi was assassinated on 24 June 1978, while
receiving a special emissary carrying a letter from Salim Rubay'i
'Ali, Chairman of the PDRY Presidential Council. The emissary
was carrying a briefcase which contained an explosive device: the
moment he opened the case, it exploded, killing both the President
and himself. Immediately a four-member Presidential Council was
formed, headed by al-Qadi 'Abd al-Karim al-'Arashi.[39]

The YAR broke off diplomatic relations with the PDRY,
accusing the latter, and the USSR, of the assassination. The Soviet
media once more claimed that Saudi Arabia had been behind the
assassination, trying to subvert relations between North and South
Yemen, and using the occasion for hurling 'unbased and false
accusations' at the PDRY.[40] Perhaps the USSR considered it
possible that tension between the two Yemens could lead to war
between them; when reporting on developments in the region, the
Soviet media appeared to be preparing the Soviet public for such an
eventuality. They estimated that in such a situation South Yemeni
forces would have the upper hand.

In mid-July 1978 Major 'Ali 'Abdallah Salih was elected
President of the YAR. He was known as a 'fighter' but was less
successful in overcoming dissatisfaction and opposition. Instability
continued to prevail. On the one hand the power and authority of
the President were limited, while on the other, tribal leaders
increased their power and became less inclined to accept central
government control. A group of military officers made a series of

attempts to seize power; when these failed, they escaped to the PDRY, constantly seeking opportunities to stage a successful comeback with South Yemeni support.

When in May 1978 Major 'Abdallah 'Abd al-'Alim, Commander of the Paratroop Corps, was ousted from the Presidential Council, he attempted a coup in the south of the country, close to the PDRY border. This was soon suppressed, but fighting there continued.

On 15 October 1978 another attempted coup failed at the last moment. One of its leaders, Mujahid al-Kuhali, Commander of the Fourth Infantry Brigade, succeeded in occupying the airport, the broadcasting station and other important centres. But an armoured brigade, loyal to the President and composed mainly of members of his tribe, intervened and defeated al-Kuhali who escaped to the PDRY. Although the struggles between various Yemeni power groups and personalities were internal, they were used by foreign powers, including the USSR, in attempts to push Yemen in a direction of their choosing.

The People's Democratic Republic of Yemen (PDRY)

Military Co-operation

Soviet interest in the PDRY was reminiscent of that which Britain had once had in the port of Aden. The PDRY controls the Bab al-Mandab Straits, and therefore the southern entrance to the Red Sea and navigation there in general. It is close to the Persian Gulf oilfields and to oil transportation routes, to Saudi Arabia, Oman and the Straits of Hormuz. An increasing Soviet naval presence in the Indian Ocean, concentrated primarily in its north-western parts, put the Soviets in need of informal base rights where Soviet vessels could find Soviet technicians, equipment and spare parts, and enjoy the usual services of a base without the political disadvantages of officially calling it such. Services of this kind had been accorded to Soviet vessels and aircraft in the PDRY since the late 1960s, but the Soviet need for them was even greater in the second half of the 1970s.

With the outbreak of the Somali-Ethiopian war in 1977, the PDRY served the Soviets as a trans-shipment centre for arms to Ethiopia. The PDRY and Libya were the only two Arab states to support Ethiopia in the conflict, and PDRY forces even fought there, alongside Soviets and Cubans. It was reported that the Soviets were building a major air base on Socotra to support

Ethiopian forces. Construction was said to involve over 700 Soviet military experts and personnel,[41] but the reports and the numbers seemed exaggerated and were unconfirmed. The number of Soviet military personnel in the PDRY was actually estimated to be about 1,000. Cuban military personnel had been in the PDRY since 1972 and reports gave varying estimates of their numbers — from a few hundred to several thousand.[42]

On 13 November 1977 Somalia announced the abrogation of its friendship treaty with the Soviet Union. It ordered the expulsion of Soviet military and civilian advisers and technicians, ending the special rights of the Soviet military to keep facilities for their exclusive use and also forbidding Soviet use of Somalian military facilities, even though these had been built with Soviet aid and were operated by, or with the help of, Soviet technicians. The Soviets also lost the use of other facilities as follows:

(1) That part of Berbera which had been extended and modernized with their aid.
(2) The use of a communications centre that served as a link between their naval headquarters and their Indian Ocean squadron.
(3) A missile base that included anti-ship missiles.
(4) The use of airfields from which their planes patrolled the north-western parts of the Indian Ocean.[43]

The Soviets removed whatever they could from these facilities, and physically transferred them to the PDRY. Thus a Soviet floating dry dock was transported from Berbera and temporarily moored in Aden. The former British facilities at Aden were extended and used by the Soviets.

At the end of 1977 and the beginning of 1978 there was a massive Soviet airlift of weapons to Ethiopia via Aden. Between 200 and 300 Soviet aircraft carrying T-34 tanks, anti-tank guns, mortars, SAM-7 missiles and petroleum landed at Aden and unloaded at a military base outside the city, reported to be entirely staffed by Soviets. The number of Soviet, Cuban and East European experts in South Yemen at that time was estimated at about 4,000.[44]

President Rubay'i 'Ali was opposed to exclusive dependence on the USSR. He advocated closer ties with the Arab and Western world, and told US Congressman Paul Findley, who visited Aden in early January 1978, that the Soviet Union 'does not have and will not have a military base in Aden'. However, Soviet forces enjoyed the use of the naval facilities there. Rubay'i 'Ali was willing to enter into discussions with the USA regarding the possibility of re-establishing diplomatic relations and was reported to have sent such a message to President Carter through Findley. Findley urged the US government to resume relations with the PDRY, but the State Department did not feel that the existing situation was 'conducive' to such a move.[45]

Admiral Sergey Gorshkov, Commander-in-Chief of the Soviet Navy, arrived in Aden on 18 May 1978 at the head of a large delegation which was not limited to naval personnel alone. The visit ended on 23 May and an agreement was probably reached on even greater PDRY-USSR co-operation, with more rights and facilities granted to the Soviets in South Yemen.[46] Rubay'i 'Ali apparently turned down some of Gorshkov's demands and the Soviets recommended that the discussions should continue in Moscow with PDRY Defence Minister, Lt.-Col. 'Ali Ahmad Nasir 'Antar. Lt.-Col. 'Antar had once been close to Rubay'i 'Ali but during extended periods of study in the USSR his outlook had gradually changed.

At the beginning of June 1978 'Antar was reported to be in East Berlin talking with German Democratic Republic (GDR) Defence Minister, Gen. Heinz Hoffman.[47] A few days later, on 7 June, TASS reported that 'Antar was 'passing through' Moscow, where he held consultations with Soviet Defence Minister, Marshal Dmitriy Ustinov.[48]

Preparations were being made at this time in the PDRY for a full transfer of power to the about-to-be-established Marxist Vanguard Party and the elimination of those opposed to it. The Moscow talks probably dealt not only with the Soviet military presence in the PDRY, but also with the role of the PDRY military and that of Defence Minister 'Antar in introducing the planned changes in the regime.

A Centre for Revolutionaries

It was in the Soviet interest to strengthen revolutionary forces in the region, but generally the USSR preferred not to assist them directly in order to forestall any accusations of interference in the internal affairs of other countries. Such groups often conducted terrorist activities from which the Soviets could easily dissociate themselves. Therefore, they needed a local force that they could covertly assist and which would — on its own behalf, acting as an independent group or country — support revolutionaries or terrorists (often the same people, depending on how they were defined and what the relationship was with them).

The PDRY served such a purpose. It became a centre for revolutionaries, opposition forces and rebels in the whole region: in Saudi Arabia, North Yemen, the Gulf states, Ethiopia, and places even more distant. Here they could set up some of their offices, training grounds and hiding places. From here aid went to the PFLO and the Eritrean Liberation Front (ELF) on the other side of the Red Sea. (This aid ceased with Ethiopia's change of regime and PDRY support of Ethiopia.) It also went to Palestinian organizations: the Popular Front for the Liberation of Palestine (PFLP), headed by George Habash, and Naif Hawatimah's Popular Democratic Front for the Liberation of Palestine (PDFLP). Both organizations had their origins in the Arab Nationalists Movement (*Haraka al-Qaumiyyin al-'Arab*), the same parent organization from which the ruling group in the PDRY National Front had sprung. From the PDRY, PFLP 'foreign operations', sky-jacking in particular, were conducted. In the mid-1970s, the PFLP decided to cease its terrorist activities outside the Middle East. This was sharply opposed by Dr Wadiyah Haddad, who headed PFLP foreign operations. He decided to continue these activities independently, a great number of them from his hiding-place in the PDRY. He was reported dead in April 1978, poisoned by Iraqi intelligence.

The South Yemenis denied that they supported terrorists, but their definition of who were terrorists differed from that generally accepted in Western countries. They loudly proclaimed their support of national liberation movements, claiming that these had a right to struggle by 'all means', including those considered as terrorist in the Western world or even in the USSR.

Economic and Technical Aid

The PDRY was a poor country, undeveloped and without natural resources. It was beset with great economic difficulties and in urgent need of foreign assistance, both economic and technical. Its strained relations with neighbouring Arab states who were rich and oil-producing precluded their providing it with financial aid, and its loud anti-Westernism prevented it from receiving aid from the Western powers.

The Soviets provided economic and technical assistance. Their agricultural development aid consisted of extending farming areas under irrigation, constructing dams, digging wells, building irrigation systems and supplying agricultural equipment.[49] They also developed fishing and ports, thus supporting their naval presence in the region. PDRY students travelled to the Soviet Union and training courses in a number of occupations were organized in South Yemen, staffed by Soviet instructors.

The aid provided by the USSR to the PDRY was small compared to that given earlier to Egypt, Somalia or Syria. South Yemen had not the means to pay for the aid it received and its absorptive capacity was also small. The PDRY leaders hoped to receive more and had tried to prove their aid-worthiness by intensifying their support for the PFLO and Ethiopia, particularly the latter. This did not lead to a substantial increase in Soviet aid but rather isolated the PDRY even more in the Arab world, bringing it into conflict with the countries around it, thus leaving it little choice but to accept whatever the Soviets were ready to provide. It now had no bargaining power to make the Soviets increase their aid.

The USSR and PDRY-Saudi Arabian Relations

Some PDRY leaders, the relatively pragmatic Salim Rubay'i 'Ali in particular, made strong efforts to lead their country out of its isolation by improving relations with Arab countries, and a joint PDRY-Saudi Arabian statement issued on 10 March 1976 announced that they had agreed to establish diplomatic relations.[50] It was reported that Saudi Arabia had given the PDRY $1 billion worth of aid to bolster its economy. It also pledged to pay the salaries of the PDRY Army and police for five years and support its economy, developing the much under-used oil refinery in Aden which had been vacated by the British Petroleum Company.[51]

Initial Soviet reactions welcomed this as a positive step, but they remained non-committal by citing other sources and not presenting their own views.[52] The Soviets were worried that a normalization in PDRY-Saudi Arabian relations might lead to the Saudis 'buying off' the South Yemen regime. According to one Soviet commentator, the elements opposing the PDRY radical reforms 'still entertained hopes of restoring the old order, if only partially'. They pinned their hopes on the establishment of political and commercial relations between Aden and Riyadh, believing that this might lead to a 'de-ideologization' of the PDRY regime, and to 'the erosion of the revolution'.[53] But the most important Soviet consideration was that improved relations between the PDRY and Saudi Arabia might bring about the establishment of USSR-Saudi Arabian relations — something that the Soviets had long desired. To achieve this end they were even prepared to go as far as to endanger relations with the PDRY.

Internal Power Struggles and Changes in Leadership

The establishment of PDRY-Saudi Arabian relations took place in March 1976, during the rule of pragmatic and relatively moderate forces in the PDRY leadership. This situation changed in mid-1977 due, *inter alia*, to developments in the Horn of Africa. The Soviets and the Cubans increased their aid to Ethiopia, sending it indirectly through Aden. Only part of this aid reached its destination; some of it remained behind in Aden. The increased Soviet presence influenced internal power struggles, leading to a strengthening of the dogmatic left. Relations between the PDRY and Saudi Arabia again deteriorated; fighting along the border was renewed and mutual attacks were once more heard in the broadcasts of both sides. Internal disputes within the PDRY leadership had existed since its members came to power. They were divided on many subjects: should they stress socialism, radicalism and ties with the USSR and other communist states, with revolutionary forces all over the world, particularly in the Middle East and the Horn of Africa? Or, without abandoning all this, should they be guided less by ideology and more by practical needs, integrating more into the Arab world in order to be able to enjoy the financial aid of conservative oil-producing Arab states, so that they would not have to lean entirely on the USSR? They could then maintain close ties with the PRC, and re-establish diplomatic relations and ties with the USA and the Western world.

As to regional problems, there was a divergence of views on relations with North Yemen — should the PDRY increase aid to those opposing the YAR regime or improve relations with that regime? Regarding relations with Oman and the PLFO, the question was whether to provide the PFLO with extensive military aid or to stop supporting it. Should the PDRY cease providing shelter and bases to international terrorist organizations and plane hijackers, or should it continue and even increase aid to them? Was it better to have minimal ties with Saudi Arabia or extend them? Should the PDRY provide aid to Ethiopia or not? Should it support Ethiopia over the problem of Eritrea, or should it remain uninvolved in order not to clash with the USSR which was acting to restore Ethiopian rule in Eritrea? On the other hand, perhaps it was better to renew long-standing PDRY ties with the Eritreans even if this meant opposing Soviet positions on this matter.

The leadership was also divided over internal policy. Should they step up the pace of revolutionary change, and struggle against remnants of the old society? They would then rebuild the regime on a Soviet pattern, concentrating power in the hands of a ruling Marxist Vanguard Party, similar to the CPSU, turning the state authorities into a rubber stamp. Or should they, perhaps, without abandoning their goal of rebuilding society along socialist lines, keep a certain balance between party and state (with some predominance of the state), compromising more with traditional tribal leaders and divisions, thus slowing down reforms and liberalizing the economy to a certain extent? The first and more radical trend was advocated by the doctrinaire Unified Political Organization National Front (UPONF) Secretary-General 'Abd al-Fattah Isma'il. The second course, with reservations, was recommended by Presidential Council Chairman Salim Rubay'i 'Ali, a relatively pragmatic man. He was prepared to include parts of the more radical suggestions in his proposals.

The rise in influence of the party increased the power of its Secretary-General Isma'il at the expense of President Rubay'i 'Ali, who also held the title of Party Deputy Secretary-General. Rubay'i 'Ali had the support of part of the military and some of the tribes, while Isma'il leaned on the party apparatus and militia. In May 1978 Isma'il was said to have ordered the arrest of 150 officers who were known to be loyal to Rubay'i 'Ali, because they had opposed the establishment of a Marxist Vanguard Party.[54] Isma'il's power increased as the Soviet, Cuban and GDR presence grew, reaching 6,000 specialists and soldiers by 1978. In late June 1978 they were said to have been joined by about 600 Cuban soldiers who were reported to have taken control of PDRY military affairs.[55] These numbers seem to be exaggerated, but even if they were much smaller the Soviets, Cubans and East Germans were in control of Aden and other central places.

Rubay'i 'Ali used the occasion of Defence Minister 'Antar's absence from the country to try to win military units in more distant places over to his side. Clashes ensued between units loyal to Rubay'i 'Ali and those of 'Antar and Isma'il, who joined forces against the President.

As described above, the President of the YAR, Lt.-Col. Ahmad Husayn al-Ghashmi, was assassinated in his office on 24 June 1978 by a bomb carried by an alleged emissary of Rubay'i 'Ali. The new YAR leadership which convened that same day accused the Aden regime of the murder and immediately broke off relations with the PDRY. Al-Ghashmi's assassination could possibly have also been instigated by Isma'il, with the following motives:

(1) To undermine Rubay'i 'Ali's position, on the eve of his removal from power, by preventing him from receiving aid from Saudi Arabia and the YAR, with whom he had good relations.
(2) Al-Ghashmi was anti-PDRY, and pro-Saudi, leaning heavily on the latter, and thus indirectly on the USA. During his time in office, relations between the two Yemeni republics worsened and it appeared that opposition groups in the PDRY were again being supported by al-Ghashmi.

In South Yemen, according to the official PDRY version, an emergency UPONF Central Committee meeting was convened on the evening of 25 June 1978. Rubay'i 'Ali refused to participate and this was interpreted as his resignation. The Central Committee decided to remove him from all his positions. Rubay'i 'Ali then tried to stage a coup and seize power. Fighting continued all the next day, 26 June and an attempt to take power by forces faithful to Rubay'i 'Ali ended in failure. Rubay'i 'Ali was tried and executed.[56]

Isma'il and the Soviets had won a battle while Saudi Arabia and the USA had lost one. This was a blow to Saudi attempts to make the PDRY regime more moderate and remove the Soviets. It was more than symbolic that on 26 June 1978, the day of Rubay'i 'Ali's defeat, an American State Department delegation arrived in Aden for talks with him, perhaps as a step towards the renewal of diplomatic relations.

The Soviet media described these events in the PDRY as a plot inspired by Saudi Arabia, with American backing, whose purpose was to bring about a PDRY-YAR conflict, making possible Saudi involvement which would then lead to a change of both regime and policy in the PDRY.[57] Arab and Western media reports of Soviet, Cuban and East German involvement were naturally denied.

The Soviets Promise Support but are Careful not to Commit Themselves

The Soviets feared that events in the PDRY and the YAR at the end of June 1978 could lead to hostilities between the two Yemens, with the possible involvement of other countries. The USSR had no interest in such a situation and tried to prevent it. The PDRY leadership 'is now doing everything possible to prevent an armed conflict', said a Soviet commentator. He expressed hope that there would be no war but was careful not to commit himself or say what the Soviet Union would do if such a conflict broke out.[58] A broadcast the following day advised the PDRY to avoid conflict, recalling the good Soviet relations with both the PDRY and the YAR:

> As for the threats, the PDRY, a sovereign state, is not alone. The progressive forces will not leave it alone to face the danger. The socialist countries and all true friends of the Yemeni people . . . express the hope that the leaders of the two Yemeni states are capable of wisdom and vision and will not allow fabrications of new disputes among Arabs. The Soviet Union, which has good relations with the PDRY and the YAR, is naturally working to provide a good atmosphere between these two Yemeni states.[59]

The message, clearly addressed to the PDRY leadership, was that the Soviet Union wanted no conflict and wished the leadership to act accordingly.

A more official message from Brezhnev to 'Ali Nasir Muhammad al-Hasani, congratulating him on his appointment to the post of Chairman of the Presidential Council, was carefully worded. Brezhnev wished:

> the friendly people of Democratic Yemen . . . further success in strengthening their national independence and in implementing progressive socio-economic transformations. The Soviet people have given and will continue to give the PDRY aid and support in this matter.[60]

'The Soviet people' (not the Soviet state) would give aid and support to implement reforms. But what in case of war? Brezhnev was silent on this point.

The Soviets soon realized that the danger of armed conflict had passed, so they again began to speak of possible aid to the PDRY. However, they knew that they must not do anything to encourage conflict, so they chose their words very carefully. TASS quoted PDRY Foreign and Defence Ministers as saying:

> There is no 'Soviet interference' in the affairs of our country, there are no Soviet or Cuban troops in the PDRY, and no foreign war bases . . . the Soviet Union is giving us selfless aid. We shall keep strengthening fruitful co-operation with the USSR and other countries of the socialist community.[61]

The Soviet military daily *Krasnaya Zvezda* described a continuing threat to the PDRY. It claimed that Saudi Arabia was concentrating forces near the PDRY border and that an Iranian expeditionary force was on the eastern borders of the PDRY, helping Sultan Qabus. PDRY Defence Minister 'Ali 'Antar was quoted as saying that 'in the event of an attack . . . we shall turn to our friends'. *Krasnaya Zvezda* went on:

> As far as the Soviet Union is concerned, it is always prepared to act consistently on the side of people defending their right to independent self-determined development. The Soviet people decisively condemn the subversive activity and plots against Democratic Yemen . . . The Soviet people have given and will continue to give help and support to the PDRY to strengthen its national independence and implement progressive socio-economic transformations.[62]

Help and support were promised, implying political and moral support and arms shipments, but no direct Soviet involvement or fighting.

On 19 August 1978 'a unit of Soviet warships' arrived 'on an official friendly visit' to the port of Aden.[63] In November 1978 there were reports of Soviet combat aircraft being sent to bases in the PDRY.[64] The air base in Aden was used by Soviets, as in the past, for servicing logistic and support aircraft *en route* to Ethiopia and Mozambique.

The Western media generally tended to exaggerate the numbers of Soviets and Cubans in the PDRY. It seemed that the numbers given in early December 1978 by Hodding Carter, spokesman of the US State Department, fitted the facts most closely. He estimated the total number of Soviet, East German and Cuban experts in South Yemen at 1,300, pointing out that more than half of them were civilians. The military advisers were: 300 Soviets attached to the armed forces: 300 Cubans in charge of training people's militias; and some 100 East German police in charge of reorganizing internal security.[65]

There were no Soviet military bases in a literal sense, in other words, no territory in which the Soviets had extra-territorial privileges. But extensive rights were given to Soviet ships or planes in the port of Aden and at the country's airports. The PDRY leadership was prepared to allow the Soviets the use of South Yemen's military facilities (a great number of which had been built with Soviet aid) but preferred control over them to remain in their own hands.

The Establishment of the Ruling Yemeni Socialist Party (YSP)

The PDRY was the only Arab country whose regime was similar to that of a communist country and whose relations with the USSR were based on a common ideology. As between communist countries, relations were established at various levels: between ruling parties, governments, military leadership, 'popular organizations' and others.

Close ties developed between the Unified Political Organization National Front (UPONF) and the CPSU. A programme agreed upon in Aden on 15 March 1978, outlining party links between them for 1978–9, said, *inter alia*:

The sides agreed to exchange party delegations and ideological workers . . . It is envisaged to develop co-operation in the field of training party and political cadres, to give assistance to the higher school of scientific socialism under the UPONF Central Committee in scientific-methodological and organizational-practical works.

The CPSU and the UPONF . . . will further contribute to the development of mutual contacts and ties between trade union, youth and women's organizations, friendship societies, and exchange party documents and publications.[66]

After extensive preparations and internal power struggles, the first Congress of the Yemeni Socialist Party (YSP) was convened on 11 October 1978, taking the place of the UPONF. Greetings sent by the CPSU Central Committee to the YSP Congress wished it:

> Success in achieving the task before it — the establishment of a vanguard party, guided by the principles of scientific socialism . . .
>
> In its efforts to continue the social progress and in its efforts against imperialism and reaction, Democratic Yemen can rely on the support and solidarity of the Soviet people and the CPSU in the future as well.[67]

The YSP was organized on the pattern of a communist party and could be considered as such. However, it was careful to play down its being communist or Marxist-Leninist, avoiding the use of such terms in order to prevent excessive alarm among its opponents. It was not a mass party. Cadres and militants were chosen very carefully. Membership was restricted to industrial and agricultural workers, fishermen, intellectuals and soldiers. Candidates for membership were well screened.

By the end of 1978 the party numbered about 25,000 affiliate-members and candidates (the total population of the PDRY is about 1.8 million). It controlled much larger 'mass organizations' which had tens of thousands of members: trade unions, youth and women's organizations, people's militia, farmers' and fishermens' co-operatives, and so on.

The YSP, like the CPSU, was the supreme body in the country, with the government existing merely to execute party policy and decisions. Its Secretary-General, 'Abd al-Fattah Isma'il, like Brezhnev in the USSR, was also Chairman of the Presidium of the PDRY Supreme People's Council.

Continued Internal Power Struggles

The leadership changes which took place at the end of June 1978 and the establishment of the YSP were only stages in the jockeying for positions and power. Rubay'i 'Ali's execution marked the opening of a widespread purge throughout army ranks, party apparatus and the government administration. Persons loyal to Rubay'i 'Ali's pragmatic policies and elements labelled 'rightist-reactionary' were removed from influential positions. There were reports of clashes between various power centres, such as the fighting in November 1978 between the YSP militia and military units.

The rivalries were as follows: old-guard National Liberation Front (NLF) veterans versus those who later joined the ruling party; native southerners versus those from North Yemen; city-dwellers from Aden versus people with a tribal background; civilians versus military. But stronger than all those were the personal rivalries.

Three main groups evolved:

(1) *The old guard.* This was composed of veteran members of the NLF who believed that South Yemen should follow a more moderate and pragmatic line, steering clear of total dependence on the Soviet Union — which they feared could result in the PDRY's isolation from the rest of the Arab world. They were also concerned that economic development was retarded since, in the existing circumstances, the capital investment and other aid required could come only from the Soviet bloc. But the Soviets continued to treat South Yemen with extreme parsimony. This implied that some reconciliation with Saudi Arabia and North Yemen was in order.

Key members of the old guard included: 'Ali Nasir Muhammad al-Hasani, Chairman of the Presidential Council; Saleh Muslih Qassim, the Interior Minister; Muhammad Salih Muti', the Foreign Minister; 'Ali 'Antar, the Defence Minister, and 'Abd al-'Aziz 'Abd al-Wali, the Finance Minister.

Most of the old-guard leaders were of South Yemeni tribal origin — in other words, neither from the city of Aden nor from North Yemen. Internal rivalries in this group resulted in temporary coalitions which changed from time to time. The background to these was mainly personal.

(2) *'Abd al-Fattah Isma'il loyalists.* These people were primarily concerned with maintaining their existing positions of power. Isma'il had been able to exploit mutual jealousies and ideological differences between the other factions to his own advantage. His aim had been to bring North Yemen under South Yemen's control. His group was generally represented as being mainly of North Yemeni origin, whose members had integrated into the public life of the city of Aden. But this was only a generalization since Isma'il and a number of people loyal to him were also of the 'old guard'.

Isma'il was a Shi'a Muslim and the Saudis were well aware of this. Although a Marxist, advocating a pro-Soviet policy, he was independent enough not to accept everything that came from

Moscow. He saw himself as 'a better Marxist' than many Soviet leaders whom he considered as deviants (because of their Soviet interests) from the 'true faith'. He too was in favour of maintaining relations with Saudi Arabia, at least in order to receive financial assistance. The image he presented — and for tactical reasons he often preferred to have such an image, at least in Soviet eyes — was that of a strictly doctrinaire adherent to Marxism-Leninism, with an over-zealous inclination towards the Soviet Union.

(3) *A Communist-Ba'thist group.* This group called for the closest possible relationship with the USSR and for strict obedience to Soviet policy directives. The Ba'thists were rather more pro-Iraqi than pro-Syrian. The most influential figure in the group was 'Ali 'Abd al-Razak Ba'dhib, leader of a small communist party which united with the ruling party in 1975.

The various groups, factions and personalities, holding opposing views on foreign policy, were in fact a reflection of personal or factional power struggles. There were usually — contrary to descriptions by the Western media — no serious divisions between pro-Soviets and Marxists and their opponents. All the members of the top leadership were, to a certain extent (at least outwardly), pro-Soviets, Marxists, Arab nationalists and pragmatists. Most of the pro-Soviets were not anxious to be fully dependent on the Soviet Union, nor did they wish to be completely isolated in the Arab world. All wanted to receive foreign aid both from the USSR and from the conservative Arab states.

The divisions and rivalries among the PDRY leadership did not feature foreign relations as the top-priority issue. There were no real groups which had crystallized to any extent, but rather *ad hoc* alignments and coalitions of personalities. For the Soviets this meant that the positions over which they had acquired control in the PDRY were not certain or permanent and could be subject to possible challenges from within.

The Red Sea — 'Red' or Arab?

Plans by the conservative Arab states to proclaim the Red Sea an 'Arab lake' met with strong Soviet opposition. The Soviets saw it as an attempt to oust them from that area and, even worse, as a threat to their navigation, since the sea route from the Black Sea, through the Mediterranean, Red Sea and Indian Ocean is one of the main links between the European part of the USSR and the Soviet Far East, much as the Panama Canal serves the USA.

The Soviets had long been established in the PDRY and Somalia, but in early 1977, when war broke out between Somalia and Ethiopia, they strengthened their ties with the latter. This posed new problems for them: how to maintain good and balanced relations with both countries without losing either. As a first step they put much effort into attempts to effect a reconciliation between their friends, the two enemies.

The USSR proposed the establishment of a federation of the region's pro-Soviet countries. The idea was put forward in March 1977 at a meeting in Aden between Fidel Castro and the heads of the PDRY, Somalia and Ethiopia, Salim Rubay'i 'Ali, Muhammad Siad Barre and Mengistu Haile Mariam, respectively. Castro suggested a federal union of the three states, and also an autonomous Eritrea and Djibouti (the latter became independent on 27 June 1977). However, Somalia rejected the proposal.[68]

An Arab counter-proposal suggested a regional organization (without clearly defining its form) which would include both the PDRY and the YAR, and, on the other side of the Red Sea, Somalia, Sudan, Djibouti and Eritrea. This organization was aimed mainly against the USSR, in an attempt to remove it from this region, but it was also against Ethiopia which had been exluded and, of course, Israel.

On 22–23 March 1977, about a week after Castro's tour, a quadripartite summit conference of the heads of state of the PDRY, the YAR, Sudan and Somalia was held in Taiz in North Yemen. The concluding statement described in general terms the subjects on which all the participants in the meeting were agreed.[69] There was no talk of removing the great powers from the Red Sea, since the PDRY and Somalia would not have accepted an anti-Soviet declaration. However, the mere fact that ties had been established between the participants was significant. Saudi Arabia, which was actually behind the conference, was ready to increase its financial aid in order to persuade the PDRY and Somalia to reject the Soviet-Cuban proposals and to work instead towards making the Red Sea an Arab lake.

The Soviet media sharply attacked these plans,[70] and a hidden struggle developed for the control of the Red Sea and its character. On one side stood Saudi Arabia (backed by the USA), which used its financial resources to turn its local friends away from the USSR. On the other side stood the USSR, using local and peripheral proxies — the PDRY, Libya and Cuba — and increasing its presence in the PDRY and Ethiopia.

Iraq

Soviet Expectations and Disappointments

Iraq was isolated in the Arab world and particularly in its own area; its friends, Libya and Algeria, were far away. Closer at home, it was in conflict with Syria and continued to fear Iran, even though Iran and Iraq had signed an agreement in March 1975. When Iraq loudly proclaimed its anti-Westernism and its opposition to conservative regimes, it was immediately suspected by Saudi Arabia and the Gulf countries for this radicalism and its apparent wish to overthrow their own governments. Iraq also spoke out against Egypt when that country turned towards the USA and peace with Israel. All these factors were conducive to a certain convergence of Soviet-Iraqi interests.

The Soviet media frequently referred to the friendship and the treaty between the two countries. The USSR was Iraq's major arms supplier, and also provided economic and technical aid and political support. This led the Soviets to entertain certain expectations as to how Iraq should act and what it should do for them. In this, however, they were disappointed, and they accused Iraq of being ungrateful when it failed to fulfil these hopes. Iraq was carrying out an independent policy; thus the Soviets were unable to use Iraq for their own purposes. They were suspicious of Iraq and made no secret of this fact; they protested and tried to intervene. This resulted in Iraqi reactions and Soviet counter-reactions, all contributing to a worsening of relations.

The policies that the Soviets had tried to encourage Iraq to adopt were the following:

(1) In bilateral and international relations: strengthen ties with the USSR and adopt an exclusive orientation towards it; abandon flirtations with the USA, Western Europe, Iran and Saudi Arabia.
(2) In inter-Arab relations: improve relations with Syria; establish a radical Arab front (to include Iraq, Syria, Libya, Algeria and the Palestinians); turn against the USA and pro-

Americans (Egypt and Saudi Arabia).

(3) In the Gulf region: adopt a more active policy supporting the revolt in Dhofar and other revolutionary movements.

(4) In the Arab-Israeli conflict: accept (or at least not lead an active opposition against) Soviet initiatives for a political settlement and its attempts to convene the Geneva Conference on the Middle East (of which the USA and the USSR were co-chairmen). These Soviet initiatives ceased when President Sadat went to Jerusalem in late 1977. The USSR and Iraq then initiated a joint Soviet-Iraqi effort against the Sadat-initiated peace process.

The Soviets wanted to turn Iraq into a surrogate, acting for them in the Gulf and serving as a centre of activities against regimes there. Iraq had been prepared to do this in earlier years but without much success. Iraq abandoned this strategy in the second half of the 1970s after improving relations with Iran and Saudi Arabia.

The Soviets were ready to supply sophisticated arms, economic aid and political support because the cost to them was low. There were even certain economic advantages, as Iraq could pay in hard currency or oil. The Iraqis, however, wanted the aid and the supplies without any political strings attached. These matters were discussed with USSR Premier Kosygin, during his visit to Iraq from 29 May to 1 June 1976. An agreement on economic and technical co-operation was signed during the visit. The joint statement also referred to CPSU-Ba'th inter-party relations: 'They reaffirmed their desire and readiness to deepen and extend co-operation between the two parties at various levels.'[71] The Soviets were interested in this co-operation because it would enable them to penetrate the Ba'th Party cadres at lower level and influence them from within. The Iraqis were suspicious, however, and only paid lip-service to the subject without doing much about it.

One item which complicated Soviet-Iraqi relations was Iraq's treatment of its communists. The Soviets wished to widen the role of the Progressive National Front (PNF) that had been formed in 1973, including the Ba'th Party, the Iraqi Communist Party (ICP) and other small parties. This would prevent the persecution of Iraqi communists, a problem which put the Soviets on the horns of a dilemma — whether to intervene on behalf of the communists at the expense of good relations with Iraq, or to do nothing and lose prestige. The more active Front might also make it possible, however remotely, for the communists to influence Iraqi policy.

In Lebanon too, during the 1975–6 civil war, the USSR had been in a delicate position, with its allies fighting each other. Iraqis, Syrians, Libyans, Palestinian organizations, the Lebanese left and the communists — all of them had received Soviet aid, either directly or indirectly, but they were all involved in Lebanon on conflicting sides, fighting among themselves. To support the Iraqis would have put the USSR against the Syrians, while supporting the Syrians would have meant it was against the Palestinians, leftists and communists.

Kosygin failed to bring about changes in Iraq's policy which would have made it more to Soviet liking. He did, however, take into consideration the fact that the existing Iraqi regime was better for the Soviets than the alternatives. He knew that the Soviets had no choice but to support Iraq as it was — maintaining the existing situation and preventing any deterioration in Soviet-Iraqi relations.

Military and Economic Co-operation

A series of agreements were concluded between the two countries on military and economic co-operation. The Soviets supplied arms needing replacement, spares, ammunition, instructors and technicians. The Iraqis were careful not to provide the Soviets with any substantial independent military facilities or services — as other Arab states did — but allowed them the use of some Soviet-built bases or other facilities under Iraqi control and supervision. Soviet military personnel in Iraq at this time numbered about 1,000.

The Iraqis also attempted to lessen their dependence on the USSR by purchasing arms in Western countries — aircraft in France and naval equipment in France and Italy. Economic ties, however, continued. In July 1975 an agreement on co-operation between Iraq and the Council for Mutual Economic Assistance (CMEA, or Comecon, the communist counterpart of the Western European Economic Community) was signed in Moscow.[72]

Iraq now began to think about ambitious development projects, for whose implementation the technology of the USSR and other CMEA countries was not sufficient. The USSR could no longer cope with the multitude of projects for which Iraq paid in cash and in hard currency. Iraq wanted the best and most advanced technology, and this could only be found in Western countries, which purchased large amounts of oil from Iraq and were anxious to improve their balance of payments. These countries therefore made great efforts to extend their exports to Iraq. Their stronger economic capabilities, together with government financial support and guarantees, gave Western European countries a competitive edge over the USSR. And so Soviet economic co-operation with Iraq gradually declined, while that of the Western countries increased. This was also true for Iraqi trade with the USA, despite the lack of diplomatic relations between the two countries.

Common Interests Stronger than Differences

The Soviets now concluded that in general the regional situation was deteriorating. As far as Iraq specifically was concerned, they felt they had reached the limit of what they could get out of it, and so began to make fewer demands. Nevertheless, because of the worsening general situation, the Soviets attached greater importance to their links with Iraq. This found expression during a visit to the USSR by Iraq's 'strong man' Saddam Husayn from 31 January to 3 February 1977. The joint Soviet-Iraqi communiqué said that 'the friendly relations between the two countries had been steadily developing and growing stronger'. It mentioned military co-operation, stating that both sides 'reaffirmed their readiness to continue co-operation in the strengthening of the defence capability of the Republic of Iraq'. On economic and technical co-operation, reference was made to co-operation in oil extraction, power generation, machine manufacture and irrigation. The communiqué also specified completion of the construction of the oilfield in North Rumaylah and the building, with Soviet technical assistance, of the Lake Tartar-Euphrates River canal.

As regards Ba'th-CPSU inter-party ties: 'a useful exchange of experience . . . [was] being carried out' and continued 'to be developed successfully'. Regarding Iraq's internal politics: 'The Soviet side highly values the revolutionary experience amassed by the Iraqi people under the leadership of the progressive forces.' It was a compromise formula on the position of the communists in Iraq.[73]

Diverging Soviet-Iraqi positions also became evident regarding developments in the Horn of Africa. The Iraqis sided with Somalia against Ethiopia and, to an even greater extent, with the rebels in Eritrea against Ethiopia. They considered them an Arab national liberation movement against non-Arab rulers and so provided them with military, material and political support. The Iraqis warned the

the Soviets against military involvement on the side of Ethiopia, or any attack against the Eritrean rebels.[74]

A coup in Afghanistan on 27 April 1978 brought to power Nur Muhammad Taraki, leader of the communist People's Democratic Party (PDP). While there was no firm evidence that the Soviets had been directly responsible for installing the new Afghan regime, Iraqi leaders believed this to be the case. They feared that the Soviets might act in Iraq in a 'similar way', and moved to forestall this by arresting communists and restricting communist activities.

In May 1978 a large-scale wave of arrests among the ranks of the ICP and its cadres was carried out.[75] The communists were told they should 'know their place' and refrain from undertaking any political activities in the armed forces. These were permitted only to the Ba'thists. Communists who sinned in this respect were arrested, and some of them executed.[76]

Reports circulated of a Moscow-backed attempt to overthrow the regime in Iraq and replace it with one more loyal to the Soviet Union. The source seemed to be Ba'thist circles who sought this pretext for undertaking widespread purges in the army and for arresting many officers and soldiers on charges of collusion in the attempted coup. Iraq then reportedly closed its airspace to Soviet warplanes and suspended the use of military facilities for Soviet warships.[77]

At that time there were those in the Iraqi leadership who strongly advocated abrogating the friendship treaty with the Soviet Union as Egypt had done in 1976 and Somalia in 1977. This would have brought the country closer, if not to the West, then to a neutral and non-aligned position. The conclusion was, however, that Iraq would gain more by maintaining the treaty. The Soviets too preferred it to remain in force, even though stripped of much of its content. *Pravda* quoted Na'im Haddad, member of the Revolution Command Council, who denied reports by Western information agencies that Iraq intended to cancel the friendship treaty with the USSR. He said that such reports 'have nothing in common with reality'.[78]

Officially, friendship with the Soviet Union continued to prevail but pro-Soviets were suspect. They were removed from their positions and arrested. It was then reported that pro-Soviet officers had been dismissed, merely for having considered opposition to the Iraqi policy of diversifying arms sources so as not to be entirely dependent on the Soviet Union. About 1,000 communists were arrested and 40 of them were executed.[79]

Soviet reactions were relatively restrained. Although they hinted at their displeasure they refrained from public criticism in order to avoid a rift similar to that which occurred when the Iraqi Ba'thist regime rose to power in 1963.[80]

The matter was dealt with at a conference of 'Communist and Workers' Parties of Arab Countries' held in December 1978. A conference statement published in Damascus gave neither its venue nor a list of the participants. The statement called for a common Arab front 'against imperialism, Zionism and Arab reaction' (a slogan constantly used by the Ba'thists). This front was to include communists, Ba'thists, Nasirists, socialists, nationalists 'and also all Arab revolutionary forces'. But instead, 'a dangerous split' occurred. In Iraq repressive measures were taken against the ICP. 'The communist and workers' parties of the Arab countries condemn such methods in relations with revolutionary forces,'[81] said *Pravda*. The language was relatively mild, mostly because of Soviet pressure.

American-Egyptian-Israeli agreements were concluded at Camp David on 17 September 1978. An Arab summit conference was convened in Baghdad from 2 to 5 November 1978 in order to take action against these agreements.[82] In Soviet eyes the problem of the Iraqi communists was small compared to the importance of having Baghdad serve as a centre of activities against the American-supported peace process. From 11 to 13 December 1978 Saddam Husayn was in the Soviet Union, where he and the Soviet leaders 'strongly condemned' the Camp David agreements and the Soviet side 'highly assessed' the Baghdad conference. The joint statement said:

> The sides noted with satisfaction the steady and fruitful development of Soviet-Iraqi relations on the firm foundation of the treaty of friendship and co-operation . . .
> The sides reiterated their readiness to keep co-operating in strengthening the defence capacity of the Iraqi Republic.[83]

The statement did not mention the treatment of Iraqi communists. They had been abandoned by the Soviets in the interests of a common Soviet-Iraqi opposition to the Camp David agreements and the USA.

Although the Soviets and the Iraqis differed on a number of

issues, each felt that the other was better than nothing — 'a bird in the hand'. They had a common stand on international affairs and the Iraqis needed Soviet military supplies and political support. There was also a common opposition to the Egyptian-Israeli agreements — this released Iraq from its year-long isolation in the Arab world and enabled it to achieve a stronger position there. The Soviets were prepared — at least for the time being — to help Iraq in this. All these factors made their mutual wish to co-operate stronger than their differences.

Iran

Improve Relations while Each Country Acts against the Other

Soviet-Iranian relations in the mid-1970s and during the last years of the Shah's rule were characterized by two contradictory trends. On the one hand there was an apparent improvement of relations, embodied in official declarations of friendship, closer economic ties, increased bilateral trade and frequent reciprocal visits during which both sides expressed their hopes for still further improvement. On the other hand, each side continued along its own path in foreign policy, with Iran seeking to reduce as much as possible the Soviet presence and activity in the Middle East.

Iran's interest extended further west to the Red Sea, the Horn of Africa and the eastern Mediterranean area. It provided aid to Somalia, trying to persuade it to break with the USSR. It had also given aid to Jordan, made efforts to turn Syria away from the Soviet Union and sought to improve relations with Egypt. Indeed, it had tried not only to prevent Egypt's return to the Soviet sphere of influence, but to strengthen those in Egypt opposing any sort of return to a radical, socialist and active pan-Arab policy.

In the east and south-east, Iran was particularly concerned that the Baluchi tribes in the Iran-Pakistan border area might attempt to follow the example of Bangladesh and seek regional autonomy, or even a separate state. The Shah declared that he would not tolerate any further dismemberment of Pakistan and that such attempts would be regarded as a threat to Iran's security. Close ties developed between Iran and Pakistan, while India drew closer to the USSR, because of its concern at Iran's military build-up and increased power in the Indian Ocean. Iran now attempted to improve relations with India, in order to make it less dependent on the USSR, and in this regard it had some measure of success.

Seeing Afghanistan establishing closer links with the USSR, Iran became more suspicious of the Soviet Union, feeling that it was being encircled by the USSR and its friends.

Close ties now developed between the PRC and Iran. Chairman Hua Guofeng visited Iran from 29 August to 1 September 1978, and on that occasion a cultural agreement was signed and talks commenced regarding scientific and cultural co-operation.[84] The Iranians were careful not to criticize the USSR, which regarded the visit as being directed against itself and its interests. However, the Soviet media preferred to concentrate their attacks on the Chinese while quoting Iranian officials who praised close Soviet-Iranian relations.

The Soviet Union hoped for a weakening of the ties between Iran and the USA, Western Europe and the PRC. It also hoped for a smaller degree of Iranian intervention in the region's affairs (an end to its role as 'the region's policeman'), less Iranian accumulation of Western-made arms, and closer relations between Iran and the Soviet Union. The Soviets had previously tried hard to attract Iran with economic inducements. They were Iran's largest customer for gas, delivered to the USSR through a trans-Iranian pipeline opened in 1970. Iran had been permitted to make use of transit trade routes through the USSR to Western Europe, via Soviet land routes and from Iranian Caspian Sea ports through the Volga-Baltic network and Volga-Don Canal. There were joint development projects in the border areas and the Soviets had assisted in the establishment of a number of industrial enterprises.[85] In general, they believed that closer economic ties between them and Iran would make Iran less suspicious of the USSR's intentions and thus consent to stronger political ties.

The Soviets and the Fall of the Shah

The year 1978 saw an increase in the strength of the opposition to the Shah's regime. This eventually led to its downfall in early 1979 and to the Shah's departure from Iran.

In 1978 the religious establishment played an increasing role, becoming the rallying point for those opposing the regime. Their turn came in September of that year, when Ayatollah Khomeyni emerged as the leader of the revolution. Previously, references to the opposition generally meant leftists of various shades and the Westernized liberal centre. Little remained of the underground communist Tudeh Party which drew its support from a tiny segment of the population, mainly the intellectuals.

The Soviets adopted a careful wait-and-see policy, closely following developments as spectators from the outside. Their media avoided any direct criticism of the Shah's regime and tried not to be seen as intervening in Iranian internal affairs. Only by mid-1978 did they begin to report the existence of opposition, or demonstrations and 'unrest'. But then, too, they gave mainly news, generally quoting others, without adding comments or presenting their own positions.

By September 1978, the Soviet media had become more favourable to the opposition forces. Their use of phrases such as 'the popular struggle', 'clashes between the population and the police' and 'mass actions of the working people demanding democratic liberties' showed the direction in which they wanted developments to go. Religious slogans, which played a major role, were dismissed by the Soviets as something marginal and unimportant. They claimed that the religious circles were only 'joining' but not leading, and that the causes of the unrest were social and economic.

In November of that year, the Soviet media departed from their policy of reporting only news of the situation in Iran. They now began to express opinions as well. Western press reports of possible Soviet involvement in the events in Iran were denied by the USSR, which spoke with increasing frequency of possible American intervention. In a statement in *Pravda* on 19 November 1978 Brezhnev said:

> The Soviet Union, which maintains traditional good neighbourly relations with Iran, emphatically declares that it is against outside interference in Iran's internal affairs by anyone, in any form and under any pretext. What is happening in Iran is a purely internal affair and the issues involved must be solved by the Iranians themselves . . .
>
> It should also be clear that any, particularly military, interference in the affairs of Iran, a state directly bordering on the Soviet Union, would be regarded by the Soviet Union as affecting the interests of its security.[86]

The Brezhnev statement was meant to give warning of American intentions to intervene in Iran and, by doing so, to claim the credit for preventing this. The Soviets believed that a weakening of American positions in Iran would bring about an increase of

Soviet influence.

The Soviet media also described a situation of general revolt against the regime and against American control of the country. They claimed that the Shah's regime was able to survive only because of the American presence. The opposition would have to end this state of affairs if it wished to succeed. Day after day Soviet reports appeared, describing American preparations to intervene in Iran. They were not only meant to incite the Iranian opposition groups against the USA. The Soviets genuinely believed that American intervention was imminent. They expected this and prepared their own public for it. There were no statements or even hints as to what the USSR would do if the USA did indeed intervene. In all probability the Soviets would have protested, published statements and condemnations, but no more.

The Soviet conclusion was that the Shah could still control the situation if he took strong measures against the opposition. Had the Soviets found themselves in such a situation they would undoubtedly have done the same. They knew the Shah was heeding American advice to avoid bloodshed. However, they did not interpret American policy in terms of human rights, as seen in the West, but as an American attempt to weaken the Shah, forcing him to pay more attention to internal affairs, and making him less independent, so that they could control him even more.

During the last months of 1978, Soviet commentators on Iran spoke of 'anti-government demonstrations' but refrained from direct criticism of the Shah, even avoiding quoting what others had said. They made no mention of opposition hopes of overthrowing the Shah and ending the monarchy. This meant that the Soviets still thought it possible for the Shah to stay in power. However, by the end of the year the Soviets had grown increasingly aware that the Shah's rule was doomed. Their media began to report demonstrations demanding his abdication — events which they had earlier refrained from describing. Even now, these reports were infrequent and not published in the central press.

The Soviets expected a repetition of the 1953 situation — a military coup with American assistance to restore the Shah. They also believed that some Americans were clandestinely supporting Khomeyni, considering that as a religious man he was anti-communist, 'naturally' making him pro-American. This would then prevent the rise of the communist Tudeh Party or of a radical military leader potentially dangerous to the USA, like Libya's

Mu'ammar al-Qadhdhafi. This made the Soviets adopt a passive position until the end of 1978 and even early 1979, to wait and see which forces would gain the upper hand in Iran, and then adapt themselves to the situation.

Notes

1. Aryeh Yodfat, 'The USSR and the Persian Gulf Area', *Australian Outlook*, vol. 33, no.1 (April 1979), pp. 60–72; David Lynn Price, 'Moscow and the Persian Gulf', *Problems of Communism*, vol. 28, no. 2 (March–April 1979), pp. 1–13; Alvin Z. Rubinstein, 'Soviet Persian Gulf Policy', *Middle East Review*, vol. 10, no. 2 (Winter 1977–8), pp. 47–55.

The importance of the Persian Gulf is shown by the following presentation of the dependence on Persian Gulf oil (1977).

	United States	Western Europe	Japan
Oil as percentage of total energy consumed	47%	55%	73%
Percentage of oil imported	49	96	100
Percentage of oil imported from Persian Gulf	34	61	72
Persian Gulf oil as percentage of total energy consumed	8	32	53

(Reported by John M. Collins and Clyde R. Mark, *Petroleum Imports from the Persian Gulf: Use of US Force to Ensure Supplies* (Library of Congress, Congressional Research Service, 1979). Cited from *Armed Forces Journal* (July 1979), p. 24. About the report, see Drew Middleton, 'Report says risks would rule out US armed action in the Persian Gulf', *New York Times*, 15 July 1979).

2. A. Sergeyev, *Krasnaya Zvezda*, 10 April 1975.

3. Aryeh Y. Yodfat and Yuval Arnon-Ohanna, *PLO Strategy and Tactics* (Croom Helm, London, and St. Martin's Press, New York, 1981).

4. Moscow radio in English to North America, 10 Sept. 1976. In FBIS, USSR, 14 Sept. 1976, pp. B9–B10.

5. Moscow radio in Arabic, 13 Feb. 1977. In FBIS, USSR, 16 Feb. 1977, pp. F6–F7.

6. V. Kudryavtsev, *Izvestia*, 11 April 1978.

7. Andrei Stepanov, *New Times*, no. 26 (June 1978), pp. 24–5. See also A. Vasil'yev, *Pravda*, 15 June 1978.

8. Pavel Davydov, 'Imported Labour in the Persian Gulf', *New Times*, no. 33 (Aug. 1978), pp. 25–7.

9. The Lebanese communist *An-Nida* described an October 1975 conference of Communist Parties of Saudi Arabia and Iraq and the Bahrain National Liberation Front on the situation in the Persian Gulf and Arabian Peninsula. It said that the National Liberation Front of Saudi Arabia had changed its name to SACP and held its first congress 'recently'. (Cited by Agence France Presse (AFP), 23 Oct. 1975).

10. Moscow 'Peace and Progress' in Arabic, 1 Oct. 1976. In FBIS, USSR, 4 Oct. 1976, p. F7.

11. A. Vasil'yev, *Pravda*, 15 June 1978.

72   *Soviet Retreats and Advances in the Region (1975–1978)*

12. Moscow radio in Arabic, 8 July 1975. In FBIS, USSR, 10 July 1975, pp. F3–F4. See also Moscow radio in Arabic, 23 Sept. 1977. In FBIS, USSR, 26 Sept. 1977, pp. F5–F6.
13. Moscow radio in Arabic, 19 Feb. 1978. In FBIS, USSR, 23 Feb. 1978, pp. F9–F10.
14. *Izvestia*, 12 Nov. 1978.
15. *Pravda*, 1 Sept. 1976.
16. *Izvestia*, 2 Sept. 1976.
17. L. Koryavin, ibid., 7 May 1977.
18. *Pravda*, 6 Dec. 1975.
19. *Al-Anba'*. Cited by Qatar News Agency (QNA), 5 Dec. 1976 and 5 April 1977. In FBIS, ME, 6 Dec. 1976, p. C1 and 5 April 1977, p. C1.
20. *Pravda*, 1 March 1978.
21. Emile A. Nakhleh, *Bahrain: Political Development in a Modernizing Society* (Lexington Books, Lexington, Mass., 1976).
22. 'Abdallah Rashid, 'Bahrain: Fighting for Liberation', *World Marxist Review*, vol. 21, no. 10 (Oct. 1978), pp. 64–8.
23. Moscow radio in Arabic, 29 Aug. 1975. In FBIS, USSR, 3 Sept. 1975, pp. F8–F9.
24. A. Malyshkin and V. Vinogradov, *Krasnaya Zvezda*, 13 Feb. 1977.
25. Anuar Akhmedov, 'Qatar. The Past and the Present', *Asia and Africa Today*, no. 6 (Nov.–Dec. 1979), pp. 46–8.
26. Yuri Tyssovsky, 'United Arab Emirates. What Was Once the Pirate Coast', *New Times*, no. 19 (May 1977), pp. 23–5.
27. V. Vinogradov, 'Oil Emirates of the Persian Gulf', *Krasnaya Zvezda*, 11 Aug. 1978.
28. A. Sergeyev, *Krasnaya Zvezda*, 10 April 1975.
29. 'Peace and Progress' in Arabic, 10 June 1975. In FBIS, USSR, 11 June 1975, pp. F5–F6.
30. Capt. Y. Gavrilov and V. Vinogradov ('Dhofar: The Fight for Freedom', *Krasnaya Zvezda*, 2 Nov. 1975) described PFLO fighting. They said that the PFLO 'have been using the latest equipment for the first time, including highly efficient anti-aircraft missiles'. They did not say that such equipment came from the Soviet Union and that the PFLO was supported by the Soviets. The only hint of this could be gleaned in their ending that the PFLO was 'not alone' in its struggle.
31. *Pravda*, 3 March 1976.
32. Moscow radio in Persian to Iran, 25 May 1977. In FBIS, USSR, 2 June 1977, pp. F1–F2.
33. Eric Rouleau's interview of Sultan Qabus, *Le Monde*, 19 Nov. 1976.
34. L. Mironov, *Krasnaya Zvezda*, 6 Jan. 1977; A. Malyshkin and V. Vinogradov, ibid., 13 Feb. 1977.
35. *People's Daily* (Peking), 27 May 1978.
36. Soviet offers of military aid including MiG-21 aircraft and T-54 tanks to replace the YAR's MiG-17s and T-34s. (*Washington Post*, 4 Aug. 1975; *International Herald Tribune*, 29 April 1976).
37. 'Peace and Progress' in Arabic, 1 Nov. 1977. In FBIS, USSR, 3 Nov. 1977, pp. F2–F3.
38. 'US military sales to North Yemen are now rising from $2.6 million in fiscal 1977 to an estimated $5 million this year . . . In addition, the United States allocated $16 million in economic aid to North Yemen in 1977 and $6.2 for this fiscal year.' (*Washington Star*, 25 July 1978).
39. San'a Domestic Service, 24 June 1978. In FBIS, ME, 26 June 1978, pp. C7–C8.
40. *Pravda*, 28, 29 June 1978; *Krasnaya Zvezda*, 27 June 1978.

41. *Al-Anba'*, 30 November 1977.

42. *The Christian Science Monitor* (14 Jan. 1976) cited Western intelligence sources estimating that there were between 3,000 and 4,000 Cubans in South Yemen. According to the *South China Morning Post* (Hong Kong, 16 Jan. 1976), 'US officials confirmed the presence of Cuban troops' in the PDRY, 'but estimated the number in hundreds'.

43. Aryeh Yodfat, 'The Soviet Union and the Horn of Africa', *Northeast African Studies*, vol. 2, no. 1 (1980), pp. 31–57.

44. AFP, 10 January 1978; *Sunday Telegraph*, 15 Jan., 5 Feb. 1978; *Afro-Asian Affairs*, no. 60, 15 Feb. 1978; *Al-Hawadith* (Beirut), 9 June 1978.

45. *Financial Times*, 16 Jan. 1978; *Al-Qabas*, 19 Jan. 1978; *Washington Post*, 25 Jan. 1978.

46. *Krasnaya Zvezda*, 18 May 1978; TASS in English, 23 May 1978. In FBIS, USSR, 24 May 1978, p. F4; *Afro-Asian Affairs*, no. 65, 15 June 1978.

47. East German News Agency (ADN), 2 June 1978. In FBIS, East Europe, 5 June 1978, p. E4.

48. TASS in English, 7 June 1978. In FBIS, USSR, 8 June 1978, p. F3.

49. *Selskaya Zhizn* (Moscow), 20 May 1977.

50. Riyadh Domestic Service, 10 March 1976. In FBIS, ME, 11 March 1976, p. C2.

51. *As-Siyasah*, 13 March, 24 April 1976; *New African Development* (London) (June 1977), pp. 472–3.

52. Moscow radio in Arabic, 11 March 1976. In FBIS, USSR, 12 March 1976, pp. F1–F2.

53. V. Alexandrov, 'Dynamic Progress', *New Times*, no. 42 (Oct. 1976), pp. 14–15.

54. *As-Siyasah*, 25 May 1978; *Al-Hawadith* (Beirut), 9 June 1978.

55. *Al-Anba'* and *Al-Liwa'* (Beirut), 28 June 1978. The *Al-Anba'* report was immediately denied in *Pravda*, 29 June 1978.

56. This version also appeared in the Soviet media: *Pravda*, 27, 28 June 1978. See also Jean Gueyras, 'South Yemen. Cuba of Arabia', *Le Monde*, 27,28 Feb. 1979; Fred Halliday, 'Yemen's Unfinished Revolution: Socialism in the South', *MERIP Reports*, no. 81 (Oct. 1979), pp. 3–20.

57. Y. Glukhov, *Pravda*, 2 July 1978.

58. TASS in English, 5 July 1978. In FBIS, USSR, 6 July 1978, p. F7.

59. Moscow radio in Arabic, 6 July 1978. In FBIS, USSR, 7 July 1978, pp. F6–F7.

60. *Pravda*, 7 July 1978.

61. TASS in English, 9 July 1978. In FBIS, USSR, 11 July 1978, p. F3.

62. Maj. Y. Gavrilov and V. Vinogradov, *Krasnaya Zvezda*, 9 July 1978.

63. TASS in English, 19 Aug. 1978. In FBIS, USSR, 22 Aug. 1978, p. F6.

64. *San Diego Union*, 1 Dec. 1978.

65. Cited by Jean Gueyras in *Le Monde*, 28 Feb. 1979.

66. *Pravda*, 17 March 1978.

67. Ibid., 12 Oct. 1978.

68. Interview given by President Siad Barre to *Al-Ahram*, 19 May 1977; *Financial Times*, 24 April, 2 May 1977; *Washington Post*, 17, 26 May, 9 June 1977.

69. San'a radio, 23 March 1977. In FBIS, ME, 24 March 1977, p. C6; Colin Legum, *Observer*, 20 March 1977; *Financial Times*, 2 May 1977; *Neue Zurcher Zeitung*, 21 April 1977.

70. V. Kudryavtsev, 'Shadows over the Red Sea', *Izvestia*, 16 April 1977.

71. Joint Soviet-Iraqi statement, *Pravda*, 1 June 1976.

72. Ibid., 5 July 1975. A Soviet comment described the economic co-operation of that time between Iraq and the CMEA countries:

With the assistance of CMEA countries, Iraq has already built or is in the process of building upwards of 200 industrial establishments, power plants, transport installations, and so on. This is helping to consolidate the state sector of the country's economy. The large national oilfields in North Rumaylah, developed with the assistance of the USSR and other CMEA countries, who supplied part of the equipment, are already yielding an annual 18 million tons . . .

Trade between the socialist countries and Iraq is going ahead on the basis of long-term agreements, under which Iraq supplies petroleum, consumer goods, foodstuffs, etc.

(Y. Zhuravlov, *New Times*, no. 31 (Aug. 1975), p. 17).

73. *Pravda*, 4 Feb. 1977.
74. Aryeh Yodfat, 'The Soviet Union and the Horn of Africa', *Northeast African Studies*, vol. 1, no. 3 (1979–80), pp. 1–17; vol. 2, no. 1 (1980), pp. 31–57; vol. 2, no. 2 (1980), pp. 65–81; *An-Nahar al-'Arabi wa ad-Dawli*, 20 May 1978.
75. *As-Siyasah*, 24 May 1978.
76. *An-Nahar al-'Arabi wa ad-Dawli*, 3 June 1978.
77. *Al-Anba'*, 6 June 1978.
78. *Pravda*, 10 June 1978.
79. *Al-Anba'*, 8 June 1978.
80. Aryeh Yodfat, *Arab Politics in the Soviet Mirror* (Halsted Press, John Wiley & Sons, New York and Toronto, 1973), pp. 165–72.
81. *Pravda*, 13 Jan. 1979.
82. Yodfat and Arnon-Ohanna, *PLO*.
83. *Pravda*, 14 Dec. 1978.
84. Aryeh Yodfat, *Between Revolutionary Slogans and Pragmatism: The PRC and the Middle East* (Centre d'Etudes du Sud-Est Asiatique et de l'Extrême Orient, Brussels, 1979), pp. 100–3.
85. A description of Soviet-Iranian economic relations, published in *Pravda* after the Shah's downfall, summed up the situation at the end of the era of the Shah's rule:

In terms of the level of trade exchange, Iran has recently ranked second or third among the USSR's customers from the developing states. In turn the Soviet Union has ranked first in Iranian exports (excluding oil).

Economic and technical co-operation has assumed considerable scope. In all, Soviet organizations have taken part in the building of 147 installations: commitments for 88 of them have already been fulfilled. To a considerable extent this co-operation is being effected on the basis of Soviet credits granted to Iran under preferential terms.

. . . among the largest installations . . . the Esfahan metallurgical plant — the largest enterprise in the country, employing 10,000 people; the machine-building plant in Arak . . . grain elevators . . . a hydro-electric system and water supply dam on the Araks River . . .

The Soviet Union has constructed the northern sector of the 487-kilometre trans-Iranian main gas pipeline through which gas extracted in south Iran is supplied to Soviet Transcaucasia. In the first eight years of this pipeline's operation almost 70 billion cubic metres of gas have been supplied . . . Revenue from the sale of natural gas is used to pay for Soviet services in construction of the various enterprises . . .

(P. Demchenko, *Pravda*, 6 April 1979).

86. *Pravda*, 19 Nov. 1978.

3

SHADOW GAME IN THE GULF
(January 1979 – September 1980)

Iran — Khomeyni's Islamic Republic

Initial Stage — the Soviets Propose Co-operation
(January – April 1979)

The fall of the Shah in Iran marked a turning-point not only in Iran but in the whole area. Iran's old regime had played the role of 'the region's policeman', trying to keep stability and order there, preserving existing regimes, ensuring the regular flow of Gulf oil, and containing advances of the Soviets and their friends. With the collapse of that regime, a vacuum developed — with no other regional power able to take over the role. Moreover, Iran's new Islamic leadership called for revolutions and changes in the whole Islamic world, and particularly in Shi'a-populated regions bordering their country. The Soviets took no part in these developments, considering the risk too great. A revival of Islam could spread to Muslim-populated areas in the USSR, near Iran. They adapted themselves as best they could to the situation, using it wherever they could to their own advantage.

On 16 January 1979 the Shah left Iran and the Soviet media, which until then had generally refrained from attacking him, now broke with the Shah, denouncing him as a corrupt monarch who had brutally oppressed his people — a 'criminal' a 'gangster', and so on.[1] They described the religious leadership heading the revolution as 'objectively progressive', meaning that even if they were 'subjectively' reactionary, anti-communist and anti-Soviet, 'objectively' their activities served the Soviet Union. This might result in 'progress' and should therefore be welcomed.

Ayatollah Ruhollah Mosavi Khomeyni's return to Iran on 1 February 1979 was favourably reported in the Soviet media. So was his appointment on 5 February of Mehdi Bazargan as head of the provisional government. The Soviets adapted themselves to the new regime, with their media stressing what they saw as the positive aspects and ignoring the negative ones, praising much and avoiding criticism. They hoped that events were developing favourably for them.

Brezhnev referred in his 2 March 1979 election speech to 'the

75

people's anti-imperialist national liberation revolution in Iran'. He made no mention of the revolution's religious character. He said:

> We . . . welcomed the victory of this revolution which put an end to the despotic oppressive regime . . . We wish new revolutionary Iran success and prosperity, and hope that relations of good neighbourliness between the peoples of the Soviet Union and Iran will be fruitfully developed on the firm basis of mutual respect, goodwill and non-interference in each other's internal affairs.[2]

A *Pravda* comment said 'the political changes taking place in Iran reveal favourable opportunities for the further development and intensification of Soviet-Iranian relations'. A number of development projects had been undertaken and installations built in Iran with Soviet aid. But:

> Although trade and economic links between the USSR developed . . . all this was not accompanied by a similar improvement in political relations. Moreover, the Iranian government frequently pursued an unfriendly policy toward the Soviet Union . . .
> Now . . . measures have been taken to end the dominance of American imperialism. The Pentagon's military bases have been abolished, the country has withdrawn from CENTO . . . All this widens the aspects of coincidence in the USSR's and Iran's political positions on the international arena.

The commentator went on to list proposals for bilateral co-operation in industry, energy and agriculture. He claimed that 'some people' had tried 'to sow mistrust' between the USSR and Iran, 'to invent stories of Soviet interference' in Iran's internal affairs.

> The USSR resolutely took the side of the Iranian revolution and did much to prevent foreign intervention in Iranian affairs and did not itself, of course, interfere and is not prepared to interfere . . . Now after the victory of the Iranian revolution the Soviet Union is prepared to make the greatest effort to strengthen and further expand Soviet-Iranian relations.[3]

Soviet appeals for co-operation were, however, ignored by Khomeyni and no Iranian response was forthcoming.

Cautious Soviet Criticism (April–November 1979)

In mid-April 1979 the Soviet attitude to Iran's regime changed. No longer was there complete and unreserved support. They now favoured the Tudeh Party more and sharpened their criticism of the Bazargan government (but not of Khomeyni). On matters of concern to the USSR they expressed their views more firmly; for instance, they no longer ignored the Iranian declarations of support for the Muslim opposition in Afghanistan.

As they had in the past, the Soviets were comparing the situation in Iran to others they had known in their own country, such as that existing after the February 1917 revolution in Russia, between the overthrow of Russia's imperial regime and the Bolshevik October revolution. The Soviets did not see any real centre power in Iran, and this had also been the case in Russia in 1917. There were the civilian Bazargan government, the Revolutionary Council, Ayatollah Khomeyni, revolutionary courts, local power centres and others, all acting in an unco-ordinated fashion, one against the other in spite of the generally accepted leadership of Khomeyni. The Soviets concluded that the situation was fluid: everything was temporary and could soon change.

The Soviet media acted as if they supported Khomeyni, pretending that the positions and aims of both countries were similar. Sometimes they reported Khomeyni's declarations not as he intended them, but as they would have wished them to be. On the other hand, criticism was evident — albeit careful and indirect, and not of the regime, or of Khomeyni himself. It generally concerned someone of lower status — a senior religious personality, say, but not one of the inner circle around Khomeyni — or perhaps a junior cabinet member, a senior official or a journalist. However, the criticism was not of what this person had said; rather, it pertained to what Khomeyni had said. The comments took the form of broadcasts and TASS reports. Khomeyni continued to be called 'the leader of the Iranian revolution', enjoying popularity among the people and proclaiming slogans similar to those of the Soviets. But there were reports of pro-Shah, 'pro-imperialist', 'reactionary' and other elements who wanted to bring Khomeyni round to their way of thinking. The people of Iran were called upon to be vigilant, and to distinguish between friends and enemies.

The Soviet Union, the Soviet media said, was a friend which desired nothing from its southern neighbour for its own benefit, but only what was good for Iran.

In *Pravda* on 2 May 1979 an article by P. Demchenko took on a different tone from that of his 6 April article quoted above. One could discern the beginnings of worry, dissatisfaction and disappointment. But there were hopes too — for changes which the Soviets desired.

Growing reservations regarding developments in Iran were expressed in the Soviet media, although not by official Soviet spokesmen. The Soviets believed that the regime was gradually leaning more and more towards a reconciliation with the USA and improved relations with West European countries. The Iranian government imposed restrictions on Tudeh Party activities, supported the Muslim revolt in Afghanistan and called for more freedom for Muslims in the USSR. Sales of natural gas from Iran to the USSR were reduced and its price was raised. The volume of Soviet-Iranian trade was now less than it had been during the Shah's rule.

Usually, as before, Soviet criticism of the regime or Khomeyni was indirect. But now, direct comments were also starting to be heard, such as that made by Aleksandr Bovin, a well-informed senior commentator, in early September 1979. He said that in Iran 'hopes have been replaced by anxiety and alarm, uncertainty and disappointment'. The country's economy was being led by 'economist-theologians' who promised much but merely brought unemployment, inflation and chaos. He went on:

> All publications which have expressed views at variance with the official religious theological doctrine have been closed down and banned. People advocating progressive social transformations . . . are being persecuted . . . the fratricidal war in Kordestan is continuing . . . Those demanding equality and autonomy are declared traitors, they are executed and the religious fanaticism of the Shi'ite masses is being aroused against them . . . Nobody can deny the Iranian clergy's positive role in the anti-Shah revolution . . . [and their] right to . . . participate in the country's political life. But there is obviously room for doubt that a theocratic concept of state will help Iran to become a modern and flourishing country.

It is obvious to me that the feeling of religious fanaticism,

anti-communist hysteria and a desire to misrepresent the policy
and intentions of a friendly country [the USSR] will not benefit
the Iranian people . . .

The coalition of political movements, forces and groups which
secured victory for the revolution has already disintegrated. The
provisional government — a government without power and
without a desire for power — is virtually paralysed . . .

Repression of the extreme left of the political spectrum automatically strengthens the extreme right and creates favourable
soil for outside pressure . . .

All this is making the situation in the country unstable and
fraught with conflicts and unexpected surprises.[4]

Sharp criticism of this kind was, however, rare. The Soviets
wanted to improve relations with Iran, no matter who was in power
and how the Soviets felt about them. This, they continued to
believe, they could achieve more easily by praise and flattery. They
also felt that the regime would, in spite of its difficulties, remain in
power so they decided once more to try to improve relations. They
were prepared to ignore aspects of Iran's politics unfavourable to
them, as long as they believed that Iran shunned the Western
world. However, now it seemed to them that things were otherwise.
TASS cited a *New York Times* report that the US administration
and the Iranian government were discussing the resumption of
American arms deliveries and spares, and a new programme for
training Iranian servicemen by American specialists.[5]

On 1 November 1979 Prime Minister Mehdi Bazargan had talks
in Algiers with American President Carter's National Security
Adviser, Zbigniew Brzezinski; and Iranian Foreign Minister
Ebrahim Yazdi; then attending the UN General Assembly session
in New York, he talked with US Secretary of State Cyrus Vance.
Agreements were concluded on bilateral matters, such as renewal
of supplies of spares, ammunition, and other much-needed
equipment for the Iranian military forces.

On 9 November 1979 the Iranian government decided to
abrogate Articles 5 and 6 of the February 1921 friendship treaty
with the Soviet Union, as well as the co-operation agreement with
the United States;[6] these permitted Soviet and American military
intervention in Iran, respectively, under certain conditions.
Undoubtedly, the Soviets viewed this most unfavourably, but
refrained from any direct reaction or comment on the matter.

This was one of the last decisions made by the Bazargan government. Bazargan had asked to be allowed to resign numerous times
but Khomeyni refused and he remained in office. However, in early
November 1979 Khomeyni finally accepted his resignation and on 6
November 1979 the provisional government was dissolved and its
power transferred to the Islamic Revolutionary Council which was
composed of religious personalities. The Soviets were happy to
watch the fall of the Western-educated 'liberal bourgeoisie'
favoured by the Americans, and the rise of those who called for
fighting the Western world and its influence. However, the Soviets
failed to remember that they were regarded by Iranian religious
fundamentalists as part of the Western world, and communism was
seen as an alien Western ideology.

The Issue of the American Hostages

On 4 November 1979 Iranian students, 'followers of the line of
Imam Khomeyni', seized the US embassy in Tehran and took its
personnel hostage. As a condition for their release the students
demanded that the deposed Shah (then in the United States for
medical treatment) and all his wealth be turned over to them. They
also insisted on a formal apology by the American administration
for 'wrongs' done to Iran, including an undertaking to refrain from
interference in Iranian internal affairs. The USA was also required
to accord formal recognition to the new regime and to lift all
restrictions on Iranians and Iranian property in the USA.

The initial Soviet reaction was to suspend criticism of the
Khomeyni regime, although only temporarily and partially. They
wanted to use the occasion to foster a *rapprochement* with Iran.
Their propaganda machine increased its praise of Iran's leadership
and its steadfast stand against 'imperialism', and supported Iran's
'just demands'.

The Soviet media warned of American threats to Iran and
preparations to use force against it, but refrained from linking
these with the issue of the hostages. They were silent as to their own
intentions in the event of an American blockade or intervention.
They even avoided referring to what the Iranians were saying about
possible Soviet aid in the event of American intervention, fearing
that this might be interpreted as a commitment on their part. Their
media repeatedly warned of impending American intervention but,
although the Soviets expected it, they were prepared to do nothing
except protest loudly.

The hostage issue had many disadvantages for the Soviets. It aroused American public anger and strengthened the 'hawks', creating a favourable climate for increasing American military appropriations and the strengthening of American military power. It also contributed to the suspension of US-USSR talks on reduction of forces in the Indian Ocean and was a factor in the increase of American naval forces there. On the other hand, it was able to serve the Soviet propaganda machine, which portrayed the USA as exploiting the occasion in order to threaten the whole area. But such propaganda was counter-productive since the Americans were usually accused of being undetermined, weak and yielding. The Soviets were also careful to avoid direct praise of the act of seizing hostages — it could happen to a Soviet embassy as well.

At the end of December 1979, after Soviet intervention in Afghanistan, they threw off their earlier restraint and spoke less about respecting diplomatic immunity. They sharply attacked the USA as an enemy of Iran, preparing for military intervention and trying to overthrow Iran's revolutionary regime in order to restore the old one. This, it was said, would be done by trying to sow discord among Iran's nationalities and between the forces that overthrew the Shah. On 13 January 1981 the USSR vetoed a UN Security Council resolution calling for economic sanctions against Iran.

The hostage issue led to a break-down in Iranian-American relations which the Soviets believed was to their advantage. The Tudeh Party leader Kianuri said: 'As long as we keep the hostages we will prevent a normalization of relations with the United States, a condition about which some Iranian politicians are dreaming.'[7]

The attempt on 24 April 1980 to rescue the hostages was a target for sharp Soviet propaganda attacks, but, as before, there were no official comments or promises of Soviet support.

Again and again the Soviet media repeated that the Americans were not interested in solving the hostage problem, and were using it as 'a pretext' to increase their military presence in the region. They constantly played up stories of American plans to attack Iran and release the hostages by force. This Soviet propaganda intensified during the last days of the Carter administration, when it appeared that the problem was about to be solved. The Soviet aim was to undermine the talks, weakening those in Iran who wanted a settlement and strengthening those opposed to it.

On 17 January 1981, when negotiations for the hostages' release were nearing their close, *Pravda* continued to sound the alarm of 'the threat of armed US intervention' that had been hanging over Iran. It said that, under cover of negotiations on the hostage problem:

> The Pentagon is preparing a new 'intimidating' operation against Iran. This dangerous adventure can be executed at any moment . . . It must be recalled in this connection that the Soviet Union repeatedly stressed the inadmissibility of any foreign interference in Iran's domestic affairs . . .[8]

Comments of this nature were meant to 'warn' Iran of an American 'trap' and to enable the Soviets to claim later that their warning had 'saved' Iran and prevented an American military incursion.

The American hostages were released on 20 January 1981, the day Ronald Reagan took office as US president. The Soviet media repeated their warning that the new administration would not honour the terms of the American-Iranian agreement, namely, not to interfere in internal Iranian affairs and to transfer to Iran the Iranian assets which had been frozen in the United States. They claimed that America could have solved the problem much earlier but had not wished to because it 'needed a pretext' to send aircraft-carriers to the Persian Gulf. The hostages left Iran but the American warships did not return to the ports from whence they came.[9]

Izvestia described the USA as the 'main opponent' of the Iranian revolution. Jointly with its allies the USA had massed over 60 warships and 200 aircraft in the Persian Gulf and had set up military bases in Egypt, Somalia, Kenya, Oman and Bahrain. 'In the United States itself and in Egypt the so-called Rapid Deployment Force is undergoing training in conditions close to those of the Iranian deserts. All this creates a direct threat to the Iranian revolution.' The USA, *Izvestia* said, was seeking a pretext for military intervention.[10]

Day after day sharp attacks on the USA and its policy towards Iran were heard in the broadcasts of the USSR-based 'clandestine' National Voice of Iran (NVOI).

'Neither East nor West'

The Soviets generally believed that the more anti-West Iran's regime, and the more strained the relations between Iran and the Western world, the greater were the chances for Iran to move closer to the USSR. They believed that if a conflict broke out between Iran and the USA, Iran would have no choice but to turn to the Soviet Union. The prevailing Iranian position after the Islamic revolution was that it need not worry about the USSR and the USA, because the rivalry between the two superpowers neutralized both. Neither would allow the other to occupy Iran.

However, experience of the history of previous Russian-British agreements made some of the leading Iranians think otherwise. For Islamic fundamentalists, the East-West, communism-capitalism controversy was a Western 'family affair'. All were regarded as infidels, all wanting the same thing — to exploit Iran and introduce it to their wicked ways of life from which the righteous must turn away. Questions were asked as to whether there was in reality an American-Soviet agreement over Iran, with both sides merely pretending to have differences. It could be, Khomeyni said, that the United States was 'playing games' with the USSR, manipulating it to do what was good for the Americans and against Iran's revolution.[11]

The slogan 'neither East nor West' was the key motif in Iran's foreign relations. Tehran radio said, '[Khomeyni] has always emphasized the dictum of following neither East nor West and only the heavenly path of Islam . . . Both the capitalist imperialism of the West and the social imperialism of the communist world are to be equally rejected.'[12]

Khomeyni described the Soviet Union as an arch-Satan. On 9 August 1980, addressing representatives of world liberation movements, he referred to 'this big satanic power, the USSR, which is exerting all its power to suffocate Afghanistan'.[13] The Soviets did not react.

A message sent on 11 August 1980 by Iranian Foreign Minister Sadeq Qotbzadeh to USSR Foreign Minister Andrey Gromyko adopted an equally sharp tone in attacking the Soviets. Qotbzadeh noted that the Iranian revolution had a long list of accounts to settle with the USSR, some of which he listed: 'Our Imam has described the United States as a great satan. Unfortunately, you, too, have proved in practice that you are no less satanic than the United States.'

Qotbzadeh raised questions that had been put to the Soviets during the term of the Bazargan government and 'to which no answer was ever given'. The question referred to large quantities of Soviet-made weapons discovered in Kordestan, and Soviet money getting to the Kurds. Also, Soviet satellites were taking photographs of Iranian military positions in Kordestan, and the photographs were being made available to 'counter-revolutionaries'. Qotbzadeh also accused the Soviets of sending agents to Iran to:

> reorganize your fifth column . . . propagating your views in your name, and sparing no financial or moral support for them . . . Members of your embassies and consulates, as well as other institutions, have not spared any efforts in establishing contacts with the enemies of our revolution and in gathering information . . . a great many of your officials, rather than attending to normal and current matters handled by a genuine embassy, are engaged in espionage operations.

In conclusion he said, 'We wish for the establishment of friendly and truly neighbourly relations,' and offered the following proposals:

> (1) A withdrawal of Soviet troops from Afghanistan.
> (2) The Soviet embassy in Tehran, Soviet consulates and other Soviet institutions in Iran 'should abstain from any irregular activities contrary to the interests of the Islamic Republic of Iran'.
> (3) A reciprocal reduction of embassy staff in both countries; the opening of an Iranian consulate in Dushanbe or, alternatively, the closure of one of the Soviet consulates in Iran. The Iranian consulate in Leningrad would be closed.
> (4) To refrain from supporting the Tudeh Party.[14]

Gromyko's reply was brief. He said the USSR did not intervene in the internal affairs of Iran or other countries:

> The Soviet Union wants to have good and neighbourly relations with Iran that are based on respect for independence, sovereignty, territorial integrity and non-interference in each other's internal affairs. At the end of your letter, you also expressed your views in favour of this in a general way. If words are manifested in

specific deeds, this will, of course, be very favourably received by us.[15]

The appointment in August 1980 of Muhammad 'Ali Raja'i as Prime Minister served as an occasion for greetings from Soviet Premier Kosygin in which he spoke of good-neighbourly relations and co-operation.[16] Raja'i's reply was cool and restrained.[17]

Again and again the Soviets reiterated their support of Iran's revolution and their readiness to help. These efforts were ignored, and even rejected by Iran's leadership who well remembered the example of how the Soviets had helped Afghanistan.

Economic Ties

The political climate between the two countries was reflected in the negotiations over the price of the Iranian gas delivered to the USSR. Iran was asking a price five times higher than that which the Soviet Union had previously paid, but it was not ready to compromise, even though it had no other customers for the gas.[18] Part of the gas was diverted for home consumption, while a large amount was simply burnt off. The Soviets, too, were unwilling to give in, saying that before they had started purchasing the gas it was being burned uselessly away. In March 1980 the talks broke down and Iran cut off the gas supplies completely.

The Soviets countered with a refusal to permit the free transit of Iranian merchandise through their territory. For Iran this was not so much a question of current use, but rather of being able to use this route in the event of a blockade of its southern coast. Iran had needed access to the Black Sea, from the Caspian Sea through the Volga River and from there to the Mediterranean. This passage had been used by Soviet ships during the last years of the Shah's rule but after his downfall traffic was greatly reduced. The quantity of goods transported over the Volga route by Soviet ships in 1979 was only one-third of that hauled in 1978.[19] Iran was also interested in using Soviet railways for transporting its goods to Western Europe and the Far East. The Soviets concluded that by completely rejecting such proposals they would alienate Iran even further. So on 16 September 1980 an agreement was signed in Moscow permitting the transit of Iranian commercial cargoes through the USSR and of Soviet foreign trade cargoes through Iranian territory.[20]

Soviet experts remained in Iran. 'We did not withdraw a single expert from Iran,' said Semyon Skachkov, Chairman of the Soviet State Committee for Foreign Economic Relations.[21] Economic relations were, however, subordinate to political considerations. The Soviet side was ready to go much further, making economic investments in order to support political aims. They offered to conclude economic agreements giving considerable advantages to Iran, hoping that this might influence political ties. The Iranians had no reason to reject such advantageous conditions, but were not ready to yield when it came to political decisions and principles.

Ayatollah Muhammad Beheshti, head of the Islamic Republican Party (IRP) and chief of the Iranian judiciary, a man whom the Soviet media praised unreservedly (he was killed by a bomb explosion in the IRP building in Tehran on 28 June 1981), was asked how he could reconcile the activities of 3,000 Soviet specialists with co-operation with the Soviet Union, taking into account the fact that many political differences existed between the two countries, especially regarding Afghanistan. Beheshti's reply was that a distinction had to be drawn between Islamic ideology and principles and economic and political ties. As long as such a distinction could be made, the ties with the Soviets would continue. However, if a choice between the two had to be made, the principles would come first, at the expense of the economic ties.[22] The Soviets were aware of this and adapted to the situation.

Iraq

Diversification of Ties and Less Dependence on the Soviets

Iraq had ambitions to become a leading regional power, playing the role of 'policeman' in the Gulf region, a job which became vacant after the Shah of Iran was ousted. Iraq had pan-Arab aspirations of taking Egypt's place as the main Arab power. It was also ambitious to play a leading role in the non-aligned world.

Soviet-Iraqi relations gradually declined. Iraq became increasingly suspicious of Soviet attempts to increase its role in the region and intervene in its affairs. The Iraqi leadership were unhappy to see developments in this direction: from the end of 1977 to early 1978, Soviet-Cuban involvement in Ethiopia; in April 1978, the coup in Afghanistan; in June 1978, changes in leadership in the PDRY; and in 1979, the Islamic revolution in Iran. The latter brought about a condition of instability in the east of Iraq which the Iraqis feared the Soviets might use to extend their influence there and against Iraq.

The Iraqis were careful, however, not to drift too far from the Soviets. They wished to have the advantage of being able to criticize Soviet policy without having to accept Soviet advice, leaving themselves freedom of action and manoeuvre, but also receiving Soviet political support and arms. They wanted to continue to appear to the Soviets as allies, but at the same time be seen in Arab and Western eyes as non-aligned and no longer dependent on the Soviets.

This led to a certain ambiguity in Soviet-Iraqi relations. There were, of course, official declarations of friendship, such as an officially binding friendship treaty between both countries and declarations of intent to continue relations in accordance with the treaty. At the same time, the Iraqis often acted quite contrary to Soviet desires, opposing Soviet positions, policy and presence in the region.

Soviet military supplies made the Iraqis very dependent on the USSR, in spite of their attempts to diversify their sources. The Soviets were happy to continue to supply arms to Iraq and even increase the shipments. However, they did not succeed in translating arms supplies into significant political influence. Paradoxical situations often developed, where the Soviets were ready to increase arms supplies in times of strained relations between the two countries, but refused to do so when they were able to take Iraqi friendship for granted.

Economic relations with Western countries were much broader than with the USSR. Iraq preferred to work with Western companies who used far more advanced technology and had the backing of their governments. Mainly (but not exclusively) economic ties developed between Iraq and West European countries — France in particular, but also Italy, Germany and Britain. This gave Iraq a certain measure of independence from the Soviets.

Trade relations with the USA also increased. The two countries had common interests: both wanted regional stability, secure oil supplies and the containment of Soviet advances. Naturally, many differences also existed: Iraq opposed peace with Israel, and was included by the USA in its list of countries which supported international terrorism. Iraq opposed the American military presence in the region. Finally, US proposals to re-establish diplomatic relations were rejected by Iraq.

Disagreements now arose between the Soviet Union and Iraq. Conditions did not reach the stage where a break was imminent, but they strongly influenced relations between the two countries. They differed on a number of issues:

(1) *Iraqi communists.* Persecutions of communists in a country maintaining a friendship treaty and close relations (officially) with the Soviet Union embarrassed the Soviets, who had no choice but to abandon these unfortunates. In the Ba'thist view, the communists were Soviet agents, serving Soviet interests and used by them. Their persecution of the communists had the dual purpose of punishing the Soviets and serving as a declaration of independence from Moscow.

(2) *Kurds.* Iraq suspected that the USSR was manipulating the Kurds, using them to further its aims. One of Iraq's primary reasons for attempting to maintain good relations with the Soviets was to get them to stop helping the Kurds.

(3) *Arms purchases in Western Europe.* The Iraqis were trying to diversify their arms sources. The Soviets were critical of this and it served to worsen relations and increase mutual suspicion.

(4) *Gulf security.* The Iraqis called for a declaration that the Gulf was outside the influence of non-Gulf powers. The Iraqi National Charter requested moves designed to prevent the Gulf from being turned into an arena for power rivalries. It also opposed the provision of military bases and services to foreign powers. The Soviets, of course, objected.

(5) *Eritrea.* While the Soviets supported Ethiopia, the Iraqis supported the Eritrean organizations fighting Ethiopia in an attempt to establish an independent Eritrean state.

(6) *Afghanistan.* Soviet intervention increased Iraqi suspicions that they might do 'the same' in Iraq, supporting 'their own' people and bringing them to power. This led to still greater persecution of communists, who, it was feared, could play such a role.

Persecution of Communists and Soviet Attempts to Ignore it

The Soviets generally tried to ignore persecutions of communists in countries where intervention on their behalf could harm relations with those countries. Their media either ignored this matter altogether, or mentioned it indirectly, in a general way, avoiding direct criticism and references. Although this applied to Iraq as well, in this case there were many in the USSR who considered that the Soviet Union could not endlessly sacrifice principles and friends for temporary and doubtful state interests. *Pravda* quoted the Iraq communist newspaper, *Tariq ash-Sha'b*:

> The widespread persecution of communists in Iraq and repression against the Communist Party's organizations and press . . . has been continuing for a year. [The ICP] has made and is continuing to make efforts to halt the deterioration of relations with the ruling Ba'th Party and not only to preserve the co-operation between the two parties but also to develop and intensify it still further.

There was no response to this.[23]

ICP Politburo member Zaki Khayri said that some 15,000 communists had been arrested. He denounced tortures which sometimes led to deaths and said that 31 party members had been sentenced and executed 'in recent months'. At the same time, the ICP continued to be an integral part of the Progressive National Front (PNF) and two communists still sat in the cabinet.[24]

Na'im Haddad, Secretary-General of the PNF, said the ICP was circulating 'hostile propaganda' abroad against Iraq. It had, he said, begun 'underground activities' but continued to remain in the PNF. Such a situation could not continue for long and the ICP, he continued, 'must either choose alliance according to the principles put forward by the Ba'th Party or choose another course'.[25] He reported that the ICP had attempted to weaken Iraq's ties with the Soviet Union but had failed. 'Relations with the Soviet Union are developing and are unblemished.'[26]

Both Soviets and Iraqis tried to pretend that in spite of the bad feeling between the Ba'th Party and the ICP, and the persecution of Iraqi communists, relations between the two countries remained as good as ever. Soviet-Iraqi relations were developing 'in an upward direction', *Pravda* said.[27]

Relations did, however, become cooler and less cordial, although formally they remained as before. In fact, they were now restricted to the government-to-government level. CPSU-Ba'th party-to-party relations officially continued, but mostly on paper, and were restricted to exchanges of delegations and speeches about friendship and co-operation. Even such speeches were now rare and usually the Soviets preferred not to mention their relations with Iraq at all.

Between Differences and Co-operation

Saddam Husayn, Iraq's 'strong man', officially became Chairman of the Revolution Command Council and President of Iraq on 16 July 1979, when Ahmad Hassan al-Bakr resigned from those positions because of 'ill health'.

One of the first steps of the old-new leader was to suppress any potential opposition, to remove and even execute those that he believed did not fully support him. There were reports of an attempted coup, supposedly with the aid of the USSR.[28] These reports were unconfirmed, being more rumour than fact, but this was enough to make Saddam Husayn suspicious and he acted accordingly. Arrests and executions followed. In such circumstances the Soviets were careful not to refer to matters over which they had differences with Iraq. They preferred to stress what was common to both sides, and the matters in which the leadership of both countries had a common interest.[29] The Iraqis equally did not want to strain relations.[30]

The Soviet intervention in Afghanistan at the end of 1979 again increased Iraqi suspicions of the Soviets. They concluded that in certain circumstances the Soviets might also exploit the internal situation in Iraq in order to intervene, and determine the character of its regime. The justification that the Soviets gave to their intervention in Afghanistan was that it fell within the framework of the USSR-Afghanistan friendship treaty. This aroused fears in Iraq, and the possibility was raised of its reviewing its friendship treaty with the Soviet Union.[31] The Iraqis were worried that the Soviets might support some Iraqi equivalent of Babrak Karmal, who was somewhere in exile or in hiding. Another related Iraqi fear was that the crises in Afghanistan and Iran might lead to a superpower confrontation and later to a division of the region between them. This strengthened Iraqi calls to both Soviets and Americans to get out of the region.

Still another source of Iraqi anxiety was the possibility of a union of USSR-supported communists with Iraqi Shi'a supported by Khomeyni's Iran, and the prospect of a renewed Kurdish revolt supported by both of them. A coalition was reported between the Iraqi communists and the Patriotic Union of Kurdistan (PUK), headed by Jalal Talabani' (and rivalling Barzani's larger Democratic Party of Kurdistan (DPK), together with guerrillas fighting government troops in northern Iraq, although they controlled no towns or villages.

An 'unofficial' Soviet broadcast attacked 'some reactionary leaders in Iraq' who were trying to distort the struggle of the ICP 'with fabricated unfounded accusations . . . labelling them as agents and traitors and accusing them of having foreign connections and other such lies'. The commentator attacked 'the hands which were stained with the blood of scores of martyrs recently' and their hostility to communism, saying, with a party such as this, 'how is it possible for a monkey to demolish it?'[32]

In ceremonial greetings from the Supreme Soviet Presidium and Council of Ministers to Iraq's leadership in April 1980, on the occasion of the eighth anniversary of the signing of the Soviet-Iraqi friendship treaty, confidence was expressed that relations of friendship and co-operation linking the Soviet and Iraqi peoples would continue to strengthen.[33] This time, Brezhnev did not sign the message as he had done in earlier years. The event was played down in the Soviet media and no Soviet meetings marking the event were reported. It looked as if the Soviets were starting to consider the possibility of Iraq's abrogating the treaty.

This cooling-off in Soviet-Iraqi relations was not accompanied by a stronger orientation toward the USA. Official US-Iraqi diplomatic relations — broken off in 1967 — were not re-established. Nevertheless, a US Interests Section in the Belgian embassy in Baghdad was manned by more diplomats than many formal embassies in Baghdad. A similar arrangement existed in Washington with Iraqi diplomats who were officially part of the embassy of India. There were also many Iraqi students in the USA and economic ties were growing. In 1979 they exceeded $1 billion, with more than $600 million in American imports (mostly oil), and $500 million in US exports (mostly agricultural products and machinery).[34]

Both the Iraqis and the Soviets pretended that there had been no worsening of relations between them. Describing Iraqi-Soviet relations, Foreign Minister Sa'dun Hammadi said:

> There are good relations, relations of friendship. All our agreements with the Soviet Union — economic, political and military — are being implemented in a normal way.
>
> All that happened was that the Soviet Union was not satisfied with our positions on some of its international moves, including the question of Afghanistan. But the Soviet Union should have expected this position, because it knows that we are a non-

aligned country . . .

But the truth is that, despite our opposition to the Soviet move in Afghanistan, their displeasure did not reflect on our bilateral relations on the economic, political and military levels, and it did not affect the implementation of the agreements between us, either on their part or on ours.[35]

A Soviet review of economic and technical co-operation with Iraq listed the following:

With the USSR's economic and technical assistance Iraq has constructed and put into operation more than 60 various industrial, agricultural, power-engineering and other projects. These include the 38 kilometre-long canal joining Lake Tartar and the Euphrates; the 585 kilometre-long Baghdad-Basra oil product pipeline; the Luheis and the North Rumaylah oilfields; the thermal electric power station in Nasiriya, and the cement works in Samawa . . .

The Soviet Union is providing aid to Iraq in training national cadres. Thus, last February [1980] two training centres for 1,200 students were officially opened in Basra. They will provide training for highly skilled specialists for Iraq's chemical, machine-building and metallurgical industries.

Foreign trade relations between the two countries are developing at a rapid pace . . . Iraq has become the USSR's largest trading partner in Asia . . .

The USSR's staple exports to Iraq are machines, industrial equipment and transport facilities . . . The USSR's staple imports from Iraq are crude oil, dates, etc.[36]

The list included projects that had been completed many years earlier, but unlike those of earlier years, the economic and technical co-operation now had much less influence on political relations, being more and more of a purely commercial nature.

Iraqi-Iranian Conflict — Prelude to War

The USSR wanted friendly, or at least non-hostile, relations to exist between Iraq and Iran, in order to avoid having to choose between them, or finding itself in a situation where closeness to one would negatively influence relations with the other.

Correct Iraqi-Iranian relations had existed during the last four years of the Shah's reign, but after Iran's Islamic revolution they deteriorated and a series of border incidents occurred. In Iraq a predominantly Sunni Muslim leadership rules over a Shi'a majority. Baghdad accused the Iranians of seeking to export their revolution and inciting sectarian conflicts in Iraq. Iran, for its part, accused Iraq of persecuting the Shi'ites and supporting opposition groups attempting to overthrow the Khomeyni regime. Iran also claimed that Iraq was encouraging a revolt in Khuzestan and Kordestan, and committing acts of sabotage.

Iraq demanded that Iran withdraw from the three islands guarding the Straits of Hormuz (Greater Tunb, Lesser Tunb and Abu Musa), which had been occupied by Iranian forces in 1971. It also called for an amendment of the 1975 Iraqi-Iranian agreement on the Shatt al-'Arab river. Iran was not prepared either to give up the islands or to amend the agreement.

Most Arab countries supported Iraq as an Arab country in conflict with a non-Arab one, partly because Iraq was considered to be stronger and partly because they feared the spread of Khomeynism and Iranian attempts to export their revolution.

On 17 September 1980 the Iraqi Revolution Command Council decided to abrogate the agreement of 6 March 1975 with Iran. Iraq declared the Shatt al-'Arab to be a national river, completely under its sovereignty, and made it mandatory for all ships using the river for navigational purposes to fly only the Iraqi flag and follow Iraqi instructions.

Border fighting between Iran and Iraq intensified, finally developing into a full-scale war when Iraqi forces invaded Iran. The Soviets remained silent and non-committal. They appeared to be waiting to see the outcome of the clash and would then take up a position accordingly.

Saudi Arabia

The Saudis Speak Many Languages

Saudi Arabia's foreign policy and its stand on regional and international affairs were strongly influenced by Iran's Islamic revolution. The Saudis had wanted the Shah weakened enough so that he could not dominate the Gulf area, but yet strong enough to maintain stability in the region and forestall an Iraqi take-over of Kuwait. It was convenient for the Saudis to criticize Iran's policy in the name of Arab solidarity, but still enjoy the Shah's role as a barrier between them and the Soviets.

The Saudis felt encircled by the Soviets and pro-Soviets in Afghanistan, South Yemen and Ethiopia, and threatened by the Soviet naval presence in the Indian Ocean. They also feared the possibility that Iran would turn pro-Soviet. They saw the Soviets gaining influence in Syria, Libya, and the Palestinian organizations — with the latter wielding considerable influence over the many Palestinians in Saudi Arabia and the neighbouring Gulf states.

The Saudis had generally relied on American help to check Soviet advances and block threats from the region's radical forces. Seeing the Carter administration abandoning friends who relied on the US, such as the Shah of Iran (and earlier the Emperor of Ethiopia), the Saudis concluded that they must not rely exclusively on the United States, which might be unable or unwilling to help them effectively. Moreover, the Soviet threat was not considered immediate, while the danger from radical nearby Arab states and forces was imminent.

The Saudis had always followed a middle-of-the-road policy in the Arab world, siding with those who called for Arab solidarity and inter-Arab co-operation. The Camp David agreements and the signing of the Egyptian-Israeli peace treaty on 26 March 1979 caused a split in the Arab world, with most Arab states adopting 'rejectionist' positions against Egypt's actions. Saudi Arabia took the side of the majority, for one reason: it believed that, by supporting the radical Arab forces, they would be neutralized and prevented from acting against it.

US Secretary of Defense Harold Brown, who visited Saudi Arabia immediately after the revolution in Iran, attempted to reassure the Saudi leadership that his country was still a reliable ally. He proposed a formal alliance with the USA, promising an American commitment to defend Saudi Arabia and expressing a wish to establish American military bases in the Arabian peninsula. The Saudis rejected the idea, bearing in mind the example of Iran, where such conditions had existed, but nevertheless the Shah's regime had not been saved.

Thus the Saudis decided to co-operate with the Arab radicals, loudly and with much publicity, criticizing the United States and its Middle East policy. However, the Saudis also knew that they had to continue to rely on the USA and that if a Soviet threat were to materialize, the Americans would help them.

The result was a set of parallel Saudi policies to be used in different circles, according to circumstances, and each different from the other. The Saudis adapted their line to suit their partner-in-dialogue of the moment: Arab radicals, Arab conservatives, the Western world, the Americans, the West Europeans or the Soviets. For example, officially they welcomed Soviet support of the Arabs against Israel, but in fact they feared it as it strengthened Arab radicals and others they would have liked to see weakened.

The Saudis wanted the Americans close at hand, but not in Saudi Arabia itself: to be present in great numbers and strength, but to be neither seen nor heard. They needed the Americans to be available in times of trouble, but invisible at all other times. They joined those urging the Americans to leave the region, but at the same time they sought an assurance that the US would remain and help if those same radical forces, whom the Saudis had joined, were to turn against them. Some in the USA understood this double-think and tried to act accordingly. Others took the words at face value and did what they believed the Saudis wanted, although in fact is was the exact opposite.

This Saudi practice of speaking 'with a forked tongue', neither saying what they meant nor meaning what they said, was often quite confusing. Things became even worse because internal power struggles and policy considerations resulted in contradictory positions and statements coming from various members of the royal family and leading Saudi personalities.

Indirect Soviet-Saudi Dialogue

The trend towards joining the Arab radicals led some in Saudi Arabia to consider going a step further and establishing relations with the Soviet Union. The Soviets had always expressed such a wish and, as a first stage, were ready to accept official economic ties, with a permanent trade mission in Riyadh, together with a branch of the Soviet trade bank. The Saudis preferred not to permit this.

A senior Soviet commentator and Middle East specialist, writing in the Moscow *Literaturnaya Gazeta* in January 1979, called for the establishment of relations between the USSR and Saudi Arabia. He said, *inter alia*:

> The Soviet Union and Saudi Arabia have never been at war with each other and they have never had any implacable conflicts. The social systems of the Soviet Union and Saudi Arabia are indeed

different but surely this cannot be grounds for mutual
enmity . . .

In its relations with all countries the Soviet Union consistently
adheres to the principle of non-interference in other states'
internal affairs . . . After all, the question of whether Saudi
Arabia's subjects are acting correctly in adhering to Wahhabi
postulates is never raised in the Soviet Union. That is their
internal affair.[37]

Saudi Arabi's Foreign Minister, Prince Sa'ud al-Faysal was
asked whether he had read the article and 'if there are objections to
establishing diplomatic relations, would you object to the establishment of commercial relations?' His reply was: 'We have no
objection to trade transactions with any of the world's countries.
We have economic dealings with many countries in which we have
no diplomatic representation.' As to 'the establishment of Soviet
commercial agencies', the Prince replied that these were usually
established 'to facilitate existing trade and not the other way
around'.

Asked if he had replied to the message that PLO Chairman Yasir
Arafat had brought him from Soviet leaders, and 'what the
objections [were] to the establishment of diplomatic relations with
them', Prince Sa'ud al-Faysal ignored the first part of the question
and said:

> There were relations between us and the Soviets in the past, but
> they were the ones who stopped these relations. We wish to assert
> that the non-existence of diplomatic relations does not mean that
> we do not recognize the USSR or the importance of the role it
> plays in international politics. On the contrary, we have more
> than once expressed our gratitude for the positive stands it
> adopted toward Arab causes.[38]

Reacting to this interview, Moscow radio in Arabic cited the
Washington Post comment which 'pointed to the possibility of the
restoration of diplomatic relations between Saudi Arabia and the
Soviet Union'. The broadcast ignored references to trade relations.
It said that 'the statement is a recognition of the great role the
Soviet Union plays in rendering assistance and support to the Arab
countries'.[39]

A *Sovyetskaya Rossiya* article dealt at length with the matter of
diplomatic relations:

. . . Reports have appeared in the press about the possible activation of Soviet-Saudi relations . . . Saudi Arabia was the first Arab country with which the Soviet Union established diplomatic relations . . . On the eve of the Second World War, Soviet representatives working in Saudi Arabia left for the USSR and since then there have been no diplomatic missions either in Moscow or in Riyadh, despite the Soviet Union's wishes . . . Some people in Saudi Arabia mention the incompatibility of Islam and communist ideology as the main obstacle to the activation of Soviet-Saudi relations. But it is appropriate to note that the Soviet Union has good relations with many monarchist and Muslim countries which cherish the ideas of Islam as closely as the Saudis.[40]

Crown Prince and Deputy Prime Minister Prince Fahd said:

We are aware of the important role that the Soviet Union plays in international politics and we are anxious to ensure that this role supports the Arabs' just causes.

I do not believe that the absence of diplomatic relations between the countries must necessarily be interpreted as a sign of hostility. As for the re-establishment of diplomatic relations, this is an issue which will be settled in accordance with events which contribute to a decision being reached.[41]

Yevgeniy Primakov, Director of the Institute of Oriental Studies, USSR Academy of Sciences, told a Beirut journal: 'Personally at present I see no insurmountable obstacles to the development of normal Soviet-Saudi relations.'[42]

The indirect Soviet-Saudi dialogue continued, with the Soviet side trying to show restraint, ignoring Saudi attacks and accusations, in an attempt to persaude them to change their position and establish diplomatic relations.

Soviet Attempts to Attract Saudi Arabia

Although no diplomatic relations were established, mutual attacks became rare and not as sharp as they had been a few years earlier. Saudi Arabia permitted Soviet transports to fly through Saudi airspace, ferrying arms to South Yemen,[43] and allowed Soviet aircraft to fly over the kingdom once a week on the weekly Moscow-San'a-Moscow flight. It had also given Saudi businessmen the go-ahead to establish free trade relations with the Soviet Union.[44]

Twice a year, in September (on the anniversary of the establishment of a united Saudi Arabian state in 1928) and in February (the anniversary of the establishment of diplomatic relations between the two countries in 1926), greetings were exchanged between the two leaders. The Soviet media exploited these greetings, referring to past friendships between the USSR and Saudi Arabia and the need to renew them. They also said that the friendship would help both sides, since there were no differences between them.[45]

On 20 November 1979 religious extremists invaded the Grand Mosque at Mecca. This led to a two-week siege with intermittent battles. A week after the siege had ended, unrest became evident among the Shi'ites in eastern Saudi Arabia, continuing during and after the *A'shura* holy days. The Soviet media gave only news reports of the seizure of the Mosque. It was too delicate a subject to risk comment. The comments appearing about the Shi'a demonstrations showed things as the Soviets wished them to be and not as they really were:

> Unrest is going on in a number of areas of Saudi Arabia in a demand for restricting royal power, setting up a people's parliament and limiting relations with the USA . . .
>
> At the head of the mass actions are religious figures and intellectuals, members of the Shi'a community . . . Information coming from Saudi Arabia is indicative of the possibility of further aggravation of the situation in that country.[46]

The Soviet intervention in Afghanistan at the end of 1979, and later, frightened the Saudis, who saw it as being a direct threat to the Gulf and themselves. They were among the first to announce a boycott of the Moscow Olympic Games. Saudi Arabia also agreed to act as a conduit for quiet American aid to Pakistan.[47]

Igor Belyayev, who in January 1979 had called for the establishment of Soviet-Saudi relations, repeated his appeal in July 1980. He claimed that the USA had tried to frighten Saudi Arabia by disclosing a Soviet plan to occupy the region, their intervention in Afghanistan being the first step. He denied the existence of such a threat and said that: 'Moscow has always supported and continues to support the Wahhabi kingdom's independence and territorial integrity. No disputed issues whatever have arisen between our countries.' He went on to say that there was 'a definite similarity of standpoints' between the USSR and Saudi Arabia on the Arab-Israeli conflict.

In Belyayev's view, Saudi Arabia was becoming increasingly dissatisfied with the USA. He claimed that the American mass media were 'circulating the most fantastic rumours about Saudi Arabia' concerning its internal situation and the royal family.

> Some members of the ruling family believe it is time to resume diplomatic relations with the Soviet Union and the other socialist countries . . .
>
> The Soviet Union has always respected Saudi Arabia's sovereignty and continues to do so . . . The source of mounting pressure on Saudi Arabia is Washington not Moscow . . . It is the American, not the Soviet mass media that are today waging a 'war of nerves' against Saudi Arabia.[48]

The Soviets continued to appeal to Saudi Arabia, attempting to bring about the establishment of relations, but such appeals were generally ignored or rejected outright. The Soviets did not tire of the game and continued to voice their repeated enticements.

The Saudi Arabian Communist Party

The Saudi Arabian Communist Party (SACP) was established on 31 August 1975, when the first constituent assembly of the party was held to draw up the political and organizational nationalist programme, determine its internal structure and elect the leading bodies.[49]

Earlier, the party's name had been Saudi National Liberation Front (SNLF), which had originated in the Popular Front for the Liberation of Oman and the Arabian Gulf (PFLOAG), later to become the Popular Front for the Liberation of Oman (PFLO). The SACP co-operated with the PFLO, the Popular Front for the Liberation of Bahrain (PFLB), and the Popular Front for the Liberation of Palestine (PFLP), headed by George Habash. The SACP centre appeared to be in Bahrain, and was joined by persecuted Iraqi communists who had escaped to Bahrain. The party was small, with a hard core consisting of Saudi Arabian Western-educated students and Palestinians who had lived long in Saudi Arabia.

An SACP statement at the end of April 1980 condemning US attempts to rescue the American hostages in Iran was published in the Lebanon-based PFLP weekly *Al-Hadaf*. This paper also published a statement issued by another organization, the Saudi Arabian Socialist Workers' Party, regarding the execution of 85 Saudis accused of membership in the organization that had attacked the Grand Mosque in Mecca.[50]

At the end of August 1980, the SACP marked its fifth anniversary and appealed for the mobilization of all opposition forces to establish 'a national democratic regime'.[51] As a small group, its activities were restricted mainly to publishing declarations. It was pro-Soviet but the Soviets preferred to ignore it in public for the time being.

'Fragile' and 'Vulnerable' — a Soviet View of Saudi Arabia

Alexei Vasil'yev, a person well acquainted with the region and visiting it often, published in late 1980 one of the rare Soviet descriptions of Saudi Arabia, its regime, society and politics.[52] He described Saudi Arabia as 'a country with a medieval and pre-medieval economy where feudal and tribal relations prevailed'; it had an 'outdated social and political system' and was a 'feudal-tribal preserve and absolute monarchy'. The ruling family, 'the Saudite clan', was described, because of its large size, as 'a ruling tribe'. There was a meaningful short reference implying that there was already a nucleus of forces that might change the regime. Vasil'yev's words were: 'A nucleus of modern industrial proletariat was formed in the country, and it has already manifested emerging class-consciousness by its actions in support of its economic and political demands.'[53]

The author tried to give a Marxist interpretation to his descriptions of various Saudi classes, the regime and the society: the ruling nobility, the commercial bourgeoisie, the middle strata of the national bourgeoisie, and others. He spoke about 'present-day Saudia Arabia as a transitional society, a "feudal-capitalist" society . . . where capitalism has been imposed on feudal-tribe relations'. The Saudi ruling class was said to have a 'dual character', to be ' "bourgeoisified" feudals inside the country and a specific financial bourgeoisie in the international arena'. As to the stability of the regime, he said:

> At first it would seem that an explosive situation has not taken shape in Saudi Arabia. The ruling class . . . has implemented some reforms . . .

This combination of reforms from above, repression, the 'bribery' of a considerable proportion of the population and the conservatism of Saudi society has secured the temporary stability of one of the most archaic regimes of the world. But the socio-economic changes in the society themselves, and even the elements of modernization that have had to be introduced from above, have broadened the base for conflict between the regime and the social classes which aspire to deeper reforms and, ultimately, to a seizure of power.

The social balance in Saudi Arabia has been destroyed, but a new one, despite all the props and partial measures, has not been created. Such a situation is unstable and fraught with social explosions in the most unexpected forms.

Describing the November 1979 Ka'ba seizure and the Shi'a demonstrations in the east of the country, Vasil'yev concluded: 'The myth of Saudi Arabia's "stability" was dispelled. The events in Mecca and the Eastern Province showed the fragility and vulnerability of the Saudi feudal regime.'[54] This description represented a view generally accepted in the Soviet Union, that an 'outdated' and 'archaic' regime such as this was doomed to an early end.

The Gulf Region — the Soviets Wish to Play an Influential Role

Kuwait

Kuwait was the only Gulf state other than Iran and Iraq to have formal ties with the USSR. The Soviet embassy there served the Soviets in their dealings with the countries with which they had no diplomatic relations.

The Islamic revolution in Iran was strongly felt in Kuwait, which had a large Shi'a population and problems very similar to those facing the Shah's regime. In early 1979 the Soviet Union sent a special envoy, Oleg Grinevskiy, to Kuwait to assert its interest in developments in the Gulf area and to affirm non-interference by the Soviet Union in the internal affairs of the countries there. Through Kuwait the Soviets wished to inform those countries with whom they had no diplomatic relations that they had had nothing to do with the disturbances in Iran and were not seeking to create tension in the area. Grinevskiy also tried to explore the views of

Kuwaiti officials on these developments.[55] He often visited the region on similar missions.

Kuwait attempted to carry out a policy that would satisfy as many countries and groups as possible, particularly those considered dangerous to its regime (Iraq, Iran, radicals, leftists, Palestinians) and, in the international arena, the USSR, USA, PRC and West European countries. It proclaimed anti-American slogans, friendship with the USSR, opposition to the Camp David agreements — all this with the purpose of neutralizing radicals in and around Kuwait.

Kuwait maintained trade relations with the USSR and purchased limited quantities of Soviet arms in order to demonstrate a certain balance in its relations with the great powers. In fact, the arms purchases had little political significance and were not accompanied by Soviet instructors.[56]

A March 1980 Moscow radio broadcast reviewed Soviet-Kuwaiti relations, saying:

> An agreement on economic, technological and cultural co-operation and an air transport agreement have been concluded between the two countries and are successfully implemented. Trade relations are developing . . . [between] the Soviet Union and Kuwait . . . attitudes toward a number of the most important issues of the time are unanimous or very similar.[57]

There was a great deal of pretence in this and similar Soviet comments relating to Kuwait. The Soviets wished to maintain relations with Kuwait's existing regime, but they also viewed it as 'archaic' and believed it would not last long. There were almost no direct official Soviet ties with Kuwaiti opposition groups — they were mostly indirect. However, with some groups direct contact did exist.[58]

Bahrain, Qatar, the UAE and Oman

Bahrain. The revolution in Iran brought renewed Iranian claims to Bahrain, 50–60 per cent of whose population were Shi'a. Ayatollah Sadeq Rohani called on Bahrain's population to topple its ruler, Shaykh 'Isa ibn Salman al-Khalifah, predicting that he would go the same way as the Shah. He claimed that the people of Bahrain 'want an Islamic Republic on the same model as Iran' and that he had sent envoys to Bahrain 'to supervise the struggle on the spot'.[59] The Emir of Bahrain, Shaykh Khalifah, said that his country had received assurances from Iran that such statements reflected the opinion of their proponents only. He described Bahraini-Iranian relations as good.[60]

In February 1980 the communist Bahrain National Liberation Front (BNLF) marked its 25th anniversary, sending a representative to Moscow to express support of the USSR and its policy.[61] An 'unofficial' Moscow broadcast devoted to the BNLF said its struggle 'brought about positive changes in the Gulf Region which fruitfully affected and influenced the conditions of Bahrain itself'. However, social and economic changes had still to come.

> The ruling clique, which is closely tied to the oil multinationals, reaps great profits from oil and banking transactions at a time when the toiling people remain in their difficult conditions . . .
>
> On the international field, the Front is fighting . . . the Camp David agreements . . . and for the return of Egypt to the fold of the Arab national liberation movement . . . It supports the Omani people's struggle led by the Popular Front for the Liberation of Oman . . . [and] welcomes any aid given by the USSR to Afghanistan . . .[62]

Officially, the Soviets avoided using such language, instead exchanging greetings with the Emir on public holidays, and hoping to establish diplomatic relations with him.

Qatar. Qatar had no diplomatic relations with the Soviet Union and its regime was also regarded by the Soviets as 'feudal' and 'archaic'. However, its Emir also used to exchange ceremonial greetings with Soviet leaders. In September 1980, on the occasion of Qatar's independence day celebrations, Brezhnev greeted the Emir, extending good wishes to him and 'the friendly Qatari people'. The Emir thanked Brezhnev and wished 'further progress to the Soviet people'.[63]

The United Arab Emirates (UAE). These countries did not have diplomatic relations with the USSR either, but the Soviet media avoided criticizing them, trying not to offend their rulers.[64] The Soviet-supported PFLO in the UAE was working against their regimes and on several occasions some of its members were arrested.[65]

Oman. Oman had no relations of any kind with the USSR — there were no exchanges of greetings and no Soviet attempts to establish official relations. The Soviet media were highly critical of Oman's regime and its Sultan, its ties with the USA and its support of Egypt's agreements with Israel. The Soviets supported the guerrilla activities of the PFLO.

A PFLO delegation headed by 'Abd al-'Aziz al-Qadhi, Chairman of the Central Executive Committee, visited the USSR from 24 to 29 April 1979, at the invitation of the Soviet Committee for Solidarity with Asian and African Countries. The Soviet statement after the visit said that during PFLO talks 'with representatives of the Soviet public', the Soviet side had expressed 'firm support' for their 'just struggle'.[66] In a statement to Moscow radio the head of the delegation stressed 'the importance and effectiveness of the assistance' of the socialist states and particularly the Soviet Union.[67]

The PFLO was not active[68] and the Soviets preferred that their contacts with it be given a low profile and no publicity.

The Soviets Call for a European Conference on the Persian Gulf

Leonid Brezhnev's election speech in Moscow on 22 February 1980 included a short reference to oil supply routes and communications in the Persian Gulf area. He said:

> In Washington they like to talk about the necessity of ensuring the safety of US oil supply routes. In a way this is understandable. But can this be achieved by turning the region of communications into a powder keg? It is obvious that the result would be the opposite.[69]

He did not elaborate further, but a TASS commentary by Nikolay Portugalov was more specific. Portugalov indicated that the oil supply routes and their security were of vital importance not only for the United States but to an even greater extent for other oil-consuming countries, and that European countries depended on Middle East oil more than the USA. He referred to a Soviet proposal to convene an all-European conference on energy, with the participation of 'all countries which have signed the Helsinki Final Act' (at the 1975 Conference on Security and Co-operation in Europe; in other words, the European states plus the USA and Canada). Portugalov proposed a correlation between 'the problem of equal and free access to oil sources with the agreement of those to whom oil belongs, and the guaranteed security of the ways of its delivery', dealing with it 'at first within an all-European framework and later at the United Nations'.[70]

One of the aims of the above was to give the USSR and its East European allies a role in any negotiations on the matter. It was not an official proposal, but rather a comment requiring no reply. No such reply was forthcoming from Western powers.

North Yemen (YAR)

Attempts to Balance the USSR and the USA

North Yemen has the largest population of any country in the Arabian peninsula, including Saudi Arabia, where over a million Yemenis are employed, sending home about $1.5 billion a year.[71] Generally, the YAR central government's control over most of the country was weak. It more or less controlled the cities, while the rest was controlled by tribes. Ever-changing tribal alliances determined the country's politics. The armed forces and the political parties were in fact tools of the tribes, some of whom were subsidized by Saudi Arabia. Others in the south of the country were oriented towards the PDRY.

Saudi Arabia wanted the YAR to be a buffer state between itself and the PDRY. It hoped for some YAR-PDRY tension, but not war. It wanted North Yemen to be strong enough to contain South Yemen, but not more than this, and not centralized. It constantly tried to keep the YAR dependent on Saudi Arabia, militarily weak and divided by internecine quarrelling. Tribal influences, under Saudi influence, controlled the country.

Saudi Arabia's position in regard to the YAR was backed by the USA and this contributed to YAR leaders' attempts to seek closer relations with the USSR. The Soviets hoped to limit Saudi Arabia's role and influence, but in order to succeed they had to invest more in the YAR and support it much more than they had done in the past. Previous experience made the Soviets hesitate to do so because their ties with the PDRY and their obligations to it limited their manoeuvrability.

YAR leaders attempted to exploit the situation, balancing East against West and using power competition to their own advantage.[72] President 'Ali Abdallah Salih came to an agreement with the PDRY, aiming to neutralize PDRY opposition to the Soviet aid which he was receiving, and which was being used to force the USA and Saudia Arabia to increase their aid and support.[73]

YAR-PDRY Fighting

The hostilities between the YAR and the PDRY which broke out on 23 February 1979, lasting until early March, began as one of many small border conflicts. South Yemeni forces succeeded, with the help of border tribes and North Yemenis who had escaped to the South, in achieving local advantages along the border.

The PDRY denied direct involvement, claiming that these were the activities of the National Democratic Front (NDF), a North Yemeni opposition group based in the PDRY. The YAR claimed it had been a planned attack with the participation of the Soviets and the Cubans. The Soviets denied any participation, and said that no Cuban technicians or advisers had been involved in the fighting on the side of South Yemen.[74]

The conflict began at a time when PDRY-Saudi Arabian talks were taking place, aiming at the eventual normalization of relations between the two countries. The PDRY Foreign Minister was then in Riyadh negotiating for a visit by 'Abd al-Fattah Isma'il. The success of the talks would have had implications for Soviet-Saudi relations, a matter on which there were serious differences of opinion in the Saudi ruling family. At that time there was an unconfirmed report that the Minister of Defence and Aviation, Prince Sultan ibn 'Abd al-'Aziz, was among those in the Saudi royal family who were against a dialogue with the PDRY and the USSR, and in favour of full co-operation with the USA. These members of the royal family encouraged the North Yemenis to stage border provocations in order to prevent a Saudi-PDRY *rapprochement*.[75]

The extent of the YAR-PDRY war was in all probability exaggerated. There were clashes, tribal wars and fighting of North Yemeni opposition forces, supported to a certain measure by the PDRY, but was there a full-scale war? The South Yemenis claimed not, and it seemed that they were, at least partly, right.

The YAR used the occasion to ask the USA for increased military aid. The Carter administration, criticized for not being firm enough and accused of leaving Iran, was now seeking an opportunity to show firmness. It wanted to reassure Saudi Arabia that the US was willing and able to help if needed. Four hundred million dollars' worth of military aid was promptly sent to the

YAR. The equipment included 12 F-5 E fighter-bombers, 64 M-60 tanks, anti-tank rockets and anti-aircraft guns. The arms were sent through Saudi Arabia, which was paying for them.

US Secretary of State, Cyrus Vance, warned the Soviet ambassador in Washington that the administration held the Soviets partly responsible for the PDRY invasion, and that unless this was called off, relations between Moscow and Washington could be adversely affected. A naval task force led by the US aircraft-carrier *Constellation* was moving from the Philippines to the Arabian Sea in order to present an implicit threat of intervention with air power.[76]

The Saudis soon learned how limited the war really was. They did not want the YAR to be strengthened or there to be direct YAR-USA arms deals, so they pressured the Americans to refrain from sending military supplies directly to the YAR. They wanted these to go through Saudi Arabia, leaving part of the American arms intended for North Yemen in their own hands, supplying them slowly — or not at all — depending on YAR policies, and using this as pressure on the YAR, to increase Saudi influence there. The Saudis also used Iraq and Syria to try to persuade the Soviets to influence South Yemen to stop fighting. The YAR concluded that if it could not receive what it needed from the USA without Saudi opposition, diminishing its dependence on Saudi Arabia, it would try to receive arms from the Soviet Union.

Arms Deals with the Soviets

Soviet arms shipments started to arrive in the YAR in September 1979, accompanied by instructors and technicians who numbered about 100 by the end of the year. The Soviets supplied 10 MiG-21 planes and 100 T-55 tanks, while the Saudis held up the delivery of American aircraft.[77]

The Saudis were reported to have asked North Yemen to ratify a protocol confirming the existing border between the two countries. This would have meant the YAR abandoning its claim to the towns of Najran and Jizan, north of the Yemen-Saudi border. Originally Yemeni, these towns had been annexed by Saudi Arabia in 1934.[78] The Saudis then asked the YAR to end its military links with the Soviets, to halt Soviet arms supplies and to expel Soviet military experts training the Yemenis on Soviet weaponry; they threatened to halt their financial support if no positive reply was forthcoming.[79] The Saudi ultimatum was rejected. Saudi Arabia appeared weakened after the incident of the Grand Mosque.

In the PDRY, Isma'il was replaced by 'Ali Nasir, with whom YAR leaders were more easily able to find a common language. They wished to strengthen the central YAR government *vis-à-vis* the tribal leaders supported by the Saudis, and work toward modernization and a strong YAR — a situation which the Saudis tried to prevent, but which the Soviets promised to help to achieve.

South Yemen (PDRY)

A Friendship and Co-operation Treaty with the USSR

The PDRY became the only Arab country to have a regime which could be termed communist, or almost so. As in other communist countries, there was inter-party co-operation between the Yemeni Socialist Party (YSP) and the Communist Party of the Soviet Union (CPSU). Since the Soviet Union was rendering military, economic and technical aid to the PDRY, it maintained a strong military presence, made up of both Soviet and Cuban personnel. The PDRY maintained installations, serving Soviet ships and planes.

The Soviet Prime Minister Kosygin visited the PDRY from 16 to 17 September 1979, on his way back from Ethiopia. He was the first top-level Soviet personality to visit there. According to the joint statement on the visit,[80] talks took place 'in an atmosphere of friendship and complete mutual understanding', in other words, each side understood why the other could not accept some of its views. Both sides were in full agreement regarding matters in distant places, and not directly concerning the PDRY, such as the situation in Vietnam or South Africa. They agreed less, or even differed, on regional matters. The USSR wanted the PDRY to present a more moderate image, a gradual PDRY approach to unity with North Yemen, and closer integration with Soviet policy in the region. Moscow also wanted greater PDRY participation in the region's affairs and improved PDRY relations with the countries of the region. The Soviets still wanted to establish relations with Saudi Arabia and the Gulf states, and PDRY extremism acted as an impediment.

The Soviets wished for even closer ties with the PDRY, to put relations on a legal basis, independent of the current leaders and personalities in power. 'Abd al-Fattah Isma'il visited the USSR from 23 to 26 October 1979, at which time the following documents were signed:

(1) A USSR-PDRY treaty of friendship and co-operation.
(2) 'A plan for contacts' between the CPSU and the YSP for the years 1980–3.
(3) A USSR-PDRY protocol on economic and technical co-operation.[81]

The friendship treaty, signed by Leonid Brezhnev and 'Abd al-Fattah Isma'il, was reminiscent of similar Soviet treaties with Ethiopia, Angola, Mozambique, Afghanistan and other Third World countries.

Article 1 indicated the 'unbreakable friendship between the two countries' and was meant to give the treaty a long-term aspect and permanence.

Article 2 stipulated that the parties would co-operate to ensure conditions 'for the safeguarding and further development of the socio-economic gains of their peoples'. This could mean Soviet commitment to intervene in case of danger to such 'gains'. It brings to mind the Brezhnev Doctrine[82] and Soviet intervention in Czechoslovakia in 1968. Perhaps even more so, it is reminiscent of the Soviet intervention in Afghanistan at the end of 1979, two months after the friendship treaty had been signed.

Article 3 said that the parties would 'exert efforts to strengthen and expand mutually advantageous economic, scientific and technical co-operation between them'.

Article 4 spoke about co-operation in science, culture, the arts, the press, radio, television, and so on. It also referred to direct ties at various levels, including the lower ranks. Such ties would enable the Soviets directly to influence PDRY groups and personalities, and, through them, to put pressure on the PDRY leadership.

Article 5 stipulated that the parties would 'continue to develop co-operation in the military field on the basis of the relevant agreements concluded between them for the purpose of strengthening their defence capacity'. It stipulated co-operation and not aid, indicating an agreement between two equal sides. This might have been flattering to PDRY leaders, but it was obvious that there could be no equality in military co-operation between a superpower and a small, very poor and highly underdeveloped country. It meant that each side would have to make its own contribution, in other words, the PDRY would have to give the Soviets something in exchange for arms and training. They had no financial means of paying for the aid, but could provide services to Soviet planes and ships, and allow them to use their military facilities. They could also contribute to Soviet efforts in the region (as they had done by sending troops to help Ethiopia in 1977–8).

Article 8 was against 'colonialism and racism in all their forms and manifestations' and in favour of co-operation and support 'of the just struggle of peoples for their freedom, independence, sovereignty and social progress'. In its wording, the article allowed the parties to be against Sultan Qabus, Saudi Arabia, Israel, Egypt — in fact, against everyone that each side wished.

Article 11 said that the parties would 'consult each other on major international questions directly affecting the interests of the countries'. 'Regular consultations' were not mentioned as they had been in other Soviet treaties. In situations 'threatening peace or violating international peace' (it was not clear who would decide that such a situation existed), the parties would 'strive to enter into contact with each other without delay, for the purpose of co-ordinating their positions in the interests of removing a threat to peace or restoring peace'.

Article 12 said that neither party would enter into military or other alliances, or 'groupings of states or actions and undertakings' directed against the other party.

Article 14 stipulated that the treaty was to remain in force for 20 years.[83]

There were reports that the treaty included secret clauses and that the Soviets had committed themselves to support and defend the PDRY regime 'under all circumstances', even in the event of it being threatened by a 'world power', in other words, the USA. If true, this would have made the treaty similar to other Soviet treaties with Warsaw Pact countries, but this seems highly improbable. The USSR had certain advantages in ties with the PDRY, but not enough to risk being involved in a war on its account. PDRY Foreign Minister Salim Salih Muhammad denied that the treaty had any secret clauses, saying that 'all its clauses and provisions were made public'.[84]

Military Ties

Soviet naval units had begun converging on PDRY ports from early 1979. In March there were reports that about 17 warships and three submarines were clustered around the entrance to the Bab al-Mandab Straits. At the huge air force base complex near al-Mukalla, MiG-23, MiG-25 and MiG 27 aircraft were in evidence, piloted by Soviets. Soviet amphibian reconnaissance aircraft began to guard and survey the PDRY, the coast-line of the Gulf and the Arabian peninsula from the bases in the PDRY.[85]

Soviet military personnel in the PDRY were estimated at between 300 and 1,500. US intelligence analysts were cited in early 1979 as saying that there were between 800 and 1,000 Soviets, between 500 and 700 Cubans and more than 100 East Germans acting as military and economic advisers. Some unconfirmed reports said that Cuban pilots were operating South Yemen's Soviet-supplied MiG-21s.[86] The Soviets trained the 20,000–25,000-strong military; the Cubans trained the militia, numbering about 55,000 and used by the YSP for internal security; while the East Germans trained the security services.

From time to time there were visits by Soviet naval units and military delegations. In mid-June 1979 a visit took place by General A. A. Yepishev, Chief of the Main Political Directorate of the Soviet Army and Navy.[87] His visits to friendly non-Soviet military forces were often meant to ascertain to what extent such forces were 'reliable' and could be used by the Soviets. There were Western reports of Soviet intentions of establishing a local military force for possible use in the Gulf area. Perhaps the possibility had been examined, but in any event, nothing seemed to have been done about it.

There were also reports of the 'rapid construction' of military installations by the Soviets. Soviet ships were said to be bringing 'voluminous amounts' of arms to the PDRY, much more than its army could use. Large military supply depots were said to have been set up, making an airlift unnecessary, at least in the beginning, to build up stocks in the event of a regional conflict.[88]

Soviet experts were reportedly engaged in building bases for Soviet submarines in South Yemeni territorial waters, 'which the submarines will use for their long-range patrols in the Arabian Sea and Indian Ocean'.[89] The Soviets were said to have completed setting up a military base on Socotra Island, containing sophisti-cated electronic surveillance systems and a communications centre for maintaining artificial satellite transmissions, long-range missile-launchers and ports for warships and submarines.[90] This report was not confirmed by other sources and was probably quite exaggerated, like many earlier reports of Soviet activities on Socotra.

President 'Ali Nasir Muhammad al-Hasani denied the existence of any Soviet bases in the PDRY.[91] During his meeting with King Khalid of Saudi Arabia in Riyadh, he tried to convince the king not to attach too much importance to the military equipment (surface-to-surface missiles, MiG-23 aircraft and T-62 and T-72 tanks) obtained by Aden from Moscow. The king stressed the need to maintain the principle of barring the presence of foreign forces in the region.[92]

Economic Co-operation

Neither the Soviets nor the South Yemenis gave much publicity to USSR-PDRY military co-operation, but they loudly played up the economic and technical co-operation, whose extent was actually much smaller, and very little compared to the considerable needs of the PDRY.

According to TASS, the aid was given in the field of agriculture and fisheries, as follows: building eight water-supply dams, drilling and putting into operation 100 water-wells for the irrigation of more than 4,000 hectares in the Hadramawt Valley, helping to build a fish cannery in al-Mukalla with a capacity of eight million fish cans a year. In Aden a port was to be built, with berths for fishing vessels, refrigerators, storehouses and repair shops with a floating dock.[93]

An earlier *Pravda* report mentioned, in addition to this list, supplies of Soviet ships, Soviet geologists prospecting for oil and hard minerals, and Soviet instructors training PDRY national cadres:

> With the help of Soviet friends many Yemenis have acquired new professions, hundreds of young men and women are studying in educational establishments in the USSR and other socialist countries, and centres for training construction workers, fishermen and highly skilled workers are operating in Aden and al-Mukalla with the assistance of Soviet specialists. A repair base is being set up . . . for training irrigation specialists.[94]

All this was not much, even for a small country like the PDRY which needed and asked for more, but the USSR did not accede to these requests. A great part of Soviet aid was concentrated in fields advantageous to the USSR. The establishment of an infrastructure for the PDRY fishing fleet was also useful to Soviet fishing vessels and the Soviet Navy in the Indian Ocean. This was also true in the case of the extension of the port of Aden, which provided the Soviets with much-needed services. When the fish cannery was completed, a large part of its production was shipped to the USSR as payment for the construction and other services. Soviet geologists learned to know the country, and PDRY students in the USSR and participants in Soviet-operated courses in the PDRY were constantly subjected to Soviet political indoctrination.

Further Changes in the PDRY Leadership

On 20 April 1980 the Secretary-General of the YSP and Chairman of the Presidium of the Supreme People's Council, 'Abd al-Fattah Isma'il, resigned from all his posts 'for health reasons'. The YSP Central Committee accepted his resignation and appointed him to an honorary position as party chairman. 'Ali Nasir Muhammad al-Hasani took his place, in addition to his position as Chairman of the Council of Ministers.[95]

Isma'il's resignation eased the situation between the PDRY and neighbouring states. Isma'il had tried to outdo Moscow in Marxism-Leninism and adherence to its doctrines, but his extremism had only succeeded in isolating the PDRY and ruining its economy. The USSR was now forced to invest in the PDRY and help it in this time of crisis, but it meant that it was doing so at the expense of its relations with other countries in the region. It impeded the establishment of ties between the Soviets and conservative Arab states.

The Soviets usually went in on the side of the winners, but this time they had reason to prefer 'Ali Nasir Muhammad al-Hasani over Isma'il, because he was acting to improve relations with the Arab countries. He was also in favour of a *rapprochement* with the YAR and the renewed flow of economic aid from conservative Arab states. He was less supportive of international radical (and terrorist) groups and opposed their training in the PDRY. He gave less aid to the PFLO and to the opposition groups in the YAR. His provision of aid to Ethiopia was also restricted. This resulted in fewer reservations regarding the PDRY in the Arab world. This indirectly strengthened the Soviet position and diminished fears of the Soviet 'bogey'. But, at the same time, the Soviets were fearful that the PDRY might turn away from them and that its greater interaction in the Arab world was part of this trend.[96] The PDRY assured the Soviets that this was not the case and that the changes in leadership were only of a personal nature, with no policy shifts envisaged. One of the aims of 'Ali Nasir Muhammad al-Hasani's visit to the USSR from 27 to 29 May 1980 was to convince the Soviets of this. According to the joint communiqué after the visit, 'the talks passed in an atmosphere of cordiality and complete mutual understanding'. During the visit, agreements were signed concerning the establishment of a permanent commission for economic and technological co-operation, co-operation in the construction of a thermal power station, and a protocol 'on the further expansion of economic and technological co-operation'.[97]

The PDRY leadership began to speak in more moderate tones, but actual changes in policy were few, and also slow in implementation. The PDRY continued to be Soviet-oriented, being dependent on its aid and protection and needing its relatively efficient security services to prop up the regime.

A Decline in Soviet Positions

The Soviets succeeded in achieving positions around the Gulf which gave the impression that they were attempting to encircle it. Their mere proximity to the Gulf region gave them advantages over the other more distantly situated powers.

To the east there was the Soviet presence in Afghanistan, which encountered growing resistance, giving the Soviets problems in pacification of the country. Muslim countries turned against the USSR, although this did not automatically mean that they favoured the USA to a greater extent.

To the west the Soviets maintained a presence in Ethiopia, propping up the regime and providing it with military aid needed to counter the Eritrean revolt and other attempts to tear away parts of the country. But Ethiopia also needed considerable economic aid, of which the Soviets provided very little. Further to the west the Soviets were co-operating with Libya. They also held positions in Syria, and their support of the Palestinian organizations gave them a certain measure of influence over these as well.

On the whole, the Soviet position was weak, dependent to a great extent on their local friends. Previously, the Soviets had invested much more in the region, but those in whom they had invested so heavily had now turned away from them, as in the case of Egypt and Somalia. This led the Soviets to conclude that they should risk less and look for more immediate benefits. But this contributed to a further decline of their position and caused local leaders to rely on them less.

The Soviets tried to exploit the Arab-Israeli conflict to their advantage, using Arab opposition to the peace between Egypt and Israel and supporting those acting against it, and attempting to turn attention away from the Muslim revolt in Afghanistan and in the direction of anti-Israel slogans and support of the PLO. However, this too helped the Soviets less than it had done previously.

The war which broke out in September 1980 between Iraq and Iran further complicated the Soviet situation in the region and contributed still more to a decline in its positions there, particularly in the Gulf region.

Notes

1. The Shah died of cancer in a Cairo hospital on 27 July 1980.
2. *Pravda*, 3 March 1979.
3. P. Demchenko, 'The USSR and Iran: Horizons of Co-operation', ibid., 6 April 1979.
4. Aleksandr Bovin, 'With Koran and Saber!!!', *Nedelya* (weekly supplement to *Izvestia*), no. 36, 4 Sept. 1979, p. 6.
5. TASS in English, 22 Sept. 1979. In FBIS, USSR, 24 Sept. 1979, p. H2.
6. Tehran Domestic Service, 5 Nov. 1979. In FBIS, ME, 6 Nov. 1979, pp. R16–R17.
7. Kianuri to Eric Rouleau, *Le Monde*, 18 April 1980.
8. Pavel Demchenko, *Pravda*, 17 Jan. 1981.
9. Boris Orekhov, 'International Review', ibid., 25 Jan. 1981.
10. *Izvestia*, 11 Feb. 1981.
11. A reasoning of this kind appeared in a Tehran radio commentary. It stated that during the Islamic revolution the Soviet Union became 'a toy in the hands of the United States, and, following the green light it received to occupy Afghanistan, it has now begun indirectly to help the US interests in Iran and to help the counter-revolutionary elements in Iran'. In Iraq, the USSR provided military aid but that did not pave a way for Soviet influence but 'works toward safeguarding US interests in harming Iran's revolution', (Tehran Domestic Service, 14 Aug. 1980. In FBIS, South Asia, 15 Aug. 1980, pp. 16–17.)
12. Tehran radio in English to Europe, 9 July 1980. In FBIS, South Asia, 10 July 1980, pp. 12–13.
13. Tehran Domestic Service, 9 Aug. 1980. In FBIS, South Asia, 11 Aug. 1980, pp. I12–I14.

14. Tehran Domestic Service, 14 Aug. 1980. In FBIS, South Asia, 15 Aug. 1980, pp. 12–16, and (correction) 18 Aug. 1980, p. 122.

15. Moscow radio in Persian to Iran, 28 Aug. 1980. In FBIS, USSR, 29 Aug. 1980, pp. H1–H2.

16. Moscow radio in Persian to Iran, 22 Aug. 1980. In FBIS, USSR, 25 Aug. 1980, p. H2.

17. Tehran Domestic Service, 25 Aug. 1980. In FBIS, South Asia, 25 Aug. 1980, p. H2.

18. Iran charged $3.80 for each 1,000 cubic feet of gas, whereas formerly the figure was 76 cents.

19. Moscow radio in Persian to Iran, 27 June 1980. In FBIS, USSR, 1 July 1980, pp. H2–H3.

20. *Pravda*, 17 Sept. 1980.

21. *Keyhan*, 21 June 1980.

22. *As-Safir* (Beirut), 21 Aug. 1980.

23. *Pravda*, 10 Jan. 1979. According to *Le Monde* (23 Feb. 1979), 1,913 Iraqi communists had 'disappeared' since 1 Jan. 1979, plus 2,125 in Kurdistan alone: 'Party leaders are very worried about them.' Under the heading 'Stop the Repressions and Persecutions' in the international communist *World Marxist Review* in March 1979, it was said:

> More than twenty activists and friends of the ICP were executed. Communists, including party leaders, were persecuted, and the ICP organizations and press were harassed . . .
>
> Since May 1978 more than 10,000 persons have been arrested and subjected to physical and mental torture. They were held in prison from a few days to several weeks, while nothing is known to this day of the fate of scores of detainees.
>
> (Naziha Duleimi, Representative of ICP, *World Marxist Review* (March 1979), p. 86).

24. *Le Monde*, 6 April 1979.

25. The ICP was later expelled from the PNF. (*Ath-Thawrah*, Baghdad, 12 Sept. 1980).

26. Iraqi News Agency (INA), 22 April 1979. In FBIS, ME, 23 April 1979, pp. E1–E2.

27. *Pravda*, 22 Jan. 1979. See also Y. Korshunov, 'The Republic's Horizons', *Izvestia*, 15 July 1979. The article included a summary of Soviet-Iraqi economic and technical co-operation.

28. *Al-Mustaqbal* (Paris), 1 Sept. 1979.

29. V. Konstantinov, 'USSR-Iraqi Friendship, Co-operation,' *Izvestia*, 9 Sept. 1979.

30. Some 200 Iraqi Army officers arrested and charged with being communists were reportedly released and promised that they would be reinstated in their units. The decision was reported to be linked to a Baghdad visit of a Soviet military delegation. (*Al-Hawadith*, London, 23 Nov. 1979).

31. *Al-Siyasah*, 6 Jan. 1980.

32. 'Peace and Progress' in Arabic, 6 March 1980. In FBIS, USSR, 7 March 1980, pp. H3–H4. See also interview with ICP First Secretary 'Aziz Muhammad in the London communist *Morning Star*, 28 Dec. 1979.

33. *Pravda*, 11 April 1980.

34. Bernard Gwertzman, *International Herald Tribune* (Paris), 7 Aug. 1980.

35. *Monday Morning*, 14–20 July 1980.

36. Alexander Borovikov, *Foreign Trade* (Aug. 1980), p.23.

37. Igor Belyayev, 'Saudi Arabia: What Next?', *Literaturnaya Gazeta*, 31 Jan. 1979.

38. Interview given by Saudi Arabia's Foreign Minister Prince Sa'ud al-Faysal to Salim al-Lawzi, *Al-Hawadith* (London), 2 March 1979.

39. Moscow radio in Arabic, 5 March 1979. Cited in BBC SU/6060/A4/2, 7 March 1979. Published in part in *Izvestia*, 6 March 1979.

40. N. Morozov, 'Around the Arabian Knot', *Sovyetskaya Rossiya*, 27 March 1979.

41. Le Monde, 15 May 1979.

42. *Monday Morning*, 2–8 July 1979.

43. President Anwar al-Sadat to the Egyptian Parliament on 28 Jan. 1980.

44. *As-Siyasah*, 29 Oct. 1979.

45. For a typical Leonid Brezhnev-King Khalid exchange of ceremonial greetings, see *Pravda*, 28 Sept. 1979. Soviet wishes to establish diplomatic relations with Saudi Arabia were voiced in Moscow radio broadcasts in Arabic, 23 Sept. 1979 and 17 Feb. 1980. Cited in FBIS, USSR, 24 Sept. 1979, pp.H4–H5, and 20 Feb. 1980, pp. H5–H7.

46. TASS in English, 13 Feb. 1980. In FBIS, USSR, 20 Feb. 1980, p. H5.

47. *The Times*, 20 May 1980.

48. Igor Belyayev, 'Just who is threatening Saudi Arabia?', *Literaturnaya Gazeta*, 9 July 1980.

49. *An-Nida*, 17 Sept. 1980.

50. *Al-Hadaf* (Beirut), 3 May 1980.

51. *L'Humanité*, 2 Sept. 1980.

52. Alexei Vasil'yev, 'Saudi Arabia Between Archaism and Contemporaneity', *Aziya i Afrika Segodniya*, no. 8 (Aug. 1980), pp. 19–21; no. 9 (Sept. 1980), pp. 17–21. The English edition (which did not include most of the September 1980 part of the Russian edition) was entitled 'Emirs and Theologians of the Oil Kingdom', *Asia and Africa Today*, no. 6 (Nov.–Dec. 1980), pp. 20–3.

53. Ibid., English edn., p. 20.

54. Ibid., Russian edn., no. 9 (Sept. 1980).

55. *As-Siyasah*, 31 Jan. 1979.

56. Kuwaiti military manoeuvres using Soviet-made ground-to-ground Luna-type missiles were reported in February 1980. (Kuwait News Agency (KUNA), 9 February 1980. In FBIS, ME, 11 Feb. 1980, p. C2).
The Soviet ambassador to Kuwait said that the Soviet Union had supplied Kuwait with weapons, including ground-to-ground missiles, without preconditions. He added that co-operation in the arms field was taking place 'on a purely business basis' and that the Soviet side was satisfied with this co-operation. (KUNA, 15 May 1980. In FBIS, USSR, 16 May 1980, p. H3).

57. Moscow radio in Arabic, 11 March 1980. In FBIS, USSR, 13 March 1980, pp. H2–H3.

58. See, for example, Aryeh Y. Yodfat and Yuval Arnon-Ohanna, *PLO Strategy and Tactics* (Croom Helm, London, and St. Martin's Press, New York, 1981), p. 99.

59. AFP, 24 Sept. 1979. In FBIS, ME, 25 Sept. 1979, p. R8.

60. *Ar-Ra'y al-'Amm*, 24 April 1980.

61. 'Peace and Progress' in Arabic, 22 Feb. 1980. In FBIS, USSR, 27 Feb. 1980, p. H5.

62. 'Peace and Progress' in Arabic, 16 Feb. 1980. In FBIS, USSR, 20 Feb. 1980, p. H9.

63. *Izvestia*, 6 Sept. 1980.

64. See M. Vasil'yev, 'UAE. What will the "Golden Rain" Bring?', *New Times*, no. 50 (Dec. 1979), pp. 14–15.

65. *An-Nahar al-'Arabi wa ad-Dawli*, 4–10 Aug. 1980.

66. *Izvestia*, 1 May 1979.

67. Moscow radio in Arabic, 27 April 1979. In FBIS, USSR, 2 May 1979, p. H2.

68. Iranian forces who helped the Sultan to fight the PFLO left Oman after Iran's Islamic revolution, and the PFLO then established ties with Iran. A PFLO delegation visited Iran in May 1979 and had a long meeting there with Ayatollah Khomeyni. (*An-Nahar al-'Arabi wa ad-Dawli*, 28 May 1979). Highly exaggerated reports appeared about the arrival of 5,000 to 7,000 Egyptian soldiers who replaced the Iranians. (*An-Nahar*, 13 March 1979).

69. *Pravda*, 23 Feb. 1980.

70. TASS in Russian, 29 Feb. 1980. In FBIS, USSR, 3 March 1980, p. G1.

71. *Washington Star*, 20 Feb. 1980.

72. Patrick Seale, 'Yemen's Balancing Act', *The Observer*, 21 Oct. 1979; Daniel Southerland, 'Yemen Arms Deal: Red Faces for the US, Jitters for Saudis', *Christian Science Monitor*, weekly int. edn., 3 Dec. 1979.

73. YAR President 'Ali Abdallah Salih said in early 1979:

We should keep our republic away from links with either of the superpowers . . .

Our desire is to diversify sources of arms so that we will not become the captive of one particular side. We are in fact now receiving limited quantities of US arms but we have not obtained all we want. We also have weapons from the Soviet Union.

(*As-Siyasah*, 29 Jan. 1979).

74. Moscow radio in English to North America, 11 March 1979. In FBIS, USSR, 12 March 1979, pp. F11–F12.

75. *Events*, 23 March 1979, p. 19.

76. William Beecher, *Boston Globe*, 10 March 1979; *The Economist*, 23 Feb. 1980, pp. 43–4; Y. Glukhov, *Pravda*, 12 March 1979.

77. *The Economist*, 23 Feb. 1980.

78. *Reuters* (London), 8 Feb. 1980. In FBIS, ME, 11 Feb. 1980, p. C4.

79. Ibid.; *October* (Cairo), 17 Feb. 1980.

80. *Pravda*, 19 Sept. 1979.

81. Ibid., 27 Oct. 1979.

82. See Charles T. Baroch, 'The Soviet Doctrine of Sovereignty (The So-Called Brezhnev Doctrine)', *Bulletin* (Institute for the Study of the USSR, Munich), Aug. 1979, pp. 7–25; Waring Herrick, 'The "Brezhnev Doctrine" Revisited', *Radio Liberty Research* (Munich), part I, 6 Dec. 1971; part II, 27 Dec. 1971; Sergey Kovalev, *Pravda*, 26 Sept. 1968.

83. *Pravda*, 26 Oct. 1979. The PDRY later signed similar friendship treaties with the GDR on 17 Nov. 1979 (*Neues Deutschland*, East Berlin, 19 November 1979) and with Czechoslovakia on 14 Sept. 1981 (*Rude Pravo*, Prague, 15 Sept. 1981).

84. *Ar-Ra'y al-'Amm*, 9 Dec. 1979.

85. *Al-Hawadith* (London), 16 March 1979.

86. *Washington Post*, 27 Feb. 1979.

87. *Krasnaya Zvezda*, 12 June 1979.

88. Manfred Rowold, *Die Welt* (Bonn), 7 Sept. 1979.

89. *Al-Hawadith* (London), 3 Nov. 1979.

90. *Al-Ahram*, 17 May 1979, citing the South Yemeni opposition United National Front.

91. *Al-Majallah*, 3–17 June 1980.

92. *An-Nahar al-'Arabi wa ad-Dawli*, 21 July 1980, p. 37.

93. TASS in English, 29 Aug. 1980. In FBIS, USSR, 2 Sept. 1980, p. H3.

94. *Pravda*, 8 July 1979. For Cuban economic and technical assistance, see *Granma*, 21 Dec. 1980, p. 12.

95. Aden Domestic Service, 21 April 1980. In FBIS, ME, 22 April 1980, pp. C1–C2.

96. People arriving from South Yemen reported that Isma'il had been removed 'because his colleagues felt that Aden has become increasingly isolated as a result of the inclination toward Moscow and of the Russians' failure to fulfil their commitments on giving Aden adequate aid'. They said it was a step towards lessening reliance on Soviet support and towards a *rapprochement* with Arab countries. (*Ash-Sharq al-Awsat*, 25 April 1980).

97. *Pravda*, 31 May 1980.

4 BETWEEN STABILITY AND UPHEAVAL
(September 1980 – Early 1982)

The Iraq-Iran War — Disadvantageous to the Soviets

On 22 September 1980 Iraqi forces began a full-scale war against Iran. The Soviets attempted to take advantage of the occasion in order to improve their relations with Iran and appear strictly neutral. They were even reported to have indirectly passed Iraq's secret plans for an offensive to the enemy. Iran's preoccupation with internal power struggles caused its leaders to view the reports with suspicion, and they refused to believe them.[1]

President Saddam Husayn expected a quick victory, leading to the overthrow of the Khomeyni regime. He hoped to seize Khuzestan within a few days, then incite successful revolts in Kordestan, and in Iran's armed forces and among the population. None of this took place. In fact, the opposite occurred — the external danger strengthened Iran's regime and brought it the support of many who had previously opposed it.

The Soviets found themselves in the delicate situation of 'damned if we do, damned if we don't'. Anything they did or said about the conflict could be interpreted by either of the warring parties as taking sides. Providing aid to Iraq would strain relations with Iran as well as Syria and Libya, which had close ties with the Soviets. On the one hand, no aid at all would damage Soviet relations with Iraq, forcing it to look elsewhere for arms — which it was doing in any case. On the other hand, direct Soviet arms supplies to Iran (if the latter requested them) would result in the Soviets being expelled from Iraq — as had happened in Egypt and Somalia.

The war came at a bad time for the Soviet Union. It was by now deeply involved in Afghanistan and faced a complicated situation in Poland. Its leadership was also preoccupied with internal matters, such as economic difficulties and preparations for the 26th CPSU Congress due to convene in February–March 1981. The war also coincided with the American election campaign, in which Soviet involvement in foreign countries was a major issue.

Iraqi Deputy Prime Minister Tariq 'Aziz visited Moscow on 22 September 1980 for talks with CPSU Secretary Boris Ponomarev and First Deputy Foreign Minister Viktor Maltsev.[2] No high-level meetings were held with Soviet officials of equal rank and position to Tariq 'Aziz's and no mention was made of the Soviet-Iraqi treaty of friendship.

When asked whether he had requested any sophisticated weapons or fresh supplies, Tariq 'Aziz replied, 'We have been buying arms for twelve years and we would not have waged a war in which we would be in need of arms within five minutes of waging it. Our arms are stockpiled and will suffice us for a long war.' He stated that the aim óf his Moscow visit was to inform the Soviets that it was in their own interests to watch the situation on the Iraq-Iran border and understand what was happening without intervening, as long as the conflict was confined to Iraq and Iran.[3]

The next day, 23 September, the Supreme Soviet Vice-President Inamadzhan Usmankhadzhayev received the Iranian ambassador Muhammad Mokri, at the latter's request.[4] The ambassador reported to his superiors that he had told the Soviets that they should condemn the Iraqi action.

> They replied: 'We are taking a neutral stand which we shall endeavour to maintain.' I told them: 'We are neither satisfied with nor consent to your neutrality, which is like giving a dagger to one of two men in a fight, then standing back and saying 'I am neutral.'[5]

Ambassador Mokri reported that the Soviet government had formally assured him that Moscow intended to remain neutral. The Soviets had refused further military aid to Iraq and maintained that Tariq 'Aziz's visit to Moscow 'was a failure'.[6]

At a Kremlin dinner in honour of Sanjiva Reddy, the Indian President, on 30 September 1980, Brezhnev said:

> The world has just become a witness to an armed conflict between Iran and Iraq — two neighbouring countries which are friendly to the Soviet Union . . .
>
> Neither Iraq nor Iran will gain anything from mutual destruction and bloodshed and undermining each other's economy. It is only the third side, the USA, to which the interests of the peoples in that region are alien, which stands to gain.
>
> As far as the Soviet Union is concerned, we are for Iran and Iraq settling disputable issues between themselves at the table of

negotiations. It would be good if they were to settle in the spirit of concord what can be settled now, but were to put off till tomorrow, when a settlement possibly comes easier, what they cannot settle today.[7]

Brezhnev described Iran and Iraq as being equally friendly to the USSR — ignoring the Soviet-Iraqi treaty and Soviet arms supplies to Iraq. He called for negotiations on what was possible, delaying the remainder indefinitely, until a time when it was easier to reach an agreement.

The Soviet's objective was to try to gain influence with both sides. This was what they had done in 1965, after the Indo-Pakistani war, when Premier Kosygin, acting as mediator, had succeeded in bringing the two adversaries to the negotiating table in Tashkent. The Soviets had tried the same tactic in the Ethiopian-Somali conflict in 1977, but failed. To have a foothold in both Iran and Iraq was, of course, to their advantage, but it seemed that if forced to choose, the Soviets were prepared to abandon their positions in Iraq, opting for influence in Iran, since, in any case, their power in Iraq was on the wane. This was similar to what had happened in the Ethiopian-Somali conflict, where the Soviets abandoned gains in Somalia for what seemed to them a more advantageous position in Ethiopia.

Brezhnev again referred to the Iraq-Iran war on 8 October 1980, at a dinner in the Kremlin for Syria's President Hafiz al-Asad. He said: 'We are not going to intervene in the conflict between Iran and Iraq. We stand for its earliest political settlement by the efforts of the two sides. And we resolutely say to the others: Hands off these events.'[8] Brezhnev said this on the very day that he and Asad had signed a Soviet-Syrian friendship treaty. Baghdad interpreted this as an anti-Iraqi action, coming at a time when Syrian-Iraqi relations were strained.

Although Soviet reports of the fighting tried to be even-handed, it was possible to discern indirect criticism of Iraq as the guilty party. The war did not go well for Iraq. Iranian forces succeeded in stopping the Iraqi advance and recaptured a great part of the territory occupied by Iraq. Needing a face-saving achievement after failing to obtain his objectives, Saddam Husayn said he was ready to withdraw from Iranian territory if Iran would accept full Iraqi sovereignty over the Shatt al-'Arab. The Iranians, however, insisted on full unconditional Iraqi withdrawal. Through all this, the Soviets were still hoping for an end to the war that had put them in such a delicate position and was certainly not to their advantage.

Iran

Soviet Offers of Aid are Rejected

The Soviets made repeated attempts to attract Iran, which continued to be very suspicious of them. Iran considered that both the Soviets and the Americans were behind Iraq's moves, each side hoping to benefit from an Iraqi victory. The Soviet ambassador to Iran, Vladimir Vinogradov, met the Iranian Prime Minister Muhammad 'Ali Raja'i and was reported as saying, 'We can co-operate in various fields and are prepared to help you with military equipment.' Raja'i rejected the proposal.[9] The text of the conversation was published the next day by Tehran newspapers. The Soviets protested, and TASS denied that the Soviet Union had offered Iran Soviet arms: 'There have been no proposals from the Soviet side to Iran concerning arms deliveries and, consequently, the Iranian Premier had nothing to reject.'[10]

A few days later, on 11 October 1980, the Iranian President Bani-Sadr met the Soviet ambassador and strongly protested about Soviet aid to Iraq. The ambassador replied that his government had been committed to a policy of neutrality since the war began. He added that his country was seeking to establish good and friendly relations with Iran, but protested at Iran's announcement of the Soviet offer to supply it with arms. He stated that this was untrue and had caused great embarassment to the USSR.[11]

Co-operation Continues in Bilateral Economic Relations

In bilateral economic relations no new Soviet-Iranian agreements were concluded, but in some of the projects that had been agreed upon in the past, protocols were being implemented.[12] Western economic sanctions, and difficulties in the use of Persian Gulf ports because of the war, increased the importance of northern inland routes through the Soviet Union. A Soviet-Iranian transit agreement was signed in September 1980 and ratified by Iran's Majlis in December. This provided for the use of Soviet territory for the transit of goods purchased by Iran from European countries, as well as for the transit of Iranian-manufactured goods to European countries.

According to an official in the Soviet State Committee for

Foreign Economic Relations, traffic between the Soviet Union and Iran moved by sea, rail and road. By the end of 1980, more than 250 wagons per day, carrying various products, were reaching the rail station at the Julfa border from the Soviet Union. Iranian export goods and other commodities were transported through this border station to the Soviet Union and other countries. Soviet river-sea vessels carried goods from Western Europe and from the Soviet Union to the Caspian Sea ports of Nawshahr and Enzeli.[13] The Trans-Siberian railway was used to transfer goods from Japan to Iran.

No agreement was reached regarding the export of Iranian gas to the Soviet Union. The Soviets wished to purchase it, but had not agreed to the price proposed by Iran, which stood firm on its price.[14] As Iranian oil exports dropped, negotiations on the subject were delayed.

Soviet Views of the Iranian Regime

The Soviet media, especially those directed at Iran, made great efforts to increase Iranian suspicions of the USA and prevent an Iranian-American *rapprochement*. They sharply criticized those Iranians pressing for an agreement with the USA to solve the problem of the American embassy hostages. Soviet commentators repeated over and over again that the USA was not interested in settling the issue, but only in using it as 'a pretext' to increase its military presence in the region.[15] They constantly repeated stories of American plans to attack Iran and release the hostages by force.[16]

The anti-Americanism of the Khomeyni regime won considerable praise in the USSR and was given wide coverage in the Soviet media, which extolled the entire regime for this one facet of its policy. This then led to a paradoxical situation where the Soviet Union was supporting those very groups that it had once scorned as being 'reactionary'. These same groups gave a blanket rejection to Western culture and concepts, and included communism as part of them. But in supporting them, the Soviets now found themselves in opposition to others who had adopted an outlook closer to their own, favouring modernization and relative secularization. This led to discussions in the Soviet Union as to whether — against all their principles — they could come to terms with such a regime simply because of its anti-Americanism, or whether there was a limit to the extent to which they could adapt themselves to situations.[17]

As they had done many times previously, the Soviet media met the challenge by presenting matters as they would have liked them to be, emphasizing those aspects of the regime which they favoured, and ignoring those that were contrary to their own outlook. The Khomeyni regime was now shown according to a Soviet ideal — completely different from what it really was.

Brezhnev's report to the 26th CPSU Congress in Moscow on 23 February 1981 included a reference to Iran:

The revolution in Iran has a special character. It was one of the major international events of recent years. With all its complications and contradictions, it is fundamentally an anti-imperialist revolution even though internal and foreign reaction is striving to change its nature. The Iranian people are seeking their own path to freedom and prosperity. We sincerely wish them success in this and we are ready to develop relations with Iran on the basis of equality and, of course, reciprocity.[18]

The Brezhnev report reflected Soviet attempts to be friendly and to attract Iran's leadership. It was, however, couched in Soviet terms, in language that did not have much meaning for the clergy ruling in Iran. This body was very suspicious of the Soviets, regarding them as 'a great Satanic power', no less dangerous than the Americans. This view assumed greater meaning because of Soviet proximity on the long border with Iran. The USSR had also intervened in Afghanistan against the Muslims and could do the same to Iran.

Officially the Soviets pretended that things were as Brezhnev had described them, ignoring Khomeyni's anti-Sovietism. However, Aleksandr Bovin, an *Izvestia* senior commentator, described the situation differently, putting into words what others in the Soviet Union were silently thinking. Describing relations between the ruling Islamic Republican Party (IRP) and President Bani-Sadr, a short time before his removal, Bovin said:

If one speaks of the religious leadership in Iran, then to judge by the chaos which exists in the country, both in the economy and in the politics — it generally, I have no doubt, is well acquainted with the Koran — the real problems facing Iran are evidently beyond the limits of its understanding. Bani-Sadr tried to reach a solution to those problems from pragmatic positions and by virtue of that he came into contradiction with the Islamic aims which now play the dominating role there.[19]

The Soviet media described President Bani-Sadr as being supported by liberal bourgeois, pro-Western and Maoist groups, thus giving a negative view of him. His dismissal by Khomeyni on 22 June 1981 was reported in the Soviet Union without comment, but as time passed he came under attack and was accused of pro-Americanism. According to Yevgeniy Primakov, Director of the Institute of Oriental Studies, USSR Academy of Sciences:

> Bani-Sadr and those groups who supported him . . . were oriented towards the United States . . . Towards the West, towards Europe . . . At the same time . . . Islamic fundamentalists . . . on a whole range of issues . . . occupy patriotic positions.

Bovin did not agree with this. He saw the Iranian anti-Americanism going hand in hand with anti-Sovietism, 'a struggle against the Eastern devil and against the Western devil'. As to the future:

> It appears that it is impossible to reorganize the country and to rebuild its social life in accordance with the principles being proposed by the fundamentalists. In other words, to return to a way of life set down in the Koran nearly 1,500 years ago. I do not think this experiment will be successful.[20]

The Soviets See the Revolution in Iran as Continuing

In a bomb explosion in Tehran IRP headquarters on 28 June 1981 64 people died, including IRP leader Ayatollah Beheshti, ministers, deputy ministers and members of parliament. Soviet reports accused the USA of staging the deed 'to destabilize the situation' and to engineer a coup in Iran similar to that in Chile against President Salvador Allende.[21] On 24 July 1981 Muhammad 'Ali Raja'i was elected President of Iran in place of Bani-Sadr. Ayatollah Beheshti's post of IRP Secretary-General was taken by Hojjat al-Eslam Muhammad Javad Bahonar. The latter was appointed Prime Minister by the Majlis on 5 August 1981. A few weeks later, on 30 August, both Raja'i and Bahonar were killed by an explosion in the office of the Prime Minister. Hojjat al-Eslam Hoseyni 'Ali Khamene'i was elected IRP Secretary-General on 31

August 1981 and on 2 October he became President of Iran. On 2 September Hojjat al-Eslam Muhammad Reza Mahdavi-Kani was nominated Prime Minister.

The Soviet media sharply attacked the USA for being behind the bombings and assassinations. They were easier on the Iranian internal opposition, accusing it of engaging in terrorist activities. On examining the reporting techniques of the Soviet media, one is able to distinguish similarities in their treatment of the present situation and the way they dealt with the one in Iran in mid-1978: on the one hand support for the Shah (or Khomeyni), but on the other, describing the great dissatisfaction of the masses with the regime. As usual, the Soviets tried to leave all their options open — remaining friendly with the regime but also avoiding antagonizing those whom they saw as having a chance of replacing the existing regime and its leadership.

Slow Soviet Penetration and Improvement in Relations

In the second half of 1981 there was some relative and limited improvement in Soviet-Iranian relations. When Iran's ambassador to the Soviet Union, Dr Muhammad Mokri, was questioned 'on the growth of relations' between the countries, he said: 'Relations are developing in a reasonable and satisfactory manner; economic and commercial relations are progressing . . . We have no arms contracts with the Soviet Union, but economic and commercial protocols previously concluded are to be renewed.'[22]

The Soviets still continued to be suspected and feared. Iran's attitude to them changed, but this too was more relative to the past than absolutely. It changed much more towards other communist countries: East European, Cuba, North Korea. This had a certain influence on Iran's view of the Soviets.

By late 1981 this attitude became evident in the IRP leadership, strengthening further in early 1982. It was not yet dominant, but was strong enough to be felt and to influence relations with the USSR. Khomeyni and his cohorts continued to fear and suspect the Soviets, whose intervention in Afghanistan was a constant reminder that this could happen to them too. In addition, the Soviet Union continued to be identified with Iran's attackers, the Iraqis. The Soviets were also suspected of being in contact with the leftist underground, the Tudeh Party and the fighting Kurds who opposed the regime. But there were those in the IRP who were becoming stronger, pressing for the government to come to some sort of working agreement with the Soviet Union in order to receive Soviet aid. Then they would be able to concentrate greater efforts against the United States, which they feared and regarded as an immediate danger. They hoped for the adoption of a policy similar to Libya's: guided by Islamic principles, but co-operating with the Soviets and receiving Soviet arms. The Soviets hoped that the people with these views would soon gain the upper hand and realize their desires. Their media often behaved as if such a situation already existed, believing that wishful thinking would bring it about.

The Soviet leaders continued their efforts to act in areas where the Iranians were ready to co-operate — technical aid, trade and military supplies through third parties — hoping that the deterioration in Iran's economic situation and its worsening relations with the USA would lead to stronger ties with the Soviet Union. Bilateral Soviet-Iranian trade increased, together with transit trade to and from Iran through the Soviet Union. From 7 to 12 October 1981 delegations of the Soviet news agency TASS and the Iranian news agency PARS held talks in Moscow regarding co-operation between them.[23] On 13 October the Chairman of the Soviet State Construction Agency met with the Iranian Minister for Housing and Urban Planning to discuss the same possibility.[24] Seven new silos for the storage of wheat were reported to have been constructed in Iran with the aid of the Soviet Union.[25] At the end of 1981 Iran rented ten Soviet locomotives, running on the Tabriz-Tehran line, driven and serviced by 19 Soviet engine-drivers, instructors and maintenance staff.[26] The railway linking the cities of Tabriz and Julfa (the latter is situated close to the Soviet border) was electrified with the help of Soviet specialists. In addition, 'several tens' of Iranian railway specialists were sent to the Soviet Union for training.[27] Each of the above-listed steps had little significance by itself, but all of them together had a cumulative effect, contributing to a slight but steady improvement in relations.

The Soviets felt that the revolution in Iran was still incomplete, with options possible in all directions. So, on the one hand, they preferred to have relations that were as close as possible with the existing regime, enabling them to maintain a presence and the ability to influence developments (or at least have first-hand information about them). On the other hand, they could watch and wait, not committing themselves to any particular preference, and then adapt themselves to circumstances and changes as they arose.

Iraq

A Cooling-off in Relations

The Soviets had officially proclaimed themselves neutral in the Iraq-Iran war, refraining from giving Iraq the military backing it expected from them. At first, when the war broke out, a few Soviet ships carrying cargoes for Iraq unloaded them in Aqaba for shipment overland through Jordan to Iraq. However, other ships *en route* for ports through which the arms could be delivered to Baghdad did not arrive at their destinations and were diverted elsewhere.[28] Some Soviet military equipment, mainly spare parts and ammunition, continued to arrive in Iraq through Arab, East European and other countries. Egypt and North Yemen also sold Iraq Soviet-made arms.

The Soviet media denied that the USSR had used Aqaba as a transit port for their arms deliveries to Iraq. They also denied claims by the former Iranian Defence Minister, Mostafa Chamran, who said that among the Iraqi troops fighting against Iran were tanks operated by Soviet military personnel. TASS dismissed as 'absolutely groundless' Iranian press reports 'alleging that Soviet specialists [were] taking part in operations of the Iraqi forces'.[29] A Soviet broadcast to Iran in mid-February 1981 said that 'the Soviet Union from the beginning of the fratricidal Iran-Iraq war had not delivered and will not deliver arms to either side in the conflict'.[30]

Later on, differences between the Soviets and the Iraqis became evident — not yet sharp enough to lead to a formal break between them, but quite sufficient to put a chill on their relations.

Iraqi persecutions of communists continued. 'Aziz Muhammad, the leader of the Iraqi Communist Party (ICP), spoke at the 26th CPSU Congress in Moscow in early March 1981, describing 'the ferocious campaign of persecution' which the ICP and the 'Kurdish people' had suffered. This had inflicted heavy losses on the ICP, but had failed, 'like all campaigns by other reactionary and dictatorial regimes'.[31] The Iraqi regime, considered 'progressive' by the Soviets a few years earlier, was now defined as 'reactionary' and 'dictatorial'. The Iraqi Ba'th Party had in the past sent representatives on such occasions, but this time no such delegation was reported as having gone to Moscow.

Avoiding Deterioration and Improving Ties

9 April 1981 — the ninth anniversary of the signing of the Soviet-

Iraqi friendship treaty — was observed in both the Soviet Union and Iraq,[32] with Moscow radio in Arabic noting the economic co-operation between the two countries.[33] *Pravda* published an exchange of greetings between Soviet and Iraqi leaders, but the cool relations were reflected in the fact that the Soviets published them on page 2 and not, as was usual, on page 1. The text was also incomplete. Both sides, however, called for friendship and co-operation. The Soviet greetings said, 'The Soviet Union is prepared to continue developing relations with Iraq on the basis of mutual interest in strengthening friendship and co-operation between our countries.' Saddam Husayn stated 'Iraq's readiness to develop the existing relations of friendship with the Soviet Union on the basis of the principles of mutually advantageous co-operation.'[34]

A delegation of the Iraqi-Soviet Friendship Society also visited Moscow and both they and the Soviets issued statements on ways 'to enhance co-operation' between the two peoples.[35] A Soviet delegation led by the Chairman of the State Committee for Foreign Economic Relations, Semyon Skachkov, came to Baghdad to attend a meeting of the permanent Soviet-Iraqi Commission on Economic and Technical Co-operation. According to a TASS report, decisions and recommendations were adopted 'for ensuring an implementation by both sides of the agreements reached earlier on Soviet-Iraqi economic and technical co-operation'. These provided for the development of co-operation in the fields of industry, trade, agriculture, irrigation, transport and training cadres.[36]

These were all signs of a desire by both sides not to permit relations to deteriorate any further. They wished to improve them as far as possible in the existing circumstances, with neither side changing its policy or its views.

On 7 June 1981 the Israeli Air Force attacked the Iraqi nuclear reactor near Baghdad, just at a time when the USA was attempting to restore relations with Iraq. This led the two countries to join together in drafting a UN Security Council resolution condemning Israel — a move not favoured by the Soviets, since it came just when they too were improving their relations with Iraq, and a few days before the visit of Iraqi Revolution Command Council member and First Deputy Prime Minister Taha Yasin Ramadan to the USSR. Ramadan was received on 18 June 1981 by Soviet Premier Nikolay Tikhonov. The Soviet statement said:

Mutual conviction was expressed that further development of relations between the USSR and Iraq on the basis of the treaty of friendship and co-operation meets the vital interests of the Soviet and Iraqi peoples. Both sides expressed the readiness to widen economic relations, trade and co-operation in other spheres on a stable basis of mutual advantage.[37]

Taha Yasin Ramadan said that in his talks he had 'achieved results in all fields of co-operation withough exception'.[38] A Soviet-Iraqi trade agreement and a protocol on trade turnover for 1981 were signed. It was decided that the Soviet Union would help Iraq build a cement factory and a thermal power station, as well as helping with the development of the West Korrina oilfield.[39]

It seems that during the visit an agreement was reached to renew Soviet military supplies, and reports were later published that Iraq was receiving renewed supplies of spare parts for its Soviet-made military equipment. There were also reports that the Soviets had supplied Iraq with advanced weapons and military equipment, including MiG-27 aircraft. They had also reportedly completed an anti-aircraft missile network designed to protect Baghdad and important Iraqi sites against air-raids. The Iraqis responded with an increase in the volume of trade with the USSR and East European countries,[40] and delegations from both sides exchanged visits.[41]

By the end of 1981 an improvement in Soviet-Iraqi relations was clearly evident, compared to what they had been at the end of 1980 and in early 1981. However, direct Soviet arms supplies were not resumed, and indirect shipments were not made in sufficient quantities to enable Iraq to replace its war losses. It was not yet a return to the earlier close relations of the early 1970s, but rather an attempt to prevent further deterioration. The Soviets were anxious to prevent any increased Iraqi gravitation towards West European countries or an improvement in Iraq's relations with the USA. The Soviets also wanted to keep their options open for the possibility of further *rapprochement* with Iraq.

Saudi Arabia

Continued Soviet Requests for the Establishment of Diplomatic Relations

The Soviet Union continued to request the re-establishment of diplomatic relations with Saudi Arabia. The press reported that the Soviets were asking Arab parties to mediate with Riyadh in this respect, saying that secret talks were under way between the Soviet Union and Saudi Arabia, either directly, or through Kuwait, the PDRY, Syria and the PLO.[42]

Saudi Arabia's Foreign Minister, Sa'ud al-Faysal, said that an ongoing dialogue did exist between Saudi Arabia and the USSR and that Saudi and Soviet diplomats were having meetings all over the world.[43]

The subject of Soviet-Saudi relations came up when PLO leader Yasir Arafat visited Moscow on 20 October 1981, to be received by Brezhnev. On his return he reported the substance of his talks to Prince Fahd in Riyadh. The latter was said to have responded by agreeing that the Soviet Union should have a part in the efforts to solve the Arab-Israeli conflict.[44]

There were also reports that the Soviets were supplying Iraq with weapons and ammunition through Saudi Arabia and that Soviet aircraft had begun to land in Badanah, north-eastern Saudi Arabia, carrying supplies to Iraq. These reports were denied by Saudi Arabia's Minister of Defence and Aviation, Prince Sultan ibn 'Abd al-'Aziz, who also denied there were any negotiations between Saudi Arabia and the Soviet Union.[45] His denials were only regarding direct dealings — but Soviet arms were arriving in Iraq indirectly and also via Saudi Arabia. The Saudis dealt through Arab suppliers. The arms would, for example, go from North Yemen through Saudi Arabian territory to Iraq.

Ceremonial greetings were exchanged between the Soviets and the Saudis on their national holidays and anniversaries. A Soviet broadcast on the occasion of Saudi Arabia's national day (23 September, the anniversary of the founding of the kingdom in 1928) said that the Soviet Union was ready to build relations with Saudi Arabia.[46] In exchanges of festive greetings between Brezhnev and King Khalid they wished each other 'prosperity and success'.[47]

The Soviets and Prince Fahd's Proposals for Settling the Arab-Israeli Conflict

In early August 1981 Prince Fahd, heir-apparent and Deputy Prime Minister (since 13 June 1982 King of Saudi Arabia), put forward a set of principles, designed to settle the Arab-Israeli conflict, which were similar to the Soviets' proposals on the same subject.[48] The proposals made no mention of peace with Israel, nor of direct negotiations with it or official recognition of its existence. They did say that 'all states in the region should be able to live in peace', but made no direct mention of Israel. The proposals called for Israel's withdrawal from all territories occupied by it in 1967, including Arab Jerusalem, and that a Palestinian state should be established with Jerusalem as its capital. It was further stipulated that Palestinian refugees should have a right to return 'to their homes', in other words, to the territory of Israel after its withdrawal from the West Bank and Gaza Strip. There was provision for a transitional period under UN auspices, meaning that there would be no direct negotiations with Israel, which would transfer the territories to the UN, which in turn would hand them over to the PLO.

The Fahd plan was similar to Soviet proposals for a resolution of the Arab-Israeli conflict, but what mattered to the Soviets was not a solution or non-solution of the conflict, but rather that their participation should be ensured in any negotiations on the matter, and that they should have a meaningful role in any implementation of the outcome of the talks. The Soviets feared a situation where the Fahd plan would be accepted by most of the Arab states and Western Europe — perhaps even the USA — and that they would all sit down and talk about it without inviting the USSR. It could even lead to a PLO-USA dialogue and an end to PLO dependence on the USSR. The Soviets suspected that Prince Fahd's aim was to bring about a split between them and the Arabs, and feared that acceptance of his proposals would act against their position in the Arab world. This led the Soviet media to attack the proposals and to welcome those in the Arab world who had opposed it.[49]

The Soviets and the Saudi Arabian Communist Party (SACP)

From time to time the SACP would issue statements on one subject or another. They were supported by the Soviets, although the latter were careful not to do so openly. An SACP statement in Beirut in January 1981 expressed support of the Brezhnev proposals on Persian Gulf security (see further),[50] and their representative attended the 26th CPSU Congress in Moscow, but if he spoke, his words went unrecorded in the Soviet press, unlike the speeches of other Arab communist representatives.

A representative of the SACP sent greetings to the 12th Bulgarian CP Congress in April 1981. He spoke mainly against the USA and its policy, but also referred to his party and its goals:

Our party has directed its efforts towards establishing a broad fatherland front, including all national and opposition forces in Saudi Arabia and abroad, with the purpose of toppling the King's regime and liquidating the influence of US imperialism and international monopolies.[51]

A statement of the SACP at the end of December 1981, marking the second anniversary 'of the uprising of residents of eastern Saudi Arabia and the Mecca mosque incident', called all domestic opposition forces to establish 'a joint national front'.[52]

The Soviets were acting in two directions — seeking to establish relations with the existing regime, but also maintaining ties with those who wished to overthrow it.

Kuwait — a Soviet Window and Door to the Gulf

Kuwait tried to be on good terms with both the USA and the USSR, believing that each of them would prevent any action against Kuwait by the other. It opposed any American military presence in the Gulf region, such as that of the planned Rapid Deployment Forces (RDF), and was also against American military bases. It considered that these would make the Soviets react in competition, thus causing conflicts between the superpowers which would also involve the countries of the region. Kuwait's arms purchases were diversified: from the USA, the USSR, Western Europe and others. Instructors and maintenance service technicians came from Arab countries owning similar weaponry.

The war between Iraq and Iran diminished the regional influence of both countries, which were now too busy with their own affairs. This increased Kuwait's regional role and influence. The war was close enough to Kuwait for it to wonder who constituted the greater danger, the Khomeyni regime in Iran, which was urging the Kuwait Shi'as (about 20 per cent of the population) to revolt against their Sunni rulers, or Iraq, which had claims to all of Kuwait but, at this stage, wanted only parts of it as a 'lease'. As Arabs, and fearing Iraq, which was closer and seemed to be stronger and more dangerous than Iran, Kuwait tended to support Iraq. But officially it remained neutral.

Kuwait was the only Gulf country to have diplomatic relations with the Soviet Union. Kuwaiti Foreign Minister Shaykh

Jabir al-Ahmad as-Sabah's visit to the USSR from 23 to 25 April 1981 was decided on after prior consultations and co-ordination with the countries of the Gulf.[53] In their speeches at a Moscow banquet on 24 April 1981 Foreign Ministers as-Sabah and Gromyko agreed 'to oppose any foreign interference or presence' in the Gulf region. Shaykh as-Sabah said that the Gulf states were capable of maintaining the security of the Gulf and wanted no 'spheres of influence in the form of military facilities or bases'. He commended the Soviet Union's stand on the Arab-Israeli conflict and on the Palestinian issue, as well as its opposition to the Egyptian-Israeli peace treaty.[54] The joint Soviet-Kuwaiti communiqué[55] conceded agreement on the Arab-Israeli conflict but not on Gulf issues. There was no mention of Afghanistan (over which their views differed) or the Gulf Co-operation Council (GCC; see further). Kuwait agreed to certain points in Brezhnev's December 1980 Gulf proposals (see further), but not to the most important ones.

There was a great deal of pretence in the formulas of both sides, as their aims and views on the Gulf situation differed widely. The Soviet Union found it convenient to maintain correct relations with Kuwait in order to show Saudi Arabia and the Gulf states that it was possible to have good relations with the Soviet Union in spite of differences in regimes; that deals with the USSR, commercial and even military, did not bring about a spread of communism, and therefore need not be suspected.[56]

In September 1981 Shaykh as-Sabah visited Bulgaria, Romania, Hungary and Yugoslavia in an attempt to underline the neutrality of Kuwait's foreign policy and to give the lie to those who claimed that Kuwait was tending more to the West. It was the only member state of the Gulf Co-operation Council that had full relations with the Soviet Union and other socialist states, so Shaykh as-Sabah said he would ask the leaders of the five other states of the Council (Saudi Arabia, Bahrain, Qatar, the UAE and Oman) 'to follow the same line and establish relations with the countries of the Eastern bloc within a policy of balance between East and West'.[57]

National holidays, both Soviet and Kuwaiti, served as occasions for the exchange of greetings between Brezhnev and the Emir, sending good wishes to the 'friendly Kuwaiti people' and the 'friendly Soviet people'.[58] These greetings were of a ceremonial nature but the Soviet media were wont to exaggerate their meaning, emphasizing the declarations of friendship, close ties, and similarity of views on world affairs.

The 'equilibrium' between East and West in Kuwait's foreign relations was due in no small measure to internal policy considerations, trying to neutralize the domestic opposition and those calling for closer ties with the East. It was also an attempt to win the friendship and support of those in the region who were Soviet-oriented.

The Soviets wanted to maintain the closest possible ties with Kuwait's rulers. But they also regarded them as 'archaic' and 'feudal', believing that they would not last long and that a Soviet presence in Kuwait would contribute positively to their relations with the succeeding regime.

Bahrain, Qatar, the UAE and Oman

The Soviets continued their attempts to establish diplomatic relations with Bahrain, Qatar and the UAE, refraining from doing anything that could be construed as interfering in those countries' internal affairs. There was limited Soviet trade with them, and greetings were exchanged between their rulers and Brezhnev on national holidays.[59] On the other hand, the Soviets supported local 'national liberation' forces, stressing their 'anti-imperialist' direction but also clearly indicating their desire to change the Gulf countries' regimes.

In early March 1981 the address to the Moscow 26th CPSU Congress by a representative of the Bahrain National Liberation Front was in line with Soviet policy. The speaker expressed support for the USSR, attacked the USA, and exhorted the Arabs 'to eliminate the US military presence and the monopolies' dominance'. He avoided direct criticism of Bahrain's regime.[60]

The Soviets now attempted to establish trade ties with Gulf countries, hoping that trade would influence political relations, but in this they were unsuccessful.[61]

Oman was openly attacked in the Soviet media, which repeatedly claimed that it was in fact dependent on the USA and Britain. These same media then continued with praise for those who acted for its 'independence' from these great powers. A Soviet commentator, at the end of 1981, described Oman as having an 'extremely reactionary regime . . . no discernible influence among neighbouring Arab countries . . . [Oman] is scarcely in a position to play a paramount role . . . [and] is not distinguished for its military or other might . . .'[62] The PFLO revolt in the Dhofar province had come to an end in 1975, but the Soviet media claimed that it was still continuing. PFLO activities were master-minded from the PDRY, where the Front had its bases and offices. This led to constant tension between Oman and the PDRY.

During the Kuwaiti Foreign Minister's above-mentioned visit to the USSR in April 1981, he tried to persuade the Soviets to exert pressure on the PDRY to ease the tension between the PDRY and Oman. The Soviet Foreign Minister replied that it was not reasonable that the Gulf states, having no diplomatic relations with the USSR, should ask it to relieve the tension in the Arabian peninsula. Why should not the Gulf states first establish relations with the USSR?, he asked.[63] The Kuwaiti Minister replied that a PDRY-Oman reconciliation would counter the circumstances and justifications that had prompted the Omanis to sign an agreement with the USA on American use of Omani military facilities, and that Sultan Qabus '[had] pledged to abrogate the facilities agreement with the Americans if his country's borders with South Yemen [were] secured by guarantee'.[64] It seems that the Soviets had used the same argument in their talks with PDRY leaders in an attempt to ease tension between the PDRY and Oman.

The Gulf states exerted pressure on Oman to reduce its military co-operation with the USA. In early December 1981 the *Washington Post* reported an offer of $1.2 billion to Oman from Saudi Arabia and the Gulf states in return for not offering military facilities on its territories to the United States. This report was denied by Saudi Arabia's Information Minister, Dr Yamani, and the Gulf Co-operation Council (GCC) Secretary-General, 'Abdallah Bisharah.[65]

Although the Soviets failed in their attempt to establish diplomatic relations with the Gulf States they did not abandon hope or diminish their efforts to this end.

North Yemen

Between Saudi Arabia and the PDRY, between the USA and the USSR

The YAR serves as buffer state between Saudi Arabia and the PDRY — with each one trying to bring it closer, or even to make it completely dependent. Each had the backing and support of the superpower towards which it was oriented: Saudi Arabia towards the USA; and the PDRY towards the USSR. Thus American policy towards the YAR was determined primarily in the context of US–Saudi relations. The YAR leadership tried to steer a more or less middle course between Saudi Arabia and the PDRY, between the USA and the USSR, and to use competition between them to its advantage.

The unstable internal situation in the YAR made this difficult. Opposing forces inside the country were trying to pull it in different directions. The government wanted a strong central government to control the whole country, while tribal leaders pressed for the opposite — a weak central government whose power would be limited to the main cities, with the tribes or groups of tribes controlling most of the country.

Saudi Arabia supported the central government on the one hand, providing it with aid amounting to hundreds of millions of dollars a year. On the other hand, the Saudis did not want the YAR to be too strong and independent, so they also provided aid to the tribes in amounts more or less equivalent to those given to the central government. The aim was to influence the San'a government through the tribes and to be able to change it or its policy in case it tried to be more independent than the Saudis would like.

As a result, the North Yemenis regarded Saudi Arabia as guilty of keeping their country weak and unstable. This, then, strengthened those among them calling for a *rapprochement* with the PDRY and more distant relations with Saudi Arabia and the USA, together with a concomitant approach to the USSR. Relations with the latter were viewed as a counterweight to Saudi influence and as a demonstration of independence from the Saudis. At the same time the North Yemenis also hoped that the Soviets would moderate the PDRY, making both the PDRY and the Soviets stop supporting YAR opposition forces. This was done carefully, trying not to lean too far towards the PDRY and the USSR, and meanwhile continuing to enjoy Saudi and American aid and political support.

The USSR and the PDRY, too, tried to play a dual political game through a contradictory policy. They made efforts to maintain good relations with the YAR, but also supported (both directly and indirectly) the opposition National Democratic Front (NDF). The latter combined most YAR opposition forces, leftist parties and groups very similar to the PDRY ruling party. It included: the Revolutionary Democratic Party, which was close to the PDRY's

National Liberation Front; the Communist Democratic Party of Popular Unity; and pro-Iraqi Ba'thists. It also included Nasirists, supporters of Libya's Colonel Qadhdhafi and others.

Fighting between the YAR government and NDF forces was reported to have broken out in December 1980, and the NDF gained control of a strip across the south of the country, along the PDRY border. The mountainous area in the south of the YAR, together with PDRY support, enabled the NDF to carry on protracted guerilla warfare. The government forces were supported by tribal and religious elements and by a Saudi-backed tribal militia. After a long fight, the NDF forces were pushed out of North Yemen into the PDRY. They had not been destroyed, however, and in April 1981 fighting was renewed along the YAR-PDRY border.[66] The revolt intensified in late 1981 and the government forces used air power against NDF strongholds in the south. The YAR suspected the Soviets of being behind the revolt and supporting it.

At the same time the PDRY-YAR talks took place, bringing agreements on economic co-operation and in other spheres. The PDRY leader, 'Ali Nasir Muhammad al-Hasani visited the YAR on 14 September 1981 and had talks with President 'Ali 'Abdallah Salih where both stressed co-operation and unity. They met again in Aden on 2 December 1981 and signed an agreement on co-ordination and co-operation. It was in the YAR's interest to influence the South Yemenis to end their support to the NDF. In this way the YAR leaders tried to show that they were to some extent independent of Saudi Arabia, and that they deserved more aid. They also wished to demonstrate to both sides that they still had the option of moving closer to the PDRY and the USSR.

A Drift Towards the PDRY and the Soviet Union

The YAR military forces had been extensively supplied by both the Soviets and the Americans for quite some time. The amount of equipment that they had on hand was much more than they were able to absorb, since they did not have sufficient manpower to operate most of it. Thus, during the first months of the Iraq-Iran war, the YAR sold Iraq substantial amounts of Soviet-made military equipment.

During 1979–80 the Soviet Union provided the YAR with some $600 million worth of major military equipment, including advanced SU and MiG aircraft, helicopters, tanks, tactical ground-to-air missiles and armoured personnel carriers, accompanied by more than 250 Soviet military advisers and technicians.[67] The deliveries made were under long-term credits and at negligible interest rates. By May 1981 reports had it that there were 600 military advisers and technicians in the country, with about 1,500 members of the YAR military forces training in the Soviet Union.[68] Most of the arms supplied were believed to have been from old stock, less sophisticated than those given to other Arab countries, and YAR-USSR economic co-operation was also quite limited.

President 'Ali 'Abdallah Salih visited the USSR from 26 to 28 October 1981. According to the official joint communiqué, talks were held 'in an atmosphere of mutual understanding and friendship'. This meant that the sides held different views on many matters. However, it also meant that both sides had an interest in talking and, equally important, showing — to Saudi Arabia, South Yemen, the USA and others — that they were in communication and that these contacts could be strengthened. The North Yemenis demonstrated their independence from Saudi Arabia by supporting the Soviet proposals, already rejected by the Saudis, regarding the Gulf and the Indian Ocean. Both sides expressed themselves in favour of convening an international conference on the Middle East, proposed by the Soviet Union, thus indicating indirect rejection of Prince Fahd's proposals. They were in favour of the Soviet proposal to declare the Red Sea 'a zone of peace'. On bilateral relations the statement spoke of 'co-operation in the economic, military, scientific, technical, trade and cultural fields, and also in the health services, education and the training of national personnel in the YAR'.[69]

The statement indicated a closer approach to the Soviet Union, away from Saudi Arabia and the USA. This was the price the North Yemenis had to pay for Soviet aid,[70] because the YAR was interested in renewed shipments of Soviet military equipment, after having sold a great part of its stock to Iraq. It was also an attempt to show the Reagan administration that if it wanted to lessen Soviet influence in the region it had to pay more attention to the YAR, appreciating its importance for itself alone, and not only in the context of US-Saudi relations.

A radical YAR leadership, capable of establishing a strong centralized government and breaking up the tribal system, could play an important role in the region, much greater than it does today. It would work for modernization, co-operation with the

PDRY, and an orientation towards the USSR. It might now represent a threat to Saudi Arabia, coming into conflict with it, and thus with the USA. This would result in an even stronger orientation toward the Soviet Union.

The PDRY — Greater Integration into the Region and Continued Reliance on the Soviets

In the course of internal power struggles and the changes in leadership which the PDRY was undergoing, 'Ali Nasir Muhammad al-Hasani strengthened his position. He concentrated into his own hands the positions of Secretary-General of the Yemeni Socialist Party (YSP) Central Committee, Chairman of the Supreme People's Council Presidium, and Chairman of the Council of Ministers. He continued the close relations between the PDRY and the USSR, but also maintained correct relations with Saudi Arabia. He tried to give the PDRY a more moderate aspect in order to be less frightening to her neighbours.

The Soviets had some doubts whether al-Hasani would be able to maintain a balance between greater integration in the region's affairs, becoming more accepted in the Arab world, and a continued orientation towards the USSR, co-ordinating his policies with those of the Soviet Union. In his talks with the Soviets he succeeded in persuading them that he was the man who could pull it off.

Close military and economic co-operation continued between the USSR and the PDRY. The Soviets strengthened their military presence there and were able, if necessary, to transfer forces from Ethiopia at short notice. In Ethiopia there were Cuban fighting units numbering about 15,000 men.[71] The PDRY served the USSR as a centre for its activities in the region.

Brezhnev's Gulf Proposals

Brezhnev's speech in the Indian Parliament in New Delhi on 10 December 1980 included references to the Iraq-Iran war and proposals for solving the Gulf conflict. His words seemed to be directed more towards Washington than towards his audience, offering Soviet strategic restraint in the region in exchange for

Western acceptance of the Soviet position in Afghanistan. He demanded a reduction in the Western presence in the region, without promising any similar withdrawal by the Soviet Union. This meant that the Soviets would remain in Afghanistan, the PDRY and Ethiopia, but that the Americans would have to vacate the Diego Garcia base, facilities in Bahrain and lose the use of Omani, Somali and other facilities. US acceptance of the proposal would put in doubt their co-operation with Saudi Arabia and other countries in the region.

'Powers situated many thousands of kilometres away from the region', said Brezhnev, had concentrated 'a miltary armada' in the Persian Gulf and Indian Ocean region, built up armaments and expanded their military bases. They justified such actions by talking about the 'Soviet threat', but 'the USSR does not intend to encroach either on the Middle East oil or its supply routes'. It has, however, an interest 'in the area which is close to our frontiers'. Brezhnev asked the United States and other Western powers, as well as China, Japan and others, to agree to 'the following mutual obligations':

(1) Not to establish foreign military bases in the area of the Persian Gulf and adjacent islands; not to deploy nuclear or any other weapons of mass destruction there.

(2) Not to use or threaten to use force against the countries of the Persian Gulf area; not to interfere in their internal affairs.

(3) To respect the status of non-alignment chosen by Persian Gulf states; not to draw them into military groupings with the participation of the nuclear powers.

(4) To respect the sovereign right of the states of the region to their national resources.

(5) Not to raise any obstacles or threats to normal trade exchange and the use of sea lanes that link the states of that region with other countries of the world.[72]

Brezhnev's first proposal was to stop the establishment of foreign military bases, but his definitions did not include the Soviet military presence in Afghanistan, the PDRY and Ethiopia, which are much closer to the Gulf than the American facilities at Diego Garcia. The proposal not to deploy nuclear weapons in the region would leave the USSR as the only nuclear power there — since Soviet nuclear weapons inside their own territory could reach the Gulf with ease.

The second proposal did not cover intervention such as that of the Soviets in Afghanistan, where they were said to have been 'invited' by 'a legitimate government'. In other places, Soviet aid to various revolts could be represented as providing aid to 'the people'.

In the third proposal, the Americans were asked to give up plans to sign bilateral security agreements with the Gulf states. The USSR, on its part, would not be giving anything up since its chances for such agreements were non-existent. The USSR had a friendship treaty with Iraq which had lost much of its content, and no relations at all with most of the Gulf states.

As regards the fourth proposal, another oil embargo on the West would bring a Western reaction. Acceptance of Brezhnev's proposals would give the USSR an excuse to denounce these reactions.

The fifth Brezhnev proposal was the only one which could interest the West: a Soviet commitment not to raise obstacles to navigation in the region.

In summary, the proposals were a call for America to abandon the region, leaving the Soviet Union victorious in the field.

Tehran radio, commenting that a lasting peace would not come about 'by a peace proposal from one superpower to another super-power', attacked both the USSR and the USA, calling for the nation to 'get out of the domination of the superpowers'.[73] Another Tehran radio comment said:

> The Soviet Union, to demonstrate its goodwill concerning its recent proposal, can put an end to its occupation of Afghanistan . . . dismantle its bases in the region . . . formally announce its neutrality and reaffirm that it does not sell arms to Iraq . . . abrogate that part of the Russian-Persian treaty of 1921 which allows for two countries to send their forces to each other's soil.[74]

Saudi Arabia's press was critical of the Brezhnev proposals.[75] So was the UAE,[76] and an Oman Foreign Ministry spokesman rejected it as well.[77] In Kuwait, however, press reports were favourable.[78] On 24 April 1981 Kuwait's Foreign Minister Shaykh as-Sabah said in Moscow that Kuwait 'has found positive points' in the Brezhnev call 'to remove foreign military forces from the Gulf region and to neutralize the region'.[79] Kuwait, however, objected to the main point — a security arrangement imposed by foreign powers.

The Soviet media repeated the Brezhnev proposals over and over again. It seemed that the Soviets had introduced them more as bargaining points for talks which they had proposed on the situation in Afghanistan. They could not have seriously believed that these proposals had a realistic chance of being accepted by the key countries of the region and by Western powers.

Soviet Attitudes to the Gulf Co-operation Council

On 4 February 1981, in Riyadh, the Foreign Ministers of Saudi Arabia, Kuwait, Bahrain, Qatar, the UAE and Oman decided to set up a Gulf Co-operation Council (GCC). Although Iraq as well as North and South Yemen wanted to join they were not invited. The two Yemens were excluded, not being immediate Gulf countries, while Iraq's non-inclusion was explained by saying that it did not wish to drag the other Gulf states into its war with Iran and therefore, by choice, did not join the GCC. Other Gulf states, in particular Kuwait, feared Iraqi attempts at 'Lebanonization of the Gulf' by its support of opposition groups in Gulf countries. Iraq also had claims on Kuwait — for example, its demand to lease Bubijan Island — but these were rejected by Kuwait.[80]

Oman advocated a joint arrangement for the defence of the Straits of Hormuz, granting the USA the use of facilities for this purpose. Other Gulf states were less inclined to accept an American military presence, fearing that this might bring a Soviet retaliation. Moreover, the immediate danger to their regimes seemed to be not so much from the outside but from internal and regional threats. Co-operation on countering such threats (such as internal security or co-ordinated action against illegal immigration) seemed to be a more urgent matter.

From the outset, the Soviet media adopted a negative attitude towards the GCC, primarily attacking Saudi Arabia as the leading country. Moscow radio said that the Riyadh conference, at which it was decided to establish the Council, had not devoted its main interest to the presence in the region of a huge naval fleet of the USA and its NATO allies. 'Every delegate was primarily concerned about internal political problems . . . what mainly interests the Saudi regime . . . is the growth of the national liberation movement.'[81]

A *Pravda* commentator described the establishment of the GCC as part of a US and NATO plan 'to create in the Persian Gulf zone a "security pact" prepared to co-operate with the West'. Such attempts, he said, 'in no way serve to stabilize the situation in the Persian Gulf region or the Arab peoples' interests'.[82]

Kuwait's Foreign Minister, Shaykh as-Sabah, said in Moscow on 24 April 1981 that the GCC 'is not directed against anybody, and is not an opponent of any bloc, nor is it a supporter of any side'.[83] Kuwait proposed a Gulf co-operation plan modelled on the European Economic Community, rather than a military security organization. The GCC initially followed this pattern, which was less objectionable to the Soviets.

Soviet comments on the meeting of the Gulf countries' head of state in Abu Dhabi at the end of May 1981 were less negative. According to TASS, Kuwait and 'some other countries' planned 'closer co-operation of the Council member countries in the economy, trade, culture, information and scientific-technical exchanges'. But the USA, 'acting through its agents', namely Sultan Qabus of Oman, was trying 'to impart a militarist character to the peaceful co-operation of the countries of the region'.[84]

The GCC Secretary-General, 'Abdallah Bisharah, denied Western press reports that the Gulf states approved of the American-European Rapid Deployment Force (RDF) for the protection of the Gulf but would not say so in public for fear of radical Arab reaction. The GCC, he said, rejected both Western offers of military protection and Soviet proposals of an international conference to make the Gulf a neutral zone:

> The neutrality of the Gulf cannot be separated from the neutrality of the adjacent areas — the Arabian Sea, the Indian Ocean and the Red Sea . . . It would be futile to neutralize the Gulf while Soviet troops are in Afghanistan and Soviet naval forces cruise the Indian Ocean or maintain facilities in various Red Sea and Arabian Sea ports.[85]

While the Soviet attitude to the GCC was generally negative, they occasionally tried to pretend that their aims and those of the GCC were similar, thus hinting at the possibility of co-operation. GCC demands regarding Gulf security 'coincided with Soviet proposals on this issue', said a Soviet broadcast, referring to the communiqué issued after the meeting of GCC foreign ministers in Ta'if, Saudi Arabia, from 31 August to 2 September 1981.[86] It was very pretentious to say this, because even when the GCC and the Soviets were proclaiming similar slogans, each gave such proclamations a quite different interpretation.

The Council was a rich men's club of conservative Arab oil-producing countries whose members wanted first of all to preserve their regimes and riches and which, with the exception of Kuwait, had no diplomatic relations with the Soviet Union. The GCC tried to adopt positions not only in regard to the Gulf but also about matters concerning the Arab world as a whole. For example, it expressed support of Prince Fahd's proposals for solving the Arab-Israeli conflict. These had been rejected by the radical, Soviet-oriented Steadfastness and Confrontation Front (which included Algeria, Libya, the PDRY, Syria and the PLO).

This strengthened Soviet opposition to the GCC. In an 'unofficial' Soviet broadcast, the Riyadh summit of 10–11 November 1981 received a negative appraisal. It was said to be under 'pressure exerted by some of the heads of those Gulf countries which revolve in the orbit of US policy'.[87]

At the end of 1981, a plot in Bahrain to overthrow the regime and seize power there was discovered. It was financed and engineered by Iran. The discovery of the plot led GCC member countries to devote more attention to internal security, giving this priority over everything else. The GCC and its members spoke about a unified security agreement and the co-ordination of security arrangements. A proposal was introduced to establish a GCC Rapid Deployment Force to intervene in any of the Council member countries, to provide them with assistance when needed.[88]

This meant that the GCC would make it more difficult for those wishing to overthrow existing regimes, including those enjoying Soviet support. The Soviets, while far from welcoming the Council, found it preferable to avoid any expressions of open or direct attack against it at this time. The USSR supported those countries in the region with a pro-Soviet orientation, encouraging them to join together as a counterweight to the GCC. One such move was the PDRY-Ethiopia-Libya co-operation treaty.

The PDRY-Ethiopia-Libya Co-operation Treaty

A PDRY-Ethiopia-Libya tripartite co-operation treaty was signed in Aden on 20 August 1981.[89] The treaty, and the subsequent meeting of representatives of the three states, received a positive Soviet appraisal.[90] The Soviets had worked for it for a long time, aiming to bring more co-ordination and co-operation among those states in the region oriented towards the USSR.

The treaty was a political declaration, having no real significance. Each of the three signatory states had conflicting interests. All of them were relatively weak and their power to act in the region was not greatly increased as a result of their alliance. Its timing was an indirect response to the establishment of the GCC, and also to US agreements with countries in the region for the use of their military facilities. An American military presence was maintained in countries in conflict with all three signatories to the treaty: in Oman (in conflict with the PDRY), Somalia (fighting Ethiopia), Egypt and Sudan (both in confrontation with Libya).

Military co-operation among the three could only be symbolic, as was the PDRY and Libyan aid offered to Ethiopia in the 1977–8 Somali-Ethiopian war. The treaty was signed during a period of Libyan-Sudanese tension which could lead to hostilities. If these began, they could not serve Ethiopia, which would not endanger its newly improved relations with the Sudan which it now saw as of great importance. In case of Egyptian-Libyan clashes, Ethiopia and the PDRY could not do much either. Regarding economic co-operation, only Libya had the means to provide aid, but had no real wish to do so.

The PDRY was anxious both to please the Soviets and to receive Libyan financial support. The South Yemenis were fearful, too, of the American use of military facilities in Oman. In fact, they were worried in general about US commitments there. The PDRY's attitude was influenced by not having been invited to join the GCC.

In joining the treaty, Ethiopia paid lip-service to the Soviets and its own radicals. Its leadership was preoccupied with internal problems — the revolt in Eritrea, continued fighting in the Ogaden, and economic difficulties. Ethiopia was in urgent need of economic aid and Libya had perhaps promised to help; however, even if such promises existed, very little aid was actually given. At the time the treaty came into force, Ethiopia was improving relations with the Sudan and Kenya, and also with some West European countries. There were even certain beginnings, albeit small, of improved ties with the USA. Ethiopia was not interested in putting a stop to all these.

Libya was increasingly fearful of possible American attempts to overthrow its regime, and of US support of Egypt and the Sudan. It had the financial means to provide aid to Ethiopia and the PDRY, and to pay the Soviets for arms. But although all three countries believed that Libya would make such agreements, it did not.

The Gulf states saw the Soviet Union as standing behind the PDRY-Ethiopia-Libya co-operation treaty and suspected that it might use the signatories to act against them and their regimes, bringing instability and upheavals once more to the region.

Trends and Considerations

Between Ideology and National Interests

Soviet policies and attitudes towards the countries of the Arabian peninsula and the Persian Gulf are far from consistent. They are not based on a centrally controlled 'master plan' or steps that have been calculated in advance but result from *ad hoc* decisions and improvised acts. Soviet behaviour is often a reaction to developments that have nothing to do with specific situations or events that have taken place in this particular region. This lack of consistency and frequent use of improvisation in dealing with the Persian Gulf countries stand in marked contrast to the planned approaches used toward many other regions.

Soviet foreign relations, like those of other countries, often reflect internal policies and power rivalries. What really matters most to Soviet leaders is their position within the power structure of their own country. It is difficult, therefore, to separate the views of Soviet leaders on any particular foreign issue from internal Soviet influences. In addition, the opinions held by the leadership are often far from unanimous. To say 'the USSR wants' or 'the Soviets think' is a gross over-simplification. On many issues, some Soviet representatives may call for moderation at the same time that others support extreme positions.

In examining Soviet policy a distinction must not only be made between tactical moves and long-range strategy, but also between doctrinal-ideological considerations of the Soviet Union as the leading communist power and the political, military and economic interests of the USSR as a state and superpower, even though in some instances doctrinal and national interests may coincide. Doctrinal-ideological considerations make the USSR see itself as head of the world's revolutionary forces, protecting and supporting 'just wars', revolutionaries and revolutions. The Soviets speak about an alliance between the USSR and other communist countries, communists in the Western world and Third World 'national liberation movements'.

Positions of this kind were advocated by Mikhail Suslov, second-in-command in the Soviet hierarchy, who was in change of ideology and world communism. His death on 25 January 1982 may bring about a change in the emphasis of Soviet policy. Most of the top leaders of today will soon have to be replaced because of their advanced age or poor health. Currently, a power struggle is going on in the Kremlin that may take a long time to resolve — until the rise of a new group of leaders. The outcome of this struggle will decide whether Soviet policy will be determined by doctrinal-ideological considerations or whether it will follow more pragmatic lines.

But even today Soviet policy is decided primarily by national interests, although Soviet leaders employ revolutionary phraseology and their declared aims and policies appear close to a doctrinal-ideological posture. In reality, Soviet policy is far from being the outcome of a purely doctrinal approach. It reflects immediate Soviet national interests and, consequently, is pragmatic and cautious.

Soviet policy should, therefore, be viewed not only in the light of what the Soviets say but also by what they do. The revolutionary or doctrinal phraseology used by the Soviets often conceals or compensates for actions that are quite different — or for no action at all, despite the Soviet rhetoric.

Interests and Considerations

The Soviet Union has a constantly growing interest in the Gulf region because of its strategic location, huge oil resources and proximity to the USSR. All these factors make it important to the USSR that the region south of its borders and close to its territory should be friendly. The USSR does not want the presence in that area of anti-Soviet forces: American, West European, Chinese or any other.

USA-USSR Competition. The Arabian peninsula and the Persian Gulf countries are a major arena in which the USSR and the USA compete, either directly or by proxy. Three trends are discernible in the methods used by the Soviets in this competition. Although each of the three is different, they supplement and complement each other. At any particular time, one trend may be given priority and the greatest emphasis.

(1) *Use of opportunities.* The Soviets frequently try to extend their influence and expand their presence by sending military and civilian advisers, supplying military equipment and providing economic aid. This occurs when it is the Soviet perception that the USA does not wish to risk a confrontation and would prefer to retreat. This trend is apparent in the Soviet interventions — directly or by proxy — in Afghanistan, Ethiopia, Angola and other places.

(2) *Caution.* The Soviets attempt to avoid direct intervention in local conflicts that might involve them in a confrontation with the USA. This trend becomes evident when the USSR concludes that the USA has the will and determination to oppose the Soviets, by force if necessary, and that such clashes might escalate into direct USA-Soviet conflict. This was the situation in Iran, South Yemen, Lebanon and other places.

(3) *Soviet-American condominium.* The Soviets would like to establish joint Soviet-American control of the region or else divide it into spheres of influence. Soviet spokesmen have expressed their readiness to contribute to stability and order in the region if they can participate in the implementation of any programme of this type. This trend appears in Soviet proposals to solve the Arab-Israeli conflict — the idea of a Geneva conference on the Middle East with the USA and the USSR serving as co-chairmen. (Soviet proposals on this matter are similar to those made by the USA and King Fahd of Saudi Arabia, except for the roles and tasks to be performed by the Soviets. The USSR wants a position equal to that of the USA, joint guarantees to any agreement and joint administration of the agreement's implementation; the USA does not want any Soviet participation.)

USSR-PRC Competition. The Gulf region is also the scene of attempts by the Chinese to erode the Soviet position and presence and to stop Soviet advances. At the same time, the Soviets are trying to remove all Chinese influence from the region.

The PRC has established close ties with a number of Middle East countries: Egypt, the Sudan, Iraq, Oman, Somalia. Most of these countries had close relations with the Soviets in the past but have changed their orientation and turned towards the West. However, they still need replacements and spare parts for their Soviet-made arms and the PRC, which uses similar equipment, can provide these countries with the supplies that they need. The Chinese view making this equipment available as a means of reducing the Soviet presence and influence in these countries.

Economic Considerations. The establishment of close relations between the USSR and Middle East countries began with the exchange of Soviet arms for local products such as cotton or oil. Although the Soviets gained certain economic advantages from the sale of arms and other military equipment, and from increasing trade with the countries of the region, their primary considerations were political and not economic. In some countries, such as Libya and Iraq before September 1980, Soviet arms were paid for with hard currency or crude oil. Other countries, such as the PDRY or Ethiopia, found it difficult to pay for the Soviet equipment. Arms are the only commodity the Soviets can offer, as the USSR has difficulty competing with the more advanced technology of the USA, Western Europe and Japan when it comes to other types of goods.

Oil. At present, the Soviets have no need of Gulf oil for their own use, although they may need it in the future. The East European allies of the USSR do need oil and the Soviets, finding it difficult to meet the growing oil needs of their own country, have advised their allies to seek oil supplies directly from the Gulf countries.[91]

Internal Soviet Considerations. The Middle East is close to Muslim-populated regions in the USSR; Iran and Afghanistan border directly on them. Up to now, developments in these two countries have had no direct influence on the situation in the adjoining Soviet republics which have similar populations. Recent developments, however, have prompted Soviet authorities to watch events in nearby countries carefully and to be prepared to react if the situation so requires.[92]

The Soviet military-industrial complex advocates an active foreign policy. Any diminution of international tension is against the interests of this complex. Such a decrease in tension enables cuts to be made in the budgetary allocations for the military, and places greater emphasis on light industry, agriculture, and the production of consumer goods and services in the Soviet economy. Such changes diminish the role of the military-industrial complex. But even among this group there may be differing opinions. For example, the Navy and Tactical Air Force have an interest in installations and services in the Middle East, while the Strategic Rocket Forces and the Strategic Air Force do not.

Conservative orthodox communists tend to believe that the USSR should not rely on local Middle East nationalist leaders and should not make a heavy investment in the region. Soviet leaders who advocate a Russian character for the USSR favour foreign adventures less than those who advocate a multinational Soviet state. Discussions of this kind are a part of the internal power struggle that goes on all the time in the Soviet Union but has lately become more intense.

Aims and Motivations

Soviet aims may be long-term, intermediate or short-term. Long-term aims are strategic, far-reaching and relate to a messianic future. Intermediate and short-term goals are tactical; they are not always aims in themselves but are a way of achieving future goals and, therefore, are more apt to be flexible and realistic.

As Marxist-Leninists, Soviet leaders believe in historical determinism. They speak about stages of development and the transition of societies from one stage to another — from feudalism to capitalism, then socialism, and eventually to communism. They believe that such changes are inevitable and that communism will eventually prevail everywhere even if they do not do much to further this outcome. This belief in the inexorable course of events explains why Soviet leaders may sometimes do nothing or even act in a contrary direction, since they assume that what they want will happen under any circumstances without requiring them to work hard for its accomplishment.

Soviet theory holds that some countries are able, under favourable conditions and with Soviet help, to omit certain stages of development and pass directly from a feudal society to socialism. This, they say, happened in the Mongolian People's Republic and in the Soviet Central Asian republics. These Central Asian republics have a predominantly Muslim population and the Soviets often compare the situation there with that in the Middle East. Beginnings of the same developments, they say, are appearing in the PDRY.

Saudi Arabia, Oman, Qatar and the UAE are considered by the Soviets to have 'patriarchal-feudal' regimes. North Yemen is beginning to enter the stage of capitalism but still has a largely tribal-feudal society. Kuwait and Bahrain appear to be in the capitalist stage as they have industry, a proletariat and emergent class conflicts, thus offering more opportunuties for revolution and for changes in their regimes.

The Soviets would like to see conflicts develop between the countries of the area and the Western world, so that the influence and presence of the West would diminish in the Gulf countries. Traditional conservative pro-Western regimes would be replaced by radical revolutionary governments that would strengthen their ties with the USSR and have a pro-Soviet political orientation. As things stand now, the Soviets prefer not to act directly to advance such aims but to wait for the action of local forces — if such forces exist in the countries of the region.

Long-term Aims. These aims have little direct bearing on current Soviet conduct or policy in the Gulf region.

(1) To turn the region, or at least the countries to the south of the USSR (Afghanistan, Iran, Turkey), into a Soviet 'southern tier' of a communist commonwealth under the USSR, parallel to the 'western tier' that the USSR has in Eastern Europe. Recent events in Afghanistan could be seen as a step in this direction but the main goal was, and remains, Iran.

(2) To control Gulf oil and integrate its production into Comecon planning.

(3) To establish land links from the USSR to the Indian Ocean, to diminish Soviet dependence on passage through the Turkish Straits, the Suez Canal and around Africa; to establish a barrier between the PRC and Europe.

Intermediate Aims. These aims are only marginally feasible under present conditions.

(1) A limited Soviet military presence in the area or near it, to prevent crises, coups or other developments detrimental to the USSR's interests (or help them when they are in the Soviet interest).

(2) The establishment of local, radical anti-Western and pro-Soviet regimes, preferably ideologically close to the Soviet Union. Such regimes would nationalize Western economic interests (particularly oil), increase trade with the Soviet Union and be integrated in the Soviet defence system. (Today there are such regimes on both sides of the Gulf — in Afghanistan and in the PDRY. Ethiopia's regime is close to it. Iraq was seen by the Soviets as moving in this direction but turned away from it.)

Short-term Aims. These aims can be realized currently or in the near future.

(1) To diminish, erode (and if possible completely remove) the Western presence and influence, political, military and economic. Towards that end, to exploit differences between local leaders and the West, the USA in particular.

(2) To undermine traditional regimes that lean on the West, and assist the emergence of revolutionary pro-Soviet regimes and leaders; to turn existing regimes towards friendly relations with the USSR and, as much as possible, towards closer co-operation with it.

(3) To prevent a PRC penetration into the region and to remove China from it.

(4) To build a military infrastructure in the region or close to it; to expand wherever possible the Soviet military presence.

(5) To expand bilateral ties with the countries of the area: trade, economic and technical co-operation, cultural relations and other ties. To establish commercial air and naval links (including over-flights and refuelling rights, and the use of local facilities) — for their own sake as well as for political and military aims.

(6) To use the region as a springboard for activities in more distant places.

The main Soviet targets are Iran and Saudi Arabia. In Iran, the Soviets hope to influence developments after Khomeyni. In Saudi Arabia, they aim to establish diplomatic relations and a Soviet presence in the country.

Soviet Ties with Governments and Those who Oppose Them

While Soviet foreign relations are conducted simultaneously on more than one level, generally one of these levels is given priority. At times, the policies at the different levels are contradictory; at other times, they are mutually reinforcing.

The two main approaches used by the Soviets are:

(1) State-to-state relations by diplomatic and other official contacts.

(2) Relations with opposition and revolutionary groups or organizations, with local communist parties, with 'national liberation movements', and with organizations or parties that are

attempting to overthrow the existing regimes or to change basic aspects of their policies.

On the state-to-state level, the Soviets maintain ties with existing governments, attempt to develop such ties when none exist, and try to expand and increase the friendliness and intimacy of the ties that already exist. According to the Soviets, their relations with foreign countries have nothing to do with the internal regimes or political orientations of these countries. They cite their relations with Kuwait as proof of this, and say that Kuwait's conservative-traditional regime does not prevent that country from having close relations with the Soviet Union.

Relations with those groups which actively oppose existing regimes are generally conducted, at least officially, on an inter-party level between the Communist Party of the Soviet Union (CPSU) and a local party or organization — or by Soviet 'popular organizations' (trade unions, friendship societies, 'Peace Partisans', and so on). In the Middle East, such relations are conducted mainly through the Soviet Committee for Solidarity with Asian and African Countries, which is subordinated to the CPSU Central Committee International Department. This was the level of Soviet relations with the Popular Front for the Liberation of Oman (PFLO). Soviet aid to this group was provided indirectly through the PDRY, and Soviet political support throughout was presented as the action of the 'Soviet people' and not of the USSR government.

Palestinian organizations are viewed by the Soviets in a much wider context than the Arab-Israeli conflict. They are regarded as a revolutionary element that creates political ferment and instability; a central point around which those who want to change existing regimes could concentrate. Such a situation occurred during the Lebanese civil war of 1975–6 and its aftermath. Such similar 'Lebanonizations' may develop in those Gulf countries that have large Palestinian communities, such as Kuwait and Abu Dhabi. Whereas Soviet support for local revolutionary groups could undermine Soviet relations with the established governments of the area, it is difficult for these governments to object to Soviet support for Palestinian organizations (even those which declare that the way to Palestine leads through revolutions in Arab states), since such support cannot be depicted as intervention in a country's internal affairs.

Soviet Positions in the Region: How Stable are They?

The USSR has close relations with the PDRY and, further afield, with Afghanistan in the east and Ethiopia in the west. By enlarging their military presence in the countries that are allied with them, the Soviets have the option of using the mere threat of their power to influence the policies and actions of the countries of the region.

In the north, the USSR itself is relatively close to the Gulf states. Close to Iran's northern border, there has been an increase in the size and readiness of Soviet forces and of Soviet transportation capabilities in Soviet Transcaucasia and Central Asia. The Soviets can also use their military presence in Afghanistan to station additional forces in that country and to place Soviet fighter aircraft within range of the Gulf. In addition, the Soviet Navy maintains a constant presence in the Indian Ocean, close to the Gulf and to the transportation routes to and from that crucial area. All this gives the Gulf states the feeling that they are encircled by the forces of the Soviets and their allies.

Gulf leaders are aware of the Soviet presence but most act as if it is a matter for the USA to deal with and not one in which they have to be directly involved. Although they want an American presence in the area, they prefer it to be in neighbouring countries and not in their own. They believe that, if danger comes, the Americans will have no choice but to intervene. The Gulf countries do not take into consideration the fact that, in order to act in an emergency, preparations have to be made in advance and that effective action cannot always be improvised at the last moment.

The attention of local leaders in the Gulf countries is concentrated on local threats, which they consider to be of more immediate danger. They tend to link some of these threats to Soviet designs and policies. Such local conflicts may indeed provide opportunities for Soviet intervention on one side or the other. Some of these conflicts present the Soviets with a dilemma — whether to help both sides that are friendly with them or neither side. Either choice could seriously worsen their relations with both sides involved in the conflict. The list of such local conflicts is long: Iraq-Iran, Iraq-Syria, PDRY-Oman, PDRY-YAR, PDRY-Saudi Arabia, Somalia-Ethiopia, Syria-Jordon, Egypt-Libya, the Arab-Israeli conflict, radicals versus conservatives and Shi'a versus Sunni. The list can be lengthened.

Is there a trend towards the strengthening of the Soviet position in the region? Iran has increased its bilateral trade with the Soviet

Union and its transit trade through Soviet territory to Western Europe and Japan. Iraq once again is receiving Soviet arms, although indirectly through third parties. Soviet arms are arriving in North Yemen after that country's long dependence on the USA and Saudi Arabia. From time to time, there are reports of Saudi-Soviet contacts to establish diplomatic relations, as well as reports of a tendency to 'normalize' relations between Egypt and the USSR. Jordan has agreed to buy Soviet arms. Syria has a friendship treaty with the USSR and has expressed a wish to establish a 'strategic alliance'. The PLO co-ordinates its moves with the Soviets and receives their aid and support.

But the Soviet position in the region — gains and losses — depends heavily on local developments and on the existence of local friends or allies whose ties with the Soviets generally result from a temporary congruence of interests. The Soviets apparently believe that by signing long-term friendship treaties with Middle Eastern countries they can ensure their permanent friendship. That is not the real situation; nothing is permanent in the Middle East. Former allies become enemies and former enemies become friends.

The Soviets Wait for the Next Regimes

The USSR has no diplomatic relations with Saudi Arabia, Bahrain, Qatar, the UAE and Oman but would like to have such ties, particularly with Saudi Arabia. The Soviets do not believe that the current regimes and rulers in these countries will last for long (there are many in the West who think the same).[93] They wish to maintain a presence in the region so as to enable them to influence future developments, or at least to have a better knowledge of what is going on in the area. The Soviets believe that the next regimes will be radical, anti-Western and, therefore, friendly towards the USSR.

Whether this will occur depends largely on internal developments in these countries and on the measures they take to avoid such a situation. It will depend on American determination not to let it happen and American preparedness to act.[94]

What if the USA intervenes to save existing regimes? Will the Soviets step in to help the other side? Perhaps, but most probably not. Instead, the Soviets will protest and issue statements and declarations. They are in fact already preparing their own public for such an eventuality.

What if a Gulf leader, coming to power after a coup or a

revolution, should ask for direct Soviet support and an increased Soviet presence in his country? Will the Soviets give him such aid? Much depends on how they evaluate the situation, as well as on local and Western reactions. The more opposition they anticipate, the less ready they will be to intervene. Afghanistan has a long border with the Soviet Union, but the Gulf states are further away and this means less Soviet interest in them. The Soviets want gains and are ready to take risks and pay a price — but not a very high one.

For the time being, the Soviets are interested in having a presence in the Gulf region or somewhere nearby, and as broad as possible a diplomatic representation. They are trying to create a situation that will enable them to influence developments in their favour at a time of dramatic internal changes which, they believe, will come within the next few years.

Notes

1. Eric Rouleau, *Le Monde*, 6 Jan. 1981; Giancesare Flesca, *L'Espresso* (Rome), 26 Oct. 1980.

2. TASS, 22 Sept. 1980. In FBIS, USSR, 23 Sept. 1980, p. H1.

3. *Ash-Sharq al-Awsat*, 30 Sept. 1980.

4. TASS in English, 23 Sept. 1980. In FBIS, USSR, 24 Sept. 1980, p. H3.

5. Interview with Ambassador Mokri, *Ettela'at*, 2 Dec. 1980.

6. AFP in English, 23 Sept. 1980. In FBIS, USSR, 24 Sept. 1980, p. H3.

7. *Pravda*, 1 Oct. 1980.

8. Ibid., 9 Oct. 1980.

9. Tehran Domestic Service, 5 Oct. 1980. In FBIS, South Asia, 6 Oct. 1980, pp. I8–I9.

10. TASS in English, 8 Oct. 1980. In FBIS, USSR, 9 Oct. 1980, p. H10.

11. Flesca, *L'Espresso*; KUNA, 27 Oct. 1980. In FBIS, South Asia, 27 Oct. 1980, pp. I17–I18; Tehran radio in Arabic, 12 Oct. 1980. In FBIS, South Asia, 14 Oct. 1980, p. I11.

12. Ambassador Mokri interview, *Keyhan*, 11 Nov. 1980.

13. Moscow radio in Persian, 13 Dec. 1980. In FBIS, USSR, 15 Dec. 1980, pp. H2–H3.

14. Tehran Domestic Service, 12 Dec. 1980. In FBIS, South Asia, 15 Dec. 1980, p. I20.

15. Moscow radio in Persian to Iran, 4 Nov. 1980. In FBIS, USSR, 5 Nov. 1980, pp. H1–H2. See also Moscow radio in Persian to Iran, 19 Nov. 1980. In FBIS, USSR, 20 Nov. 1980, pp. H1–H2.

16. Ibid., 17 Jan. 1981. In ibid., 19 Jan. 1981, pp. A2–A3; Pavel Demchenko, *Pravda*, 17 Jan. 1981.

17. A discussion of this between Aleksandr Bovin, *Izvestia* senior political observer, and Yevgeniy Primakov, Director of the Institute of Oriental Studies, USSR Academy of Sciences, appeared on Moscow television. The former stressed the regime's religious character and anti-Sovietism, while the latter stressed its anti-

Americanism. (Moscow Domestic Television in Russian, 'Studio Nine' Programme, 27 Dec. 1980. In FBIS, USSR, 5 Jan. 1981, pp. CC7–CC9.)

18. *Pravda*, 24 Feb. 1981.
19. Moscow radio in Russian, 13 June 1981. In FBIS, USSR, 15 June 1981, p. H1.
20. Moscow radio in Russian, 25 July 1981. In FBIS, USSR, 30 July 1981, pp. CC10–CC11.
21. Moscow radio in Persian to Iran, 29, 30 June 1980. In FBIS, USSR, 1 July 1981, pp. H2–H3.
22. *Ettela'at International* (Tehran), 16 Sept. 1981.
23. *Izvestia*, 13 Oct. 1981.
24. *Pravda*, 20 Oct. 1981.
25. Moscow radio in Persian to Iran, 8 Dec. 1981. In FBIS, USSR, 9 Dec. 1981, p. H4.
26. *Izvestia*, 15 Dec. 1981.
27. TASS in English, 6 Jan. 1982. In FBIS, USSR, 7 Jan. 1982, p. H5.
28. *Financial Times*, 11 Nov. 1980.
29. *Pravda*, 11 Oct. 1980; TASS in English, 8, 9, 11 Oct. 1980. In FBIS, USSR, 9 Oct. 1980, pp. H11–H12; 10 Oct. 1980, p. H5; 15 Oct. 1980, p. H3; TASS, 3 Nov. 1980, In BBC SU/6567/A4/1, 5 Nov. 1980.

V. Romanov denied *Krasnaya Zvezda* (15 Jan. 1980) reports of 'participation of Soviet specialists in Iraq troop operations against Iran' and of deliveries of Soviet tanks to Iraq.

30. Moscow radio in Persian to Iran, 16 Feb. 1981. In FBIS, USSR, 19 Feb. 1981, p.H1.
31. *Pravda*, 2 March 1981.
32. A soirée was held in the Moscow House of Friendship on that occasion. (Moscow radio in Arabic, 9 April 1981. In FBIS, USSR, 14 April 1981, pp. H2–H3). *Pravda* reported a Baghdad meeting in which Iraqis spoke about friendship with the Soviet Union. (*Pravda*, 21 April 1981.)
33. Moscow radio in Arabic, 11 April 1981. In FBIS, USSR, 14 April 1981, pp. H3–H4.
34. *Pravda*, 11 April 1981.
35. INA, 18 April 1981. In FBIS, USSR, 24 April 1981, p. H3.
36. TASS in English, 21 April 1981. In FBIS, USSR, p. H2; Baghdad Domestic Service, 21 April 1981. In FBIS, ME, 22 April 1981, p. E1.
37. TASS in English, 18 June 1981. In FBIS, USSR, 19 June 1981, p. H1.
38. *Ash-Sharq al-Awsat*, 28 June 1981.
39. *Izvestia*, 24 June 1981; Moscow radio in English, 19 June 1981. In FBIS, USSR, 22 June 1981, p. H6.
40. *Al-Majallah*, 12–18 Dec. 1981, p. 7; *The Economist*, 3 Oct. 1981, p. 50; *8 Days*, 11 July 1981, p. 3, and 21 Nov. 1981, pp. 40–1.
41. A Supreme Soviet delegation visited Iraq from 30 November to 5 December 1981 (statement on vistit, *Pravda*, 10 Dec. 1981).
42. *Al-Khaleej* (Ash-Shariqah), 2 April 1981.
43. Foreign Minister Sa'ud al-Faysal to '*Ukaz*, 26 May 1981.
44. Noram Kirkham, *Sunday Telegraph*, 15 Nov. 1981; Voice of Palestine, 21 Nov. 1981. In FBIS, ME, 23 Nov. 1981, p. A9.
45. *Al-Jazirah* (Riyadh), 13 Dec. 1980.
46. A telegram from Brezhnev to King Khalid dated September 1981 included greetings to him and to the people of Saudi Arabia. In his reply, the King expressed his gratitude for the greetings and conveyed 'his best wishes' to Brezhnev and 'wishes of further success to the Soviet people'. (*Izvestia*, 27 Sept. 1981). Similar greetings were exchanged by Brezhnev and King Khalid on the occasion of the Soviet

October revolution anniversary. (Ibid., 14 Nov. 1981.)

47. Moscow radio in Arabic, 12 Aug. 1981 (in FBIS, USSR, 13 Aug. 1981, p. H1) said that the Saudi proposals 'conform in practice with the main principles of the Soviet programme for the settlement of the Middle East crisis'.

48. The full text of Prince Fahd's proposals was given in Riyadh Domestic Service, 7 Aug. 1981. In FBIS, ME, 10 Aug. 1981, pp. C4–C5.

49. V. Kudryavtsev, 'The New East. The Webs of a New Plot', *Izvestia*, 23 Aug. 1981.

50. Moscow radio in Persian to Iran, 30 Jan. 1981. In FBIS, USSR, 5 Feb. 1981, p. H1.

51. *Rabotnichesko Delo* (Sofia), 9 April 1981.

Pravda (13 Nov. 1981) reported that the CPSU had received greetings from the SACP on the occasion of the Soviet October revolution day. No text was published.

52. Moscow radio in Mandarin to China, 28 Dec. 1981. In FBIS, USSR, 31 Dec. 1981, pp. H6–H7.

53. Manama Gulf News Agency, 25 April 1981, citing *Al-Khaleej* (Ash-Shariqah).

54. 'Shaykh as-Sabah said that Kuwait supports the right of the Afghan people to choose the regime they want without any pressure from anybody . . . Kuwait also supports the efforts . . . to end the war between Iraq and Iran. He also paid tribute to Soviet-Kuwaiti relations, saying that these relations have developed in the past in a manner which takes into consideration the interests of both friendly peoples.' (KUNA, 25 April 1981. In FBIS, USSR, 29 April 1981, pp. H1–H3).

55. *Pravda*, 26 April 1981.

56. Kuwait purchased arms from the Soviet Union. A Kuwaiti military delegation paid a visit to the Soviet Union in June 1981, 'held initial negotiations and acquainted itself during the visit with samples of all weapons'. (*Ar-Ra'y al-'Amm*, 6 July 1981; KUNA, 5 Aug. 1981. In FBIS, ME, 6 Aug. 1981, p. C8).

57. *Al-Qabas*, 21 Sept. 1981. Asked whether the principle of 'international equilibrium' that Kuwait was following also embraced the economic domain, the Emir said:

> We do not restrict our major projects to a certain country or to firms of a specific international nature. Rather we announce our tenders to all and our choice is determined by the price offered by these firms, regardless of their nationality. He who observes our local projects will find a diversity in the firms currently implementing them, from Eastern and Western countries and also from Third World countries.
>
> During this tour, we bought government bonds from the socialist countries that we toured within our economic co-operation with these countries.

58. See, for example, *Izvestia*, 12 Nov. 1981.

59. *Pravda*, 17 Dec. 1981; *Izvestia*, 12, 13 Nov. 1981.

60. *Pravda*, 4 March 1981.

61. Dubai bought Soviet cars, timber, alcoholic beverages, chemicals and rubber products. The Soviets participated in commercial exhibitions in the UAE in a bid to gain a foothold on the local market. (*Khaleej Times*, Dubai, 27 July 1981.)

62. V. Pustov, 'The United States: Dangerous Intrigues in the Near East', *Krasnaya Zvezda*, 22 Nov. 1981.

63. Saudi Arabia's Foreign Minister, Prince Sa'ud al-Faysal, in an interview with *'Ukaz*, 26 May 1981.

64. *Al-Hadaf* (Kuwait), 7 May 1981, citing a Soviet Foreign Ministry official.

65. *As-Siyasah*, 4 Dec. 1981; Riyadh Domestic Service, 3 Dec. 1981. In FBIS, ME, 4 Dec. 1981, p.C9.

Al-Qabas said that GCC members had asked Oman to reduce its military co-operation with the USA. Oman was offered a pledge that the Council would intervene with the PDRY to stop meddling in Omani affairs. Oman specified that it wanted the PDRY to cease extending aid to guerrillas in the Dhofar area; to cease its anti-Sultanate press and radio campaigns; and to extend diplomatic recognition to the Omani regime. Oman was also reportedly offered $2,000 million in development aid. (Cited by AFP, 4 Dec. 1981. In FBIS, ME, 7 Dec. 1981, p. G1.)

66. *Al-Watan* (Kuwait), 26 Jan. 1981; *As-Siyasah*, 6, 7 Sept. 1981; 'North Yemen. Everybody's Friend or Nobody's', *The Economist*, 4 April 1981, p. 51; Deborah Smith, 'The Yemens Start to Talk', *8 Days*, 26 Sept. 1981, p. 6.

67. US Congress, 97th Congress, 1st sess., House Committee on Foreign Affairs, *US Security Interests in the Persian Gulf*, Report of a Staff Study Mission . . . 21 October – 13 November 1980 . . . 16 March 1980 (Government Printing Office, Washington D.C., 1981), p. 37.

68. *8 Days*, 30 May 1981.

69. *Pravda*, 29 Oct. 1981.

70. During President 'Ali 'Abdallah Salih's Moscow visit, the Soviet Union had exempted North Yemen from the repayment of a $265 million loan received by San'a in the forms of arms and ammunition.

The YAR President had requested $1 billion from Saudi Arabia to pay for new Soviet arms and to finance construction projects. Saudi Arabia had not agreed and negotiations were conducted to reduce the figure. (*An-Nahar al-'Arabi wa ad-Dawli*, 6 – 12 Dec. 1981, p. 17.)

71. For a summary of Soviet economic aid to the PDRY, see Pyotr Alkhimov, 'Soviet Assistance to Southern Yemen in its Economic Development', *Foreign Trade*, no. 9 (Sept. 1981), pp. 36 – 40.

At the end of 1981 reports spoke about the construction of missile bases by Soviet experts in the PDRY, aiming to have bases stretching from the outskirts of Aden to the borders with North Yemen. Their purpose was the protection of the Soviet, Cuban and South Yemeni headquarters against possible attacks from the sea. Other reports said that the Soviets were supervising a military training school in the Ma'allah area in Aden. (*Al-Hawadith*, London, 11 Dec. 1981, p. 11.)

72. *Moscow News*, supp. to no. 51, 21 Dec. 1980, pp. 5 – 6; *Pravda*, 11 Dec. 1980.

73. Tehran Domestic Service, 11 Dec. 1980. In FBIS, South Asia, 12 Dec. 1980, pp. 14 – 15.

74. Tehran Domestic Service, 14 Dec. 1980. In FBIS, South Asia, 15 Dec. 1980, pp. 121 – 122.

75. Saudi Press Agency (SPA), 13 Dec. 1980. In FBIS, ME, 15 Dec. 1980, p. C3.

76. Editorial, 'Gulf Can be Protected Only by Its People', *Al-Ittihad al-Usbu* (Abu Dhabi), 11 Dec. 1980; statement by UAE Minister of State for Foreign Affairs, Rashid 'Abdallah, *Emirates News* (Abu Dhabi), 14 Dec. 1980.

77. Muscat Domestic Service, 17 Dec. 1980. In FBIS, ME, 18 Dec. 1980, p. C1.

78. *Ar-Ra'ay al-'Amm*, 11 Dec. 1980, welcomed the Brezhnev proposals.

79. KUNA, 25 April, 1981. In FBIS, USSR, 29 April 1981, pp. H1 – H3.

80. Sulayman al-Farazli, 'Iraqi-Gulf relations enter lukewarm stage', *Al-Hawadith* (London), 17 July 1981, p. 19.

According to Gulf Co-operation Council (GCC) Secretary-General, 'Abdallah Bisharah:

It is not enough to be an Arab country or a Gulf country to be in the GCC. The members of the GCC have certain characteristics . . . GCC members are countries that by and large have identical political systems, identical internal and foreign policies, identical ideologies, identical aspirations and identical human, social and political problems.

(*Monday Morning*, 20 – 26 July 1981, p. 26.)

81. Moscow radio in Arabic, 6 Feb. 1981. In BBC SU/6644/A4/2, 9 Feb. 1981.
82. Vladimir Peresada, 'On a Dangerous Course', *Pravda*, 10 Feb. 1981. The *Pravda* article received an immediate sharp reply in *'Ukaz*, 11 Feb. 1981.
83. KUNA, 25 April, 1981. In FBIS, USSR, 29 April 1981, pp. H1—H3.
84. TASS in English, 27 May 1981. In FBIS, USSR, 28 May 1981, p. H8.
85. *Monday Morning*, 20—26 July 1981.
86. Moscow radio in Arabic, 3 Sept. 1981. In BBC SU/6820/A4/1, 5 Sept. 1981. For the communiqué of the Ta'if GCC Foreign Ministers' meeting see SPA, 2 Sept. 1981. In FBIS, ME, 3 Sept. 1981, pp. C2—C4.
87. Moscow 'Peace and Progress' in Arabic, 12 Nov. 1981. In FBIS, USSR, 13 Nov. 1981, pp. H4—H5.
For the GCC Riyadh summit statement, see Riyadh Domestic Service, 11 Nov. 1981. In FBIS, ME, 12 Nov. 1981, pp. C4—C5.
88. *Wakh* (Manama), 20 Dec. 1981. In FBIS, ME, 23 Dec. 1981, pp. C1—C2.
89. The text of the PDRY-Ethiopia-Libya treaty as broadcast by Addis-Ababa Domestic Service, 1 Sept. 1981. In FBIS, ME, 2 Sept. 1981, pp. R1—R3, and BBC ME/6818/A/1-3, 3 Sept. 1981.
90. Vladimir Peresada, 'Strengthening Solidarity', *Pravda*, 23 Aug. 1981.
91. For Soviet oil policy, see Arthur Jay Klinghoffer, *The Soviet Union and International Oil Politics* (Columbia University Press, New York, 1977); Benjamin Shwadran, *The Middle East Oil and the Great Powers* (Israel Universities Press, Jerusalem, 1973).
92. The KGB Chairman of the Azerbaijan Soviet Republic, Major-General Ziya Yusif-Zade, said at the end of 1980: 'In view of the situation in Iran and Afghanistan the US special services are trying to exploit the Islamic religion . . . as one factor influencing the political situation in our country.' The Soviet state security organs, he said, 'resolutely suppress the enemy's subversive activity', had succeeded in their struggle against 'ideological subversion' and had suppressed actions by 'reactionary Muslim clergy'. (Z. Yusif-Zade, 'Guarding the Security of the State and the People', *Bakinskiy Rabochiy*, Baku, 19 Dec. 1980.)
93. A former US State Department official with intimate experience of the Persian Gulf made the following evaluation of the current Gulf regimes' probabilities of surviving through 1990 (numbers indicate percentages of probability):

Iran	—	5	UAE	—	5
Iraq	—	40	Saudi Arabia	—	25
Kuwait	—	10	Oman	—	20
Bahrain	—	10	North Yemen	—	5
Qatar	—	10	South Yemen	—	40

(Abdul Kasim Mansur [pen name], 'The Military Balance in the Persian Gulf: Who will Guard the Gulf States From their Guardians?', *Armed Forces Journal International* (Nov. 1980), pp. 44—86.)
94. Joshua M. Epstein, 'Soviet Vulnerabilities in Iran and the RDF Deterrent', *International Security* (Cambridge, Mass.), vol. 6, no. 2 (Fall 1981), pp. 126—58; Dennis Ross, 'Considering Soviet Threats to the Persian Gulf', ibid., pp. 159—80.

BIBLIOGRAPHY

Middle East and Gulf — General

Books and Pamphlets

Abir, Mordechai, *Oil, Power and Politics. Conflict in Arabia, the Red Sea and the Gulf* (Frank Cass, London, 1974)
———— *The Role of the Persian Gulf Oil in Middle Eastern and International Relations* (Leonard Davis Institute for International Relations, The Hebrew University, Jerusalem, 1976)
Agwani, Mohammed Shafi, *Communism in the Arab East* (Asia Publishing House, London, 1968)
Amirie, Abbas (ed.), *The Persian Gulf and Indian Ocean in International Politics* (Institute for International Politics and Economic Studies (IIPES), Tehran, 1975)
Amirsadeghi, Hossein (ed.), *The Security of the Persian Gulf* (St. Martin's Press, New York, 1981)
Ayoob, Mohammed, *Conflict and Intervention in the Third World* (St. Martin's Press, New York, 1980)
———— *The Politics of Islamic Reassertion* (St. Martin's Press, New York, 1981)
———— (ed.), *The Middle East in World Politics* (Croom Helm, London, in association with the Australian Institute of International Affairs, Canberra, 1981)
Becker, Abraham, *Oil and the Persian Gulf in Soviet Policy in the 1970s* (Rand Corporation, Santa Monica, Calif., 1972)
Bennigsen, Alexandre A. and S. Endres Wimbush, *Muslim National Communism in the Soviet Union* (University of Chicago Press, Chicago, 1979)
Burnell, R. M., *The Persian Gulf* (Center for Strategic and International Studies, Georgetown University, Washington, D.C., 1972)
———— and Alvin J. Cottrell, *Iran, the Arabian Peninsula and the Indian Ocean* (National Strategy Information Center, New York, 1972)
Center for Strategic and International Studies, Georgetown University, *The Gulf, Implications of British Withdrawal* (Washington, D.C., 1969)
Chubin, Shahram, *Soviet Policy Towards Iran and the Gulf*

(International Institute for Strategic Studies (IISS), London), Adelphi Papers, no. 157 (Spring 1980)

Confino, M. and S. Shamir (eds.), *The USSR and the Middle East* (John Wiley & Sons, New York and Toronto, 1973)

Cottrell, Alvin, J., *The Persian Gulf States: A General Survey* (Johns Hopkins University Press, Baltimore, 1980)

Eran, Oded, *The Mezhdunarodniki, An Assessment of Professional Expertise in the Making of Soviet Foreign Policy* (Turtledove Publishing, Ramat Gan, Israel, 1979)

Erb, Richard D. (ed.), *The Arab Oil-Producing States of the Gulf: Political and Economic Developments* (American Enterprise Institute, Washington, D.C., 1980)

Eudin, Xenia Joukoff and Robert S. North, *Soviet Russia and the East, 1920–1927. A Documentary Survey* (Stanford University Press, Stanford, 1957)

Freedman, Robert D., *Soviet Policy Toward the Middle East Since 1970* (Praeger, New York, 1975)

Fukuyama, Y. F., *New Directions for Soviet Middle East Policy in the 1980s. Implications for the Atlantic Alliance* (Rand Corporation, Santa Monica, Calif., 1980)

Golan, Galia, *Yom Kippur and After. The Soviet Union and the Middle East Crisis* (Cambridge University Press, London, 1977)
——— *The Soviet Union and the Palestine Liberation Organization. An Uneasy Alliance* (Praeger, New York, 1980)

Hunter, Robert E., *The Soviet Dilemma in the Middle East* (International Institute for Strategic Studies (IISS), London), Adelphi Papers (1969): no. 59, I, The Problem of Commitment; no. 60, II, Oil and the Persian Gulf

Hurewitz, Jacob C. (ed.), *Diplomacy in the Near and Middle East: A Documentary Record, 1914–1956* (2 vols., Van Nostrand, Princeton, N.J., 1956)
——— (ed.), *Soviet-American Rivalry in the Middle East* (Praeger, New York, 1969)
——— *The Persian Gulf* (Foreign Policy Association, New York, 1974)
——— *The Persian Gulf After Iran's Revolution* (Foreign Policy Association, New York, 1979)

International Institute for Strategic Studies (IISS), London, *Security in the Persian Gulf* (Allanheld, Montclair, N.Y., for the IISS, 1981): vol. 1, Chahram Chubin, Domestic Political Factors; vol. 2, Robert Litwak, Sources of inter-conflict; vol. 3, Avi

Plascow, Modernization, Political Development and Stability; vol. 4, Chahram Chubin, The Role of Outside Powers

Joshua, Wynfred, *Arms for the Third World. Soviet Military Aid Diplomacy* (Johns Hopkins University Press, Baltimore, 1969)

Jukes, Geoffrey, *The Soviet Union in Asia* (Angus & Robertson, in association with the Australian Institute of International Affairs, Sydney, 1973)

Kelly, J. B., *Arabia, the Gulf and the West: A Critical View of the Arabs and their Oil Policy* (Weidenfeld & Nicolson, London, 1980)

Khalidi, Rashid, *The Soviet Union and the Middle East in the 1980s* (Institute for Palestine Studies, Beirut, 1980)

Klieman, Aaaron S., *Soviet Russia and the Middle East* (Johns Hopkins University Press, Baltimore, 1970)

Klinghoffer, Arthur Jay, *The Soviet Union and International Oil Politics* (Columbia University Press, New York, 1977)

Kuniholm, Bruce R., *The Origins of the Cold War in the Near East: Great Power Conflict and Diplomacy in Iran, Turkey and Greece* (Princeton University Press, Princeton, N.J., 1980)

Landis, Lincoln, *Politics and Oil, Moscow in the Middle East* (Dunellen Publishing Co., New York and London, 1973)

Laqueur, Walter Z. (ed.), *The Middle East in Transition* (Praeger, New York, 1958)

—— *The Soviet Union and the Middle East* (Routledge & Kegan Paul, London, 1959)

—— *Communism and Nationalism in the Middle East* (Routledge & Kegan Paul, London, 1961)

—— *The Struggle for the Middle East* (Routledge & Kegan Paul, London, 1969)

—— *Confrontation: The Middle East and World Politics* (Quadrangle, New York, 1974)

Lederer, Ivo J. and Wayne C. Vucinich (eds.), *The Soviet Union and the Middle East: The Post-World War II Era* (Hoover Institution Press, Stanford, Calif., 1974)

Leitenberg, Milton and Gabriel Sheffer, *Great Power Intervention in the Middle East* (Pergamon Policy Studies, Elmsford, N.Y., 1979)

Lenczowski, George, *Soviet Advances in the Middle East* (American Enterprise Institute, Washington, D.C., 1972)

—— *The Middle East in World Affairs*, 4th edn. (Cornell University Press, Ithaca, N.Y. and London, 1980)

McLane Charles, B., *Soviet Middle East Relations* (Central Asian Research Centre, London, and Columbia University Press, New York, 1973)

Millar, T. B., *East-West Strategic Balance* (Allen & Unwin, London, 1981)

Niblock, Tim (ed.), *Social and Economic Development in the Arab Gulf* (Croom Helm, London, and St. Martin's Press, New York, 1980)

Novik, Nimrod, *On the Shores of Bab al-Mandeb* (Foreign Policy Research Institute, Philadelphia, 1979)

Noyes, James H., *The Clouded Lens: Persian Gulf Security and US Policy* (Hoover Institution Press, Stanford, Calif., 1979)

Page, Stephen, *The USSR and Arabia* (Central Asian Research Centre, London, 1971)

Pennar, Jaan, *The USSR and the Arabs — The Ideological Dimension, 1917–1972* (Crane, Russak & Co., New York, 1973)

Pranger, Robert J. and Dale R. Tahtinen, *American Policy Options in Iran and the Persian Gulf* (American Enterprise Institute, Washington, D.C., 1979)

Ramazani, Rouhollah K., *The Northern Tier: Afghanistan, Iran and Turkey* (Van Nostrand, Princeton, N.J., 1966)

—— *The Persian Gulf and the Strait of Hormuz* (Sijthoff and Noordhoff, Netherlands, 1979)

Ro'i, Yaacov, *From Encroachment to Involvement: A Documentary Study of Soviet Policy in the Middle East, 1945–1973* (John Wiley & Sons, New York, and Israel Universities Press, Jerusalem, 1974)

Rosen, S. J., *Soviet Strengths and Vulnerabilities in the Middle East* (Rand Corporation, Santa Monica, Calif., 1980)

—— *The Security of the Cape Oil Route* (Report of a Study Group of the Institute for the Study of Conflict, London, 1974)

Sella, Amnon, *Soviet Political and Military Conduct in the Middle East* (St. Martin's Press, New York, 1981)

Servan-Schreiber, Jean-Jacques, *The World Challenge: OPEC and the New Global Order* (Simon & Schuster, New York, 1981)

Schichor, Yitzhak, *The Middle East in China's Foreign Policy, 1949–1977* (Cambridge University Press, New York, 1979)

Shwadran, Benjamin, *The Middle East Oil and the Great Powers* (Israel Universities Press, Jerusalem, 1973)

Smolansky, Oles M., *The Soviet Union and the Arab East Under Khrushchev* (Bucknell University Press, Lewisburg, Pa., 1974)

———— *Soviet Objectives in the Middle East* (Report of a Study Group of the Institute for the Study of Conflict, London, January 1974)

Spector, Ivar, *The Soviet Union and the Muslim World, 1917–1958* (Washington University Press, Seattle, 1959)

Tahtinen, Dale R., *Arms in the Persian Gulf* (American Enterprise Institute, Washington, D.C., 1974)

Tucker, Robert W., *The Purposes of American Power. An Essay on National Security* (Praeger, New York, 1981)

U.S. Congress, House Committee on Foreign Affairs, Subcommittee on Europe and the Middle East, *US Interests In, and Policies Toward, the Persian Gulf, 1980*, Hearings, 24 March–3 September 1980 (Government Printing Office, Washington, D.C., 1980)

———— House Committee on Foreign Affairs, *US Security Interest in the Persian Gulf*, Report of a Staff Study Mission . . . 21 Oct–13 Nov 1980 . . . (Government Printing Office, Washington, D.C., 1981)

Yodfat, Aryeh, *Arab Politics in the Soviet Mirror* (Halsted Press, John Wiley & Sons, New York and Toronto, 1973)

———— *Between Revolutionary Slogans and Pragmatism: The PRC and the Middle East* (Centre d'Etudes du Sud-Est Asiatique et de l'Extrême Orient, Brussels, 1979)

———— and M. Abir, *In the Direction of the Gulf. The Soviet Union and the Persian Gulf* (Frank Cass, London, 1977)

Yodfat, Aryeh Y. and Yuval Arnon-Ohanna, *PLO Strategy and Tactics* (Croom Helm, London, and St. Martin's Press, New York, 1981)

York, Valerie, *The Gulf in the 1980s* (Royal Institute of International Affairs, London), Chatham House Papers, no. 6 (1980)

Articles

Ayoob, Mohammed, 'The super-powers and regional "stability": parallel responses to the Gulf and the Horn', *The World Today* (May 1979), pp. 197–205

Azar, Edward E., 'Soviet and Chinese Rules in the Middle East', *Problems of Communism*, vol. 18, no. 3 (May–June 1979), pp. 18–30

Berry, John A., 'Oil and Soviet Policy in the Middle East', *Middle East Journal*, vol. 26, no. 2 (Spring 1972), pp. 149–60

Campbell, John C., 'The Soviet Union and the United States in the

Middle East', *The Annals of the American Academy of Political and Social Sciences*, vol. 401 (May 1972), pp. 126–35

——— 'The Communist Powers and the Middle East, Moscow's Purposes', *Problems of Communism*, vol. 21, no. 5 (Sept.–Oct. 1972), pp. 40–54

——— 'The Soviet Union in the Middle East', *Middle East Journal*, vol. 32, no. 1 (Winter 1978), pp. 1–12

Canfield, Robert L., 'Soviet Gambit in Central Asia', *Journal of South Asian and Middle Eastern Studies*, vol. 5, no. 1 (Fall 1981), pp. 10–30

Cooley, John K., 'The Shifting Sands of Arab Communism', *Problems of Communism*, vol. 24, no. 2 (March–April 1975), pp. 22–42

——— 'Iran, the Palestinians and the Gulf', *Foreign Affairs*, vol. 57, no. 3 (Summer 1979), pp. 1017–34

Cottrell, Alvin J., 'The Soviet Union in the Middle East', *Orbis*, vol. 19, no. 3 (Fall 1970), pp. 588–98

Dawisha, Karen, 'Soviet Decision-Making and the Middle East: The 1973 October War and the 1980 Gulf War', *International Affairs* (London), vol. 57, no. 1 (1980–1), pp. 43–59

——— 'Moscow's moves in the direction of the Gulf — so near and yet so far', *Journal of International Affairs*, vol. 34, no. 2 (Fall/Winter 1980/1), pp. 219–33

——— 'Moscow and the Gulf War', *The World Today*, vol. 37, no. 1 (Jan. 1981), pp. 8–14

Eilts, Hermann F., 'Security Considerations in the Persian Gulf', *International Security*, vol. 5, no. 2 (Fall 1980), pp. 79–113

Freedman, Robert O., 'Soviet policy towards the Middle East since the invasion of Afghanistan', *Journal of International Affairs*, vol. 34, no. 2 (Fall/Winter 1980/1), pp. 283–310

Golan, Galia, 'Soviet Aims and the Middle East War', *Survival*, vol. 16, no. 3 (May–June 1974), pp. 106–14

Greig, J., 'The Security of Persian Gulf Oil', *Atlantic Community Quarterly*, vol. 18, no. 2 (1980), pp. 193–200

Griffith, William E., 'Soviet Influence in the Middle East', *Survival*, vol. 28, no. 1 (Jan.–Feb. 1976), pp. 2–9

Halliday, Fred, 'The arc of revolutions: Iran, Afghanistan, South Yemen, Ethiopia', *Race and Class* (London), vol. 20, no. 4 (Spring 1979), pp. 373–90

——— 'The Gulf Between Two Revolutions: 1958–1959', *MERIP Reports*, no. 85 (Feb. 1980), pp. 6–15

Hansen, R., 'The Strait of Hormuz and Secure Oil Routes: A Challenge to US Strategy', *Conflict*, vol. 2, no. 1 (1980), pp. 121–36

Hottinger, Arnold, 'Ferment on the Persian Gulf', *Swiss Review of World Affairs*, vol. 20, no. 11 (Feb. 1971), pp. 12–16

–––––– 'The Reopening of the Suez Canal. The Race for Power in the Indian Ocean', *The Round Table* (London), issue 256 (Oct. 1974), pp. 393–402

–––––– 'Arab Communism at Low Ebb', *Problems of Communism*, vol. 30, no. 4 (July–Aug. 1981), pp. 17–32

Hurewitz, J. C., 'The Persian Gulf: British Withdrawal and Western Security', *The Annals of the American Academy of Political and Social Science*, vol. 401 (May 1972), pp. 106–15

Ibrahim, Saad Eddin, 'Superpowers in the Arab World', *The Washington Quarterly*, vol. 4, no. 3 (Summer 1981), pp. 80–96

Khalilhad, Zalmay, 'The Superpowers and the Northern Tier', *International Security* (Winter 1979–80), pp. 6–30

Lenczowski, George, 'The Arc of Crisis: Its Central Sector', *Foreign Affairs*, vol. 57, no. 4 (Spring 1979), pp. 796–820

Luttawak, Edward N., 'Cubans in Arabia! Or, The Meaning of Strategy', *Commentary*, vol. 68, no. 6 (Dec. 1979), pp. 62–6

Maddy-Weitzman, Bruce, 'The Fragmentation of Arab Politics: Inter-Arab Affairs Since Afghanistan Invasion', *Orbis*, vol. 25, no. 2 (Summer 1981), pp. 389–407

Mansur, Abdul Kasim (pseud.), 'The Military Balance in the Persian Gulf: Who Will Guard the Gulf States from their Guardians?', *Armed Forces Journal International* (Nov. 1980), pp. 44–86

McLaurin, R. C., 'Soviet Military in the Middle East', *IDSA Journal* (Institute for Defence Studies and Analysis, New Delhi), vol. 11, no. 1 (July–Sept. 1978), pp. 1–29

Millar, T. B., 'Soviet Policies South and East of Suez', *Foreign Affairs*, vol. 49, no. 1 (Oct. 1970), pp. 70–80

Munford, J. C., 'Soviet Motivation in the Middle East', *Military Review* (Sept. 1972), pp. 40–9

Newsom, David D., 'America Engulfed', *Foreign Policy* (Washington, D.C.), no. 43 (Summer 1981), pp. 17–32

Page, Stephen, 'Moscow and the Persian Gulf Countries, 1967–1970', *Mizan* (Oct. 1971), pp. 72–88

Pipes, Daniel, 'This World is Political!!! The Islamic Revival of the Seventies', *Orbis*, vol. 24, no. 1 (Spring 1980), pp. 9–41

Price, David Lynn, 'Moscow and the Persian Gulf', *Problems of Communism*, vol. 28, no. 2 (March–April 1979), pp. 1–13

Ra'anan, Uri, 'Soviet Policy in the Middle East, 1969–73', *Midstream*, vol. 19, no. 10 (Dec. 1973), pp. 23–45

Ramazani, R. K., 'Security in the Persian Gulf', *Foreign Affairs*, vol. 57, no. 4 (Spring 1979), pp. 821–35

Record, Jeffrey, 'The RDF: Is the Pentagon Kidding?', *The Washington Quarterly*, vol. 4, no. 3 (Summer 1981), pp. 41–51

Richards, Guy, 'The Persian Gulf's Strait of Ormuz: A New Area of US-Soviet Conflict?', *East Europe* (New York), vol. 20, no. 1 (Jan. 1971), pp. 8–15

Ross, Dennis, 'Considering Soviet Threats to the Persian Gulf', *International Security*, vol. 6, no. 2 (Fall 1981), pp. 159–80

Rubinstein, Alvin Z., 'Soviet Persian Gulf Policy', *Middle East Review*, vol. 10, no. 2 (Winter 1977–8), pp. 47–55

—— 'The Soviet Union and the Arabian Peninsula', *The World Today*, vol. 35, no. 11 (Nov. 1979), pp. 442–52

—— 'The Evolution of Soviet Strategy in the Middle East', *Orbis*, vol. 24, no. 2 (Summer 1980), pp. 323–37

—— 'The Soviet Presence in the Arab World', *Current History*, vol. 80, no. 468 (Oct. 1981), pp. 313–16, 338–9

Sicherman, H., 'Reflections on "Iraq and Iran War" ', *Orbis*, vol. 24, no. 4 (Winter 1981), pp. 711–18

Smolansky, Bettie M. and Oles M. Smolansky, 'Soviet and Chinese Influence in the Persian Gulf', in Alvin Z. Rubinstein (ed.), *Soviet and Chinese Influence in the Third World* (Praeger, New York and London, 1975), pp. 131–53

Smolansky, O. M., 'Moscow and the Persian Gulf: An Analysis of Soviet Ambitions and Potential', *Orbis*, vol. 14, no. 1 (Spring 1970), pp. 92–108

—— 'Soviet Policy in Iran and Afghanistan', *Current History*, vol. 80, no. 468 (Oct. 1981), pp. 321–4, 339

Sreedhar, 'The Dilemmas of the US Policy Toward the Gulf', *IDSA Journal* (Institute for Defence Studies and Analysis, New Delhi), vol. 12, no. 1 (July–Sept. 1979), pp. 104–20

Swearingen, Will D., 'Sources of Conflict Over Oil in the Persian/Arabian Gulf', *Middle East Journal*, vol. 35, no. 3 (Summer 1981), pp. 315–30

Toole, Wyclife D., 'Soviet Interests in Arabia', *Military Review* (May 1968), pp. 91–7

Tucker, Robert W., 'Oil: The Issue of American Intervention',

Commentary (Jan. 1975), pp. 21–31
—— 'A New International Order', *Commentary* (Feb. 1975), pp. 38–50
—— 'Further Reflections on Oil and Force', *Commentary* (March 1975), pp. 45–56
—— 'Oil and American Powers. Six Years Later', *Commentary* (Sept. 1979), pp. 35–42
—— 'American Power and the Persian Gulf', *Commentary* (Nov. 1980), pp. 25–41
Van Hallen, Christopher, 'Don't Engulf the Gulf', *Foreign Affairs*, vol. 59, no. 5 (Summer 1981), pp. 1064–78
Watt, D. C., 'The Persian Gulf — Cradle of Conflict', *Problems of Communism* (May–June 1972), pp. 32–40
Yapp, M. E., 'The Soviet Union and the Middle East', *Asian Affairs* (Feb. 1976), pp. 7–18
Yodfat, Aryeh, 'The USSR and Arab Communist Parties', *New Middle East*, no. 32 (May 1971), pp. 29–33
—— 'The People's Republic of China and the Middle East', *Asian Quarterly* (Brussels), part I, 1977/3, pp. 233–6; part II, 1978/1, pp. 67–78; part III, 1978/4, pp. 295–308
—— 'The USSR and the Persian Gulf Area', *Australian Outlook*, vol. 33, no. 1 (April 1979), pp. 60–72

Iran

Abidi, A. H. M., 'The Iranian Revolution, its Origins and Dimensions', *International Studies* (New Delhi), vol. 18, no. 2 (April–June 1979), pp. 129–61
Abrahamian, Ervand, 'Structural Causes of the Iranian Revolution', *MERIP Reports*, no. 87 (May 1980), pp. 21–6
—— 'The Guerrilla Movement in Iran, 1963–1977', *MERIP Reports*, no. 86 (March–April 1980), pp. 3–15
Alexander, Yonah and Alan Nanes (eds.), *The United States and Iran: A Documentary History* (Aletheia Books, University Publications of America, Frederick, Md., 1980)
Algar, Hamid, *Constitution of the Islamic Republic of Iran* (Mizan Press, Berkeley, Calif., 1980)
Alpher, Joseph, 'The Khomeyni International', *The Washington Quarterly*, vol. 3, no. 4 (Autumn 1980), pp. 54–74
Amirie, Abbas and Hamilton A. Twitchell (eds.), *Iran in the*

1980s (Institute for International Politics and Economic Studies (IIPES), Tehran, 1978)

Atkin, Muriel, 'The Kremlin and Khomeyni', *The Washington Quarterly*, vol. 4, no. 2 (Spring 1981), pp. 50–67

Beck, Lois, 'Revolutionary Iran and its Tribal Peoples', *MERIP Reports*, no. 87 (May 1980), pp. 14–20

Bill, James A., 'Iran and the Crisis of '78', *Foreign Affairs*, vol. 57, no. 2 (Winter 1978–9), pp. 323–42

Binder, Leonard, *Revolution in Iran: Three Essays* (American Academic Association for Peace in the Middle East, New York, 1980)

Campbell, W. R. and Djamchid Darvich, 'Global Implications of the Islamic Revolution for the Status Quo in the Persian Gulf', *Journal of South Asian and Middle Eastern Studies*, vol. 5, no. 1 (Fall 1981), pp. 31–51

Chubin, Shahram, 'Leftist Forces in Iran', *Problems of Communism*, vol. 29, no. 4 (July–Aug. 1980), pp. 1–25

Epstein, Joshua M., 'Soviet Vulnerabilities in Iran and the RDF Deterrent', *International Security*, vol. 6, no. 2 (Fall 1981), pp. 126–58

Fatemi, Faramarz S., *The USSR in Iran* (Barnes & Co., New York, 1980)

Forbis, William H., *Fall of the Peacock Throne: The Story of Iran* (Harper & Row, New York, 1980)

Graham, Robert, *Iran: The Illusion of Power* (Croom Helm, London, and St. Martin's Press, New York, 1978)

Gunther, Michael M. and Sanford R. Silverburg, 'Violating the Inviolable: The Iranian Hostage Case and Its Implications', *Journal of South Asian and Middle Eastern Studies*, vol. 5, no. 1 (Fall 1981), pp. 52–76

Halliday, Fred, *Iran: Dictatorship and Development* (Penguin, London, 1978)

———— 'Iran's Revolution: The First Year', *MERIP Reports*, no. 88 (June 1980), pp. 3–5

Helms, Cynthia, *An Ambassador's Wife in Iran* (Dodd, Mead, & Co., New York, 1981)

Hirschfeld, Yair P., 'Moscow and Khomeyni: Soviet-Iranian Relations in Historical Perspective', *Orbis*, vol. 24, no. 2 (Summer 1980), pp. 219–40

Hoveyda, Ferreydom, *The Fall of the Shah* (Weidenfeld & Nicolson, London, 1980)

Jazani, Bizhan, *Capitalism and Revolution in Iran* (Zed Press, London, 1980)

Katouzian, Hama, *The Political Economy of Modern Iran: Despotism and Pseudo-Modernism 1926–1979* (New York University Press, New York, 1981)

Keddie, Nikki R., *Iran. Religion, Politics and Society* (Frank Cass, London, 1980)

—— *Roots of Revolution: An Interpretive History of Modern Iran* (Yale University Press, New Haven, 1981)

Kedourie, Elie and Sylvia G. Haim (eds.), *Towards a Modern Iran: Studies in Thought, Politics and Society* (Frank Cass, London, 1980)

Laqueur, Walter Z., 'Why the Shah Fell', *Commentary* (March 1979), pp. 47–55

Ledeen, Michael A. and William H. Lewis, 'Carter and the Fall of the Shah: The Inside Story', *The Washington Quarterly* (Spring 1980), pp. 3–40

—— *Debacle: The American Failure in Iran* (Alfred A. Knopf, New York, 1981)

Lenczowski, George, *Russia and the West in Iran, 1918–1948: A Study of Big Power Rivalry* (Cornell University Press, Ithaca, N.Y., 1949)

Moss, Robert, *The Campaign to Destabilize Iran* (Institute for the Study of Conflict, London), Conflict Studies, no. 101 (1978)

Mottahedeh, Roy Parviz, 'Iran's Foreign Devils', *Foreign Policy* (Spring 1980), pp. 19–34

Nickel, Herman, 'The US Failure in Iran', *Fortune* (12 March 1979), pp. 94–106

Pahlavi, Mohammad Reza Shah, *Mission for My Country* (McGraw Hill, New York, 1961)

Petrossian, Vahe, 'Iran's Crisis of Leadership', *The World Today*, vol. 37, no. 2 (Feb. 1981), pp. 39–44

Ramazani, Rouhollah K., *The Foreign Policy of Iran, 1800–1941* (Virginia University Press, Charlottesville, 1966)

—— *The Persian Gulf. Iran's Role* (Virginia University Press, Charlottesville, 1972)

—— 'Emerging Patterns of Regional Relations in Iranian Foreign Policy', *Orbis*, vol. 18, no. 4 (Winter 1979), pp. 1043–70

—— 'Iran's Revolution: Patterns and Problems', *International Affairs* (London), vol. 56, no. 3 (Summer 1980), pp. 443–57

Rezun, Miran, *The Soviet Union and Iran: Soviet Policy in Iran from the Beginnings of the Pahlavi Dynasty Until the Soviet Invasion of 1941* (Institut Universitaire de Hautes Etudes Internationales, Leiden, Sijtohoff, Geneva, 1981)

Roosevelt, Kermit, *Countercoup: The Struggle for the Control of Iran* (McGraw Hill, New York, 1979)

Rouleau, Eric, 'Khomeyni's Iran', *Foreign Affairs*, vol. 59, no. 1 (Fall 1980), pp. 1–20

Rubin, Barry, *Paved with Good Intentions: The American Experience and Iran* (Oxford University Press, New York, 1980)

Rubinstein, Alvin Z., 'The Soviet Union and Iran under Khomeyni', *International Affairs* (London), vol. 57, no. 4 (Autumn 1981), pp. 599–617

Saikal, Amir, *The Rise and Fall of the Shah* (Angus & Robertson, London, 1980)

Sale, Richard, 'Carter and Iran: From Idealism to Disaster', *The Washington Quarterly*, vol. 3, no. 4 (Autumn 1980), pp. 75–87

Sreedhar, 'The Role of Armed Forces in Iranian Revolution', *IDSA Journal* (Institute for Defence Studies and Analysis, New Delhi), vol. 12, no. 2 (Oct.–Dec. 1979), pp. 121–42

Steinbach, Udo, 'Iran — Half Time in the Islamic Revolution', *Aussen Politik* (English edn.), vol. 31, no. 1 (1980), pp. 52–68

Sullivan, William H., 'Dateline Iran: The Road Not Taken', *Foreign Policy*, no. 40 (Fall 1980), pp. 175–86

——— *Mission to Iran* (Norton, New York, 1981)

US Congress, Senate Committee on Foreign Relations, Subcommittee on Foreign Assistance, *US Military Sales to Iran*, A staff report . . . July 1976 (Government Printing Office, Washington, D.C., 1976)

US Congress, House Committee on Foreign Affairs, Subcommittee on Europe and the Middle East, *US Policy Toward Iran*, January 1979, Hearing . . . (Government Printing Office, Washington, D.C., 1979)

Zabih, Sepher, 'Communism in Iran', *Problems of Communism*, vol. 14, no. 5 (Sept.–Oct. 1965), pp. 46–55

——— *The Communist Movement in Iran* (University of California Press, Los Angeles, 1966)

——— *Iran's Revolutionary Upheaval: An Interpretive Essay* (Alchemy Books, San Francisco, 1979)

Iraq

Batatu, Hanna, *The Old Social Classes and the Revolutionary Movement in Iraq* (Princeton University Press, Princeton, N.J., 1979)

Dann, Uriel, *Iraq Under Qassem: A Political History, 1958–1963* (Praeger, New York, 1963)

Dawisha, Adeed J., 'Iraq: The West's Opportunity', *Foreign Policy*, vol. 41 (Winter 1980–1), pp. 134–53

—— 'Iraq and the Arab World: The Gulf War and After', *The World Today*, vol. 37, no. 5 (May 1981), pp. 188–94

Khadduri, Majid, *Republican Iraq: A Study of Iraqi Politics since the Revolution of 1958* (Oxford University Press, London, 1969)

Penrose, Edith Tilton, *Iraq: International Relations and National Development* (Westview Press, Boulder, Colo., 1978)

Stork, Joe, 'Iraq and the War in the Gulf', *MERIP Reports*, no. 97 (June 1981), pp. 3–18

Thoman, Roy E., 'Iraq and the Persian Gulf Region', *Current History* (Jan. 1973), pp. 21–5, 37–8

Wright, Claudia, 'Iraq — New Power in the Middle East', *Foreign Affairs*, vol. 58, no. 2 (Winter 1979–80), pp. 257–77

—— 'Behind Iraq's Bold Bid', *New York Times Magazine* (26 Oct. 1980), pp. 43–117

—— 'Implications of the Iraq-Iran War', *Foreign Affairs*, vol. 59, no. 2 (Winter 1980–1), pp. 275–303

Yodfat, Aryeh Y., 'Unpredictable Iraq Poses a Russian Problem', *New Middle East*, no. 13 (Oct. 1969), pp. 17–20

—— 'Russia's Other Middle East Pasture — Iraq', *New Middle East*, no. 38 (Nov. 1971), pp. 26–9

The Kurds and Kurdistan

Adamson, David, *The Kurdish War* (Allen and Unwin, London, 1964)

Chaliand, G. (ed.), *People Without a Country: The Kurds and Kurdistan* (Zed Press, London, 1980)

Ghareeb, Edmund, *The Kurdish Question in Iraq* (Syracuse University Press, Syracuse, 1981)

O'Ballance, Edgar, 'The Kurdish Factor in the Gulf War', *Military Review*, vol. 61, no. 6 (June 1981), pp. 13–20

Sim, Richard, *Kurdistan: The Search for Recognition* (Institute for the Study of Conflict, London), Conflict Studies, no. 127 (1981)

Van Bruinessen, M. M., *Agha, Shaikh and State: On the Social and Political Organization of Kurdistan* (University of Utrecht, Utrecht, 1978)

Saudi Arabia

Gaspard, J., 'Feisal's Arabian Alternative', *New Middle East*, no. 6 (March 1969), pp. 15–19

Halliday, Fred, 'Shifting Sands Behind Royal House of Saud', *Hong Kong Standard* (4 Jan. 1980)

Helms, Christine Moss, *The Cohesion of Saudi Arabia* (Johns Hopkins University Press, Baltimore, and Croom Helm, London, 1981)

Hoagland, Jim and J. P. Smith, 'Saudi Arabia and the United States: Security and Interdependence', *Washington Post* (22, 27 Dec. 1977)

Hottinger, Arnold, 'King Faisal, Oil and Arab Politics', *Swiss Review of World Affairs* (Oct. 1973), pp. 8–10

—— 'Saudi Arabia: On the Brink', *Swiss Review of World Affairs* (May 1979), pp. 8–12

—— 'Does Saudi Arabia Face Revolution?', *New York Times Review of Books* (28 June 1979)

—— 'Notes from Saudi Arabia', *Swiss Review of World Affairs* (Aug. 1980), pp. 10–20

Ochsenwald, William, 'Saudi Arabia and the Islamic Revival', *International Journal of Middle East Studies*, vol. 13, no. 3 (Aug. 1981), pp. 271–86

Quandt, William B., 'Riyadh Between the Superpowers', *Foreign Policy*, no. 44 (Fall 1981), pp. 37–56

—— *Saudi Arabia in the 1980s: Foreign Policy, Security and Oil* (Brookings Institution, Washington, D.C., 1981)

Yodfat, Aryeh, 'The Soviet Line on Saudi Arabia', *Soviet Analyst* (London) (18 Sept. 1975), pp. 4–5

The Gulf States

Abdullah, Muhammad Marty, *The United Arab Emirates: A Modern History* (Barnes & Noble, New York, 1978)

Akhmedov, Anuar, 'Qatar. The Past and the Present', *Asia and Africa Today*, no. 6 (Nov.–Dec. 1979), pp. 46–8

Alexandrov, Yevgeni and Alexander Filonik, 'Kuwait. The Country Within a City', *Asia and Africa Today*, no. 6 (Nov.–Dec. 1980), pp. 48–9

Anthony, John Duke, 'The Union of Arab Amirates', *Middle East Journal*, vol. 28, no. 3 (Summer 1972), pp. 271–87

Burrell, R. M., 'Rebellion in Dhofar: The Spectre of Vietnam', *New Middle East*, no. 42–3 (March–April 1972), pp. 55–8

Clements, F. A., *Oman: The Reborn Land* (Longman, New York, 1980)

Halliday, Fred, 'Report from Dhofar', *Black Dwarf*, no. 31 (March 1970)

Hawley, D., *The Trucial States* (Allen & Unwin, London, 1970)

Khuri, Fuad J., *Tribe and State in Bahrain: The Transformation of Social and Political Authority in an Arab State* (University of Chicago Press, Chicago, 1980)

Lunchinger, Fred, 'Rumblings in Araby: The Dhofar Rebellion', *Swiss Review of World Affairs* (Dec. 1973), pp. 18–20

al-Mallakh, Ragaei, *Qatar: Development of an Oil Economy* (St. Martin's Press, New York, 1979)

Nakhleh, Emile A., *Bahrain: Political Development in a Modernizing Society* (Lexington Books, Lexington, Mass., 1976)

O'Neill, Bard E. and William Brundage, 'Revolutionary Warfare in Oman: A Strategic Appraisal', *Middle East Review* (New York), vol. 10, no. 4 (Summer 1978), pp. 48–56

Owen, R. P., 'Developments in the Sultanate of Muscat and Oman', *The World Today* (Sept. 1970), pp. 379–83

Price, D. L., *Oman: Insurgency and Development*, Conflict Studies (London), no. 53 (Jan. 1975)

Searle, Pauline, *Dawn Over Oman* (Allen & Unwin, London, 1979)

Townsend, John, *Oman: The Making of the Modern State* (Croom Helm, London, 1977, and St. Martin's Press, New York, 1979)

Tremayne, Penelope, 'End of Ten Years' War [in Dhofar]', *RUSI* (Journal of the Royal United Services Institute for Defence Studies, UK), vol. 122, no. 1 (March 1977), pp. 44–8

Wald, Peter, 'The Pacification of Southern Oman', *Swiss Review of World Affairs* (April 1981), pp. 14–15

Ware, L., 'Turmoil in Southern Arabia', *Military Review*, vol. 59, no. 11 (Nov. 1979), pp. 51–4

Zahlan, Rosemarie Said, *The Origin of the United Arab Emirates: A Political and Social History of the Trucial States* (St. Martin's Press, New York, 1978)

North and South Yemen

Alkhimov, Pyotr, 'Soviet Assistance to Southern Yemen in its Economic Development', *Foreign Trade* (Moscow), no. 9 (Sept. 1981), pp. 36–40

Bissell, Richard E., 'Soviet Use of Proxies in the Third World: The Case of Yemen', *Soviet Studies* (Glasgow), vol. 30, no. 1 (Jan. 1978), pp. 87–106

Creekman, C., 'Sino-Soviet Competition in the Yemens', *US Naval War College Review*, vol. 32, no. 4 (July–Aug. 1979), pp. 73–82

Halliday, Fred, 'Counter Revolution in the Yemen', *New Left Review*, no. 63 (Sept.–Oct. 1970), pp. 3–25

——— 'South Yemen: Road Still Fraught with Dangers', *The Middle East* (July 1977), pp. 18–19

——— 'Yemen's Unfinished Revolution: Socialism in the South', *MERIP Reports*, no. 81 (Oct. 1979), pp. 3–20

Little, T., *South Arabia: Arena of Conflict* (Pall Mall, London, 1968)

Lynch, B., 'The Superpowers' Tug of War over Yemen', *Military Review*, vol. 61, no. 3 (March 1981), pp. 10–21

Macro, Eric, *Yemen and the Western World* (C. Hurst & Co., London, 1968)

Malone, Joseph J., 'The Yemen Arab Republic's "Game of Nations" ', *The World Today*, vol. 27, no. 12 (Dec. 1971), pp. 541–8

Novik, Nimrod, *Between Two Yemens: Regional Dynamics and Superpower Conduct in Riyad's 'Backyard'* (Center for Strategic Studies, Tel Aviv University, Tel Aviv), paper no. 11 (Dec. 1980)

O'Ballance, Edgar, *The War in the Yemen* (Faber & Faber, London, 1971)

Peterson, J. E., 'The Yemen Arab Republic and the Politics of Balance', *Asian Affairs* (London), vol. 12, part 3 (Oct. 1981), pp. 254–66

Schmidt, Dana Adams, *Yemen: The Unknown War* (Bodley Head, London, and Holt, Rinehart and Winston, New York, 1968)

Stookey, Robert W., 'Social Structure and Politics in the Yemen Arab Republic', *Middle East Journal*, vol. 28, no. 3 (1974), pp. 248–60; no. 4 (1974), pp. 409–18
——— *Yemen: The Politics of the Yemen Arab Republic* (Westview Press, Boulder, Colo., 1978)
Swanson, Jan C., *Emigration and Economic Development: The Case of the Yemen Arab Republic* (Westview Press, Boulder, Colo., 1979)
Wenner, Manfred W., *Modern Yemen, 1918–1966* (Oxford University Press, London, and Johns Hopkins University Press, Baltimore, 1967)
Wrase, Michael, 'South Yemen: A Soviet Outpost', *Swiss Review of World Affairs* (July 1979), pp. 25–7
Yodfat, Aryeh, 'The People's Republic of South Yemen', *New Outlook* (Tel Aviv) (March 1971), pp. 43–8

Afghanistan

Adamec, L., *Afghanistan's Foreign Affairs to the Mid-Twentieth Century* (University of Arizona Press, Tucson, Ariz., 1974)
Arnold, Anthony, *Afghanistan: The Soviet Invasion in Perspective* (Hoover Institution Press, Stanford, Calif., 1981)
Baloch, Inayatollah, 'Afghanistan-Pashtunistan-Baluchistan', *Aussen Politik* (Hamburg-Stuttgart, English edn.), vol. 31, no. 3 (1980), pp. 283–301
Dupree, Louis, *Afghanistan* (Princeton University Press, Princeton, N.J., 1973)
——— 'Inside Afghanistan. Yesterday and Today: A Strategic Appraisal', *Strategic Studies* (Journal of the Institute of Strategic Studies, Islamabad), vol. 2, no. 3 (Spring 1979), pp. 64–83.
——— 'Afghanistan Under the Khalq', *Problems of Communism*, vol. 18, no. 4 (July–Aug. 1979), pp. 34–50
Halliday, Fred, 'Revolution in Afghanistan', *New Left Review* (Nov.–Dec. 1978), pp. 3–44
Harrison, Selig S., *In Afghanistan's Shadow: Baluchi Nationalism and Soviet Temptations* (Carnegie Endowment for International Peace, Washington, D.C., 1981)
Heller, Mark, 'The Soviet Invasion of Afghanistan', *The Washington Quarterly*, vol. 3, no. 3 (Summer 1980), pp. 36–59

Hussain, Syed Shabbir *et al., Afghanistan Under Soviet Occupation* (World Affairs Publications, Islamabad, 1980)

Kakar, Hasan, 'The Fall of the Afghan Monarchy in 1973', *International Journal of Middle East Studies*, vol. 9, no. 20 (May 1978), pp. 195–214

Khalilzad, Zalmay, 'Afghanistan and the Crisis in American Foreign Policy', *Survival* (July–Aug. 1980), pp. 151–61

────── 'Soviet Occupied Afghanistan', *Problems of Communism*, vol. 29, no. 6 (Nov.–Dec. 1980), pp. 23–40

Monks, Alfred L., *The Soviet Intervention in Afghanistan* (American Enterprise Institute, Washington, D.C., 1981)

Negaran, Hannah (pseud.), 'The Afghan Coup of April 1978: Revolution and International Security', *Orbis* (Spring 1979), pp. 93–113

────── 'Afghanistan: A Marxist Regime in a Muslim Society', *Current History* (April 1979), pp. 172–5

Newell, Nancy Peabody and Richard S. Newell, *The Struggle for Afghanistan* (Cornell University Press, Ithaca and London, 1981)

US Department of State, *Soviet Dilemma in Afghanistan*, Special Report no. 72 (Washington, D.C., June 1980)

The Indian Ocean

Adie, W. A. C., *Oil, Politics and Seapower. The Indian Ocean Vortex* (National Strategy Information Center, Crane, Russack & Co., New York, 1973)

Alford, Jonathan, 'Strategic Developments in the Indian Ocean Area', *Asian Affairs*, vol. 12, part 2 (June 1981), pp. 141–9

Beazley, Kim C. and Ian Clark, *Politics of Intrusion: The Super Powers and the Indian Ocean* (Alternative Publishing Cooperative Ltd., Sydney, 1979)

Bowman, Larry W. and Ian Clark (eds.), *The Indian Ocean in Global Politics* (Westview Press, Boulder, Colo., and University of Western Australia, Nedlands, W.A., 1981)

Chalfont, Lord, 'Russia and the Indian Ocean: New Attitudes to Sea Power', *New Middle East*, no. 44 (May 1972), pp. 4–6

Clementson, J., 'Diego Garcia' (*RUSI,* Journal of the Royal United Services Institute for Defence Studies, UK), vol. 126, no. 2 (June 1981), pp. 33–9

Cottrell, Alvin J. and R. M. Burrell, *The Indian Ocean: Its*

Political, Economic and Military Importance (Praeger, New York, 1979)

—————— 'Soviet-US Naval Competition in the Indian Ocean', *Orbis*, vol. 18, no. 4 (Winter 1975), pp. 1109–28

Cottrell, Alvin J., Robert J. Hanks, Geoffrey Kemp and Thomas H. Moorer, *Seapower and Strategy in the Indian Ocean* (Sage Publications, London, 1981)

Ghebhardt, Alexander O., 'Soviet and US Interests in the Indian Ocean', *Asian Survey*, vol. 15, no. 8 (Aug. 1975), pp. 672–83

Haass, Richard, 'Naval Arms Limitation in the Indian Ocean', *Survival*, vol. 20, no. 2 (March–April 1978), pp. 50–7

Hickman, W., 'Soviet Naval Policy in the Indian Ocean', *US Naval Institute Proceedings*, vol. 105, no. 8 (Aug. 1979), pp. 42–52

Jukes, Geoffrey, 'The Soviet Union and the Indian Ocean', *Survival* (Nov. 1971), pp. 370–5

—————— *The Indian Ocean in Soviet Naval Policy* (International Institute for Strategic Studies (IISS) London), Adelphi Papers, no. 87 (May 1972)

Kaushik, Devendra, *The Indian Ocean* (Vikas Publications, Delhi, 1972)

Lacouture, J., 'Seapowers in the Indian Ocean: A Requirement for Western Security', *US Naval Institute Proceedings*, vol. 105, no. 8 (Aug. 1979), pp. 30–41

Menon, Rajan, 'Soviet Policy in the Indian Ocean Region', *Current History* (April 1979), pp. 176–9, 186, 192

Misra, K. P., 'International Politics in the Indian Ocean', *Orbis*, vol. 18, no. 4 (Winter 1979), pp. 1088–108

'Soviet Foreign Policy East of Suez', *Australian Outlook*, vol. 31, no. 1 (April 1977), pp. 125–213

Tahtinen, Dale R. with the assistance of John Lenczowski, *Arms in the Indian Ocean: Interests and Challenges* (American Enterprise Institute, Washington, D.C., 1977)

Wheeler, Geoffrey, 'The Indian Ocean Area: Soviet Aims and Interests', *Asian Affairs*, vol. 59, part 3 (Oct. 1972), pp. 270–4

Wise, James C., 'Access to the Indian Ocean', *Military Review*, vol. 60, no. 11 (Nov. 1980), pp. 63–70

The Horn of Africa

Abir, Mordechai, *The Contentious Horn of Africa* (Institute for the Study of Conflict, London), Conflict Studies, no. 24 (June 1972)

——— 'Red Sea Politics', *Conflicts in Africa* (International Institute for Strategic Studies (IISS), London), Adelphi Papers, no. 93 (Dec. 1972), pp. 25–41

Bowyer, Bell J., 'Strategic Implications of the Soviet Presence in Somalia', *Orbis*, vol. 19, no. 2 (Summer 1975), pp. 402–11

Chaplin, Dennis, 'Somalia and the Development of Soviet Activity in the Indian Ocean', *Military Review* (July 1975), pp. 3–9

Crozier, Brian, *The Soviet Presence in Somalia* (Institute for the Study of Conflict, London), Conflict Studies, no. 54 (Feb. 1975)

David, Steven, 'Realignment in the Horn: The Soviet Advantage', *International Security*, vol. 4, no. 2 (Fall 1979), pp. 69–90

Farer, Tom, J., 'Soviet Strategy and Western Fears', *Africa Report* (Nov.–Dec. 1978), pp. 4–8

——— *War Clouds on the Horn of Africa. The Widening Storm*, 2nd revised edn. (Carnegie Endowment, New York and Washington, D.C., 1979)

Gorman, Robert F., *Political Conflict on the Horn of Africa* (Praeger, New York, 1981)

Halliday, Fred, 'The Fighting in Eritrea', *New Left Review*, no. 67 (May–June 1971), pp. 57–67

Hamilton, David, *Ethiopia's Embattled Revolutionaries* (Institute for the Study of Conflict, London), Conflict Studies, no. 82 (April 1977)

Henze, Paul B., 'Communism and Ethiopia', *Problems of Communism*, vol. 30, no. 3 (May–June 1981), pp. 55–74

Legum, Colin and Bill Lee, *Conflict in the Horn of Africa (Africana Publishing Co., New York, 1977)*

——— *The Horn of Africa in Continuing Crisis* (Africana Publishing Co., New York, 1979)

Ottoway, David and Marina, *Ethiopia — Empire in Revolution* (Africana, New York, and Holmes and Meier, London, 1978)

Paytan, G., 'The Soviet-Ethiopian Liaison: Airlift and Beyond', *Air University Review*, vol. 31, no. 1 (Nov.–Dec. 1979), pp. 66–73

Sherman, Richard, *Eritrea. The Unfinished Revolution* (Praeger, New York, 1980)

Simes, Dimitri R., 'Imperial Globalism in the Making. Soviet Involvement in the Horn of Africa', *The Washington Review of Strategic and International Studies*, Special Supp: The Story of

Africa (May 1978), pp. 31–9

Valenta, Jivi, 'Soviet-Cuban Intervention in the Horn of Africa: Impact and Lessons', *Journal of International Affairs*, vol. 34, no. 2 (Fall/Winter 1980–1), pp. 353–67

Vanneman, Peter and Martine James, 'Soviet Intervention in the Horn of Africa: Intentions and Implications', *Policy Review* (Summer 1978), pp. 15–36

Yodfat, Aryeh, 'The Soviet Union and the Horn of Africa', *Northeast African Studies* (East Lansing, Mich.), vol. 1, no. 3 (Winter 1979–80), pp. 1–17; vol. 2, no. 1 (1980), pp. 31–57; vol. 2, no. 2 (1980), pp. 65–81.

Periodicals and Newspapers

B — Beirut	K — Kuwait	L — London
M — Moscow	NY — New York	P — Paris
T — Tehran	UK — United Kingdom	W — Washington, D.C.

Al-Ahram, Cairo

Akhbar al-Yawm, Cairo

Al-Anba', K

Arab-Asian Affairs (former *Afro-Asian Affairs*), L

Arab Report, L

Arab Report and Record, L

Asian Affairs, L

Aziya i Afrika Segodniya, M (English edn.: *Asia and Africa Today*)

Bakinsky Rabochy, Baku

Bulletin, Institute for the Study of the USSR, Munich

Christian Science Monitor, Boston

Commentary, NY

Current History, Philadelphia, Pa.

Daily Report, Foreign Broadcast Information Service (FBIS), USA

Daily Telegraph, L

Department of State Bulletin, W

The Economist, L

[Eight] *8 Days*, L

Ettela'at, T

Events, L
Financial Times, L
Foreign Affairs, NY
Foreign Policy, W and NY
Foreign Trade, M
Granma (weekly review in English), Havana
Guardian, L
Al-Hawadith, B and L
Al-Hayat, B
Horizont, East Berlin
L'Humanité, P
International Affairs, L
International Affairs, M
International Herald Tribune, P and Zurich
International Problems, Tel Aviv
International Security, Cambridge, Mass.
Izvestia, M
Jeune Afrique, P
Journal of the Gulf and Arabian Peninsula Studies, K
Journal of International Affairs, K
Keyhan, T
Al-Khaleej, Sharjah (UAE)
Khamsin (Journal of Revolutionary Socialists of the Middle
    East), L
Kommunist, M
Kommunist Tadzhikistana, Dushanbe
Krasnaya Zvezda, M
Literaturnaya Gazeta, M
Al-Majallah, L
MERIP Reports (Middle East Research and Information
    Project), W
The Middle East, L
Middle East International, L
Middle East Journal, W
The Middle East Newsletter, L
The Middle East and North Africa (Yearbook), L
Middle East Review, NY
Middle East Reporter, B
Middle Eastern Studies, L
Military Review, US Army
Mirovaya Ekonomika i Mezhdunarodniye Otnosheniya, M

Mizan, L
Monday Morning, B
Le Monde, P
Moscow News, M
An-Nahar, B
An-Nahar Arab Report, B
An-Nahar al-'Arabi wa ad-Dawli, P
Narody Azii i Afriki, M
Neue Zurcher Zeitung, Zurich
New Left Review, L
New Middle East, L
New Outlook, Tel Aviv
News from Oman & Southern Arabia, Copenhagen
Newsweek, NY
New Times, M
New York Times, NY
An-Nida, B
Observer, L
Orbis, Philadelphia, Pa.
Peking (Beijing) Review, Beijing
The Petroleum Economist (Petroleum Press Service), L
Pravda, M
Problems of Communism, W
Al-Qabas, K
Radio Liberty Research, Munich
Ar-Ra'y al-'Amm, K
Review of International Affairs, Belgrade
RIPEH (The Review of Iranian Political Economy & History), Georgetown University, W
RUSI (Journal of the Royal United Services Institute for Defence Studies), UK
Ash-Sharq al-Awsat, L
As-Siyasah, K
Sovyetskaya Rossiya, M
Soviet Analyst, L
Der Spiegel, Hamburg
SSha — Ekonomika, Politika, Ideologia, M
Summary of World Broadcasts, British Broadcasting Corporation (BBC), L
Sunday Telegraph, L
Sunday Times, L

Survival, L
Swiss Review of World Affairs, Zurich
Time, NY
The Times, L
Trud, M
'Ukaz, Jidda
US News & World Report, W
Washington Post, W
The Washington Quarterly, W
Washington Star, W
World Marxist Review, Prague
The World Today, L
Za Rubezhom, M
Zarya Vostoka, Tbilisi

INDEX

Note: The definite article *al* has been dropped from most Arabic names listed in the index. Whenever retained, it has been disregarded in the alphabetical arrangement of entries.
Italicized page numbers indicate principal references.

Index

5# Index 191

41, 50, 61, 63, 67, 94, 114, 120, 122, 132, 156–7

Ta'if 5, 145
Taiz 5, 60
Talabani, Jalal 90
Taraki, Nur Muhammed 65
Tigris River 19
Tikhonov, Nikolay 130
Transcaucasia, Soviet 21
Tudeh Party 68, 70, 78, 81, 127
Turkey 16–17, 153

Umm al-Quwain 13
Unified Political Organization National Front (PDRY) 7, 52–3, 56
Union of Soviet Socialist Republics (USSR) 23–8, 32–4; competition with the PRC 150–1; competition with the USA 149–50; economic and technical aid and co-operation 2, 6, 11, 19, 23, 40, 49–50, 62; military supplies 2–6, 13–14, 17–19, 40–1, 55–6, 62, 107–8; policy in Middle East: factors behind Soviet successes and failures 23–8, ideology and national interests 148–9. interests and considerations, aims and motivations 149–57, the Soviets wait for the next regimes 157–8; Soviet Muslims and Middle East 1, 75, 78, 162n92; trade with Middle East 1, 10–11, 30; *For USSR relations with Middle Eastern countries see individual countries*
United Arab Emirates (UAE) *13, 41–2, 103*, 152, 157, 162n93
United Arab Republic (UAR) 17, 32
United States of America (USA) 2–3, 8–10, 16–18, 22–3, 32–4, 38–9, 42–3, 45, 47–8, 51, 53, 61, 64, 68–70, 80–2, 94–5, 104–7, 110, 115, 124, 127, 131–4, 136–8, 140, 142, 144, 147, 149, 154, 157

Vance, Cyrus 79, 107
Vasil'yev, Alexei 14, 100
Vietnam 15
Vinogradov, Vladimir 123

Yazdi, Ebrahim 79

Yemen Arab Republic (YAR) *44–6*, 51, 53, 56, 60, *105–8*, 113, *137–41*, 156; attempts to balance between the USSR and the USA 105–6, 137–7; fighting between North and South Yemen 106–7; Soviet military supplies 107–8, 139–40; *see also* Yemen, North
Yemen, Civil War 2–4, 29n11
Yemen, North 1, *2–5*, 6, 26, 32, 37, *44–6*, 49, 51, 58, 105, 152, 157, 162n93
Yemen, South 4, *5–7*, 12–14, 34, 43–6, 94, 97; *see also* PDRY, PRSY
Yemeni Socialist Party *56–7*, 108, 111, 113; co-operation with the CPSU 108–9
Yepishev, A. A. 111

Zaire 37